All Was Light

The statue by Roubillac of Newton with his prism in the Ante-Chapel of Trinity College, Cambridge. Photograph by kind permission of Dr A. A. Mills.

All Was Light

An introduction to Newton's *Opticks*

A. Rupert Hall

CLARENDON PRESS · OXFORD
1993

Oxford University Press, Walton Street, Oxford OX2 6DP

Oxford   New York   Toronto
Delhi   Bombay   Calcutta   Madras   Karachi
Kuala Lumpur   Singapore   Hong Kong   Tokyo
Nairobi   Dar es Salaam   Cape Town
Melbourne   Auckland   Madrid

and associated companies in
Berlin   Ibadan

Oxford is a trade mark of Oxford University Press

Published in the United States
by Oxford University Press Inc., New York

A catalogue record for this book is available from the British Library

Library of Congress Cataloging in Publication Data
Hall, A. Rupert (Alfred Rupert), 1920–
All was light: an introduction to Newton's opticks / A. Rupert
Hall.
1. Newton, Isaac, Sir, 1642–1727.   Opticks.   2. Optics—Early
works to 1800.   3. Optics—Europe—History.   I. Title.
QC353.H35   1993   535–dc20   92-43731
ISBN 0–19–853985–1

Set by Advance Typesetting Ltd., Oxford
Printed in Great Britain
by Biddles Ltd.
Guildford & King's Lynn

Preface

Opticks or a Treatise of the Reflections, Refractions, Inflections and Colours of Light was reprinted (with a Foreword by Albert Einstein and an Introduction by Sir E. T. Whittaker) in 1934, from the fourth edition of 1730 (see Appendix I). This volume in turn was reproduced in facsimile by Dover Publications in 1952, with a new Preface by I. Bernard Cohen and an Analytical Table of Contents by D. H. D. Roller, but no index. This is the edition to which I have referred throughout, simply citing it by page-numbers at the close of quotations. The most recent edition of *Opticks* known to me is that in French published in 1989; it is a re-issue of the translation by J.-P. Marat (1787), with new material by Françoise Balibar and Michel Blay.

The orthography of the original printed editions is capricious. Capitalization of words is of no significance; sometimes the same word was printed twice within the same paragraph, once with and once without the initial capital. Newton preferred such forms as 'reflexion' but the word may be printed as 'reflection'. I have tried to follow the vagaries of the printed forms, though they tell us nothing. Many Newtonian texts can be found in printed versions carefully transcribed by modern scholars from a manuscript (or manuscripts) and also in contemporary print. In most cases it makes no difference which version is used, and I have quoted either as seemed convenient. Newton misspelled many words (especially in his early manuscripts) and commonly employed the conventional abbreviated forms such as 'pressiō' for 'pression' [pressure] as well as 'yᵉ', 'yⁿ', 'wᶜʰ', 'yᵗ' and so on. I have written abbreviations out in full in transcribing (the, then or than, which, that, etc.) just as a seventeenth-century printer would have done, retaining the idiosyncrasies of Newton's spelling otherwise. I have also kept the ampersand, as it is still in current use. Nothing is gained by slavishly copying and printing Newton's manuscripts with diplomatic accuracy except when the detailed evolution of a text is to be considered.

I have reserved double quotation marks "____" for quotations of Newton's own words, using single quotation marks for extracts from other writers. Editorial additions or alterations in quotations are, as is usual, surrounded by square brackets [____]. References to the edition of Newton's *Correspondence* as edited by H. W. Turnbull, J. F. Scott, A. R. Hall, and Laura Tilling (Cambridge University Press, seven volumes, 1959–77) are given by Letter-number and (if necessary) page.

The Bibliography lists books and articles which I have read and profited from as well as those from which I have directly quoted. It is a small selection. Larger bibliographies of relevant publications will be found in Sabra (1967), Shapiro (1984), and Mamiani (1986), as well as many other books.

It has been my aim to write an account of what kind of a book Newton's *Opticks* is; to outline its lengthy evolution into its final published form; to give some account of its meaning in contemporary context (but not to give a history of optics in the seventeenth century) and also of its reception within Newton's lifetime and shortly thereafter; to examine both the 'open' and the 'private' aspects of Newton's understanding of his subject; and to some extent to discuss his success in relation to his ambitions. I have not set out to prepare a detailed analytical narrative of Newton's long-continued experimentation and speculation in optical science and related fields, or to present an elaborate *analyse de texte* of *Opticks*, or (thirdly) to tease out of the book a reconstruction of Newton's scientific methodology. I am happy to leave such specialized investigations to others, being content here to demonstrate that *Opticks* is a book offering many points of interest and varied potential for further study.

I wish gratefully to acknowledge personal indebtedness to Paolo Casini, Judith Field, John Hendry, Alan Shapiro, William Schupbach, and especially my wife; my thanks are also due to Isaac Newton Felis for his patient companionship in my labours.

1993   A.R.H.

Contents

Vivida vis animi pervicit, et extra
Processit longé flammantia mœnia mundi,
Atque omne immensum peragravit mente animoque.

Mac. S

The apotheosis of Newton according to Owen McSwiney. An engraving by
L. Desplaces after D. M. Fratta, after G. B. Pittoni and D. and G. Valeriani
(?1741). Reproduced from the example in the Wellcome Institute Library, London,
by kind permission of the Librarian.

Introduction

To the best of my knowledge the present is the first attempt to give a general account of one of the most celebrated books in the history of science: Newton's *Opticks*. The content of that work has been summarized by many writers; Newton's experimental investigations of light and colour, and his theories in explanation of his results, have also been the subject of many books and articles. My concern, however, is not with Newton's optics as a scientific or epistemological structure, but with Newton's *Opticks* as an exposition of it. To some extent I have modelled my treatment upon Bernard Cohen's *Introduction to Newton's 'Principia'* (1971), but I have allowed myself a wider scope.

Chapter 1 considers *Opticks* in the context of Newton's other scientific writings, and of the time. It is necessary to realize that Newton's treatment of topics in the science of optics was highly idiosyncratic. His approach was physical, though (as invariably) he thought geometry essential to the construction of a sound physics. He was not much interested in problems of image-formation, for his chief pre-occupation was with the physical nature of light and its interactions—of many kinds—with matter. The writing of *Opticks* was made the more difficult because the phenomena involved were obscure and complex, and steadily increasing in range during Newton's lifetime. He believed that it was essential to investigate these various phenomena experimentally, and quantitatively if possible, before advancing theories about their explanation in terms of a postulated composition of things. Hence *Opticks* is of at least as great methodological interest as the *Principia*. Newton's idiosyncratic approach to optics was little understood by his contemporaries when it was first revealed in 1672: some of them failed to grasp the extreme precision of his experimental procedures. This incomprehension in turn affected the subsequent writing of *Opticks*.

As Newton himself hinted in the *Advertisement* to the first edition of *Opticks*, the materials upon which Newton drew (in 1687 and subsequently) in preparing his second great work for the press—at last!—had accumulated throughout his mature life; they included his own early research notes, his first series of university lectures, his correspondence with the Royal Society, and papers sent to that body. I have described the gradual evolution of a long-awaited book in Chapter 2.

When, after this long period of gestation (1670–87) Newton took up his pen with the resolution to publish a definitive account of his optical researches and the conclusions to which they had led him, he wrote with speed—but outside events postponed the fulfilment of his purpose until (probably) 1692. Then he patiently deferred publication until after the death of Robert Hooke in 1703. In Chapter 3 I review the preparation of this text published in 1704, the reasons for its achieving less than Newton had proposed to himself, and the tailing-off of the book into a series of Queries. The 1704 *Opticks* was revised and extended—particularly as to the Queries—in the Latin re-issue of 1706 and the subsequent English editions (1717, 1721, 1730). This development of the initial text is also treated in Chapter 3.

Chapter 4 is, as it were, an addendum to the story of the arrival of the text at its final form in the fourth edition (1730), for it reviews the reception of the book and its influence within Britain and upon the Continent. It appears that the histories of *Opticks* and of the *Principia* in these respects were very different, not least in the greater popularity of the former book. Even so, popularizers of Newton were rarely able to cope with the true subtleties and enigmatic convolutions of Newton's mature theories of light and colour.

ONE

The author and the background to his book

§1. Newton: the writer

The long evolution of Opticks

Isaac Newton began to prepare a new book, *Opticks, or a Treatise of Light and Colours*, from the ample materials that he had to hand, in 1687, when the pen that had written his immortal *Philosophiae naturalis principia mathematica* was barely dry. Deceptively, one might suppose that a taste for publication had come upon him. This task was broken off by the political events of the following year, and Newton's involvement in them, which led to his brief representation of the University in the Convention Parliament. That completed, Newton probably concluded his new text in 1692, but it was to remain in his drawer for a further twelve years.

Following hard upon the *Principia*, Newton's substantial draft of 1687 was, like that book, set down in Latin, under the provisional title *Fundamentum opticae*. He was by this time an experienced author in the learned language, having already prepared his *Lectiones opticae* ('Optical Lectures', 1671–2) and *Arithmetica universalis* ('Universal Arithmetic', 1684) before the *Principia*, as well as a number of large mathematical and philosophical letters. But Newton was also an experienced author in English too: his letters printed in the *Philosophical Transactions* amounted to a stout volume.

As Newton's first paper in that journal was published in March 1672, while his first attention to optics was at least seven years before that, one may ask why the composition of his mature statement upon matters considered in his youth was delayed to his old age. Historians have at various times pointed to Newton's reluctance to return to a field that Robert Hooke wished to claim as his own, his dislike of such controversies as had followed the publication of his optical letters in the 1670s, and his temperamental reluctance to part with any writings of his own. In all these points there is truth and falsehood.

It was true that the printing of *Opticks* was stayed for a dozen years till Hooke was dead. But neither Hooke nor the controversies had hindered Newton from planning an abortive book on optics in the mid-1670s. The great obstacle to publication was within Newton himself. He wrote, he was forever writing, to please himself. Sometimes he had readers in mind also, or (in the case of the Optical Lectures, the Arithmetic, and the *Principia mathematica*) he had, at least in a formal sense, a university audience to instruct. I do not think that Newton cared to form a picture of either audience and its needs—he wrote for some ideal body of auditors, perhaps composed of other Newtons. It was therefore his custom continually to revise, develop, enlarge, and improve his writings. To him the mechanical business of printing was an awkward termination of the ceaseless process of creative activity. It brought the piece of work to an arbitrary state of concreteness or definition, so that readers might interpret the work in this concrete state as giving a final view of Newton's mind upon this particular topic. He himself preferred to go on considering things before declaring his mind. We know the vicissitudes through which the *Principia* passed in their brief, incredibly swift progress to the fixity of print; *Opticks* went through a more complex evolution over a longer period of time.

Newton was never satisfied with what he had written, still less with what he had printed. The *Principia's* revision began before the ink was dry on the printer's sheets. The *Arithmetic* he would not have printed at all, but that William Whiston took the text from the Cambridge University Library. *The Chronology of Ancient Kingdoms Amended* was stolen from him. All these works were imperfect. A major reason for not completing the text of *Opticks* before 1692 or thereabouts, and for not publishing the book then prepared until after Hooke's death in 1703, was its incompleteness. Books I and II could hardly be improved, but Newton was well aware that they did not comprehend the whole range of his theme, still less tell the whole story of physical theory that he wished to tell. Recent scholars are agreed that the *Opticks* we have is a *faute de mieux* book, not the more profound and certain contribution to natural philosophy that its author had long envisaged. *Opticks* also suffered from changes in Newton's idea of what the book was to be about, and from developments in experimental optics that did not spring from Newton's own hands. It is beyond doubt that Newton's fundamental ideas of the nature of light were first formed before he had heard of (what we would call) interference, birefringence, or diffraction—all colour-forming phenomena. Newton's early framework of thought had to be adapted with reluctance and difficulty to accept these newly-discovered effects.

The tradition of optics

In short, the development of the science of optics in Newton's lifetime was not entirely under his control, for all that his own share in it was so great. For all his supreme originality, he was heir to a long tradition whose further evolution was going on around him. Christiaan Huygens, whose contributions to experimental and theoretical optics many historians place only just below those of Newton—and judge in some ways more far-seeing—was no more indebted to Newton than was Newton to him, that is, not at all. The construction of a reflecting telescope, albeit on the smallest scale, first brought fame to Newton, but the principle of such an instrument had been known for a generation or more. Newton's single most important apprehension of a new fact in Nature, that the colour of a refracted ray of light does not change as a result of a second refraction was already in print, but of this he was never aware (see below §3). As this unawareness emphasizes, the tradition of seventeenth-century optics was far richer than Newton ever realized, since he made no systematic effort to explore it (as he explored alchemy and theology through massive literary research). Appendix III gives a far from complete list of seventeenth-century optical writings, few of which found their way into Newton's own library. Books with no effect upon Newton's highly individual researches nevertheless helped to shape the environment within which Newton's publications were received.

§2. Newton and his predecessors

The history of the rainbow in optics

Seventeenth-century optics embraced many topics, some of no interest to Newton. Perspective or the optical aspects of representational painting, the anatomy of the eye and the mechanism of vision, the properties of mirrors and lenses, geometrical optics concerned with the formation and position of optical images, the computation of atmospheric refraction for the astronomer's purposes, the practical construction of optical instruments—these are not topics that come near the heart of *Opticks*, though in that book or elsewhere Newton said something about all of them, sometimes something of importance. The book is to all intents and purposes about three fundamental optical effects: reflection, refraction, and interference (I use our modern term; Newton spoke of "the colours of thin plates"). Each of these effects is associated with the appearance of colours. Each reveals something major about the nature and properties of light, and serves in its own way to account for the manifestation of natural colours. In the seventeenth-century literature of optics the clearest thread leading to the *Opticks* is the history of the rainbow (Boyer 1959), though indeed Newton comes to this topic late in the book and soon dispatches it. He was the first mathematician or philosopher to set the mathematical and physical explanation of the rainbow's position and colours within its proper context, an understanding of how the prismatic spectrum is produced. However, that there is an analogy between the natural rainbow and the colours artificially produced by shining light through a spherical water-vessel or an angular glass had been perceived in the late Middle Ages.

Descartes was the giant upon whose shoulders Newton stood in this matter and he cared little for those who had preceded Descartes. In fact, they were many. It is enough here to note Theodoric of Freiberg (*d*.1311), whose investigation of the rainbow 'is a model example of the thirteenth-century theory of experimental science in practice and a model of experimental procedure for all time' (Crombie 1953, p. 233). Theodoric explained the rainbow by supposing that the sun's rays forming it reach the eye after two refractions and one reflection within raindrops in the air, at appropriate angles; or in the case of the secondary bow, by two refractions and two reflections within the drop, in which case the order of the colours is reversed. The explanation was analogical: model 'raindrops' produced the same rainbow colours (ibid., p. 237). Theodoric had no clear explanation of how the colours come into being. He regarded the rainbow as presenting four colours, intermediate between white (sunlight) and black (darkness), each colour successively being a less brilliant, or darker, manifestation of white. The circular form of the rainbow was occasioned by the fact that the drops from which came the rays forming each band of colour had to be so situated that at each one the line to the eye and the line to the sun formed a constant angle (ibid., p. 255).

Theodoric's promising ideas do not seem to have been strongly echoed during the next three centuries and were never mentioned by Descartes. Crombie has demonstrated that they were not wholly unknown. Francesco Maurolico of Messina (1494–1575) in *Diaphaneon* (1553) may have borrowed from him indirectly the idea of reflection within the raindrops (he does not speak of refraction) and he knew that each bow is formed at fixed angles to the observer and the sun. The Croat priest Marco Antonio de Dominis (1560–1626)—who taught at Italian universities and became Archbishop of Split—also had a partial familiarity with the same set of ideas. He knew of a refraction into each drop and a reflection within and of the constancy of the angles at the drop (*De radiis visus et lucis*, Venice 1611).

In *Les Météores* (1637) Maurolico was cited by Descartes, in *Opticks* De Dominis was mentioned by Newton. (He is of particular interest to Englishmen because, like Giordano Bruno earlier, he sought refuge for a time in England, dying in the Inquisition's prison after his return to Italy; luckier than Bruno, he had died before his body was burned.) Newton, who owned a copy of *De radiis* at his death (Harrison 1978, no. 535), printed a highly flattering and inaccurate account of De Dominis's work:

For he teaches there how the interior Bow is made in round Drops of Rain by two Refractions of the Sun's Light, and one Reflexion between them, and the exterior by two Refractions, and two sorts of Reflexions between them in each Drop of

Water, and proves his Explications by Experiments made with a Phial full of Water, and with Globes of Glass filled with Water, and placed in the Sun to make the Colours of the two Bows appear in them (*Opticks* 1952, p. 169).

In the Optical Lectures some twenty years before Newton had more fairly and honestly ignored De Dominis (who had followed Theodoric, but ignored the second reflection and refraction), writing that Descartes had prepared the way for the true explanation of the rainbow "for it is due to him that we know it to be formed in falling drops of rain water" (Shapiro 1984, p. 593). If this is historically naïve, it admits Newton's personal obligation. In *Opticks* Descartes is only given the credit of having pursued "the same explanation [as De Dominis] in his Meteors, and mended that of the exterior Bow" (1952, p. 169). Not sharing Newton's animosity towards Descartes, we may record that the chief merit of his treatment of the rainbow in the *Météores* is to demonstrate geometrically why light from any part of the primary bow subtends nearly the same angle to the eye (about 42°) and similarly with the secondary bow (about 52°). True, the basic elements of his account were known to Theodoric, but Descartes went beyond analogical guess to strict proof.

The sine-law of refraction

Knowing the sine-law of refraction, Descartes could calculate the angle at which any refracted ray leaves the drop, with respect to the line of the incident ray. This law ($\sin i/\sin r = k$), bearing now the name of the Dutch mathematician Willebrord Snel (1580–1626), who discovered it near the end of his life, was first published by Descartes in *La Dioptrique* (1637) and very probably found out by him independently (Sabra 1967, p. 103). It defines the bending undergone by a ray of light in passing through the interface between two different mediums (Fig. 1). We need not here analyse in detail Descartes's rather fanciful kinematic derivation of the law, except to note that it begins from the counter-intuitive supposition that light increases in speed as it travels from a less dense to a more dense optical medium. (Dense means, strictly speaking, optically dense, that is, more refractive, but in the seventeenth century gravitational density and optical density were taken to be correlated, a notion espoused in general terms by Newton.) Thus light was supposed to travel more freely and so more swiftly in glass than in water, and in water than in air. In Descartes's rather curious mode of argument it was held that only the component of the motion of light normal to the interface between two mediums was affected by passing through it, the component parallel to the interface being unaffected, with the result that the ray was bent (when entering a denser medium) towards the perpendicular, as experience confirms. The converse is obvious.

One must, perhaps, pay an irrelevant tribute to Thomas Harriot (1560–1621), the English mathematician of genius whose application of

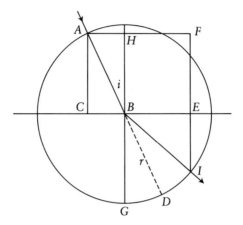

Fig. 1. Descartes's treatment of simple refraction. As the ray AB passes through the boundary *CBE* into a different medium its speed normal to *CBE* is deemed to increase or decrease, its speed parallel to *CBE* remaining constant. Suppose its speed to decrease. In the time taken by the ray to travel the distance $BI = AB$, the component of motion along AH will have reached F, while that normal to CBE has only reached I. Put $FH = n.AH$. Then $\sin i = AH/AB$, $\sin r = BE/BI$; hence $\sin r = n.AH/AB = n.\sin i$. If the ray BI is swifter than the ray AB, $FH < AH$, and $r < i$.

the sine-law as early as 1601 has only been rediscovered in the present generation, 'although no explicit formulation of it by him has as yet been found in his unpublished manuscripts' (Edward Rosen in Shirley 1974, p. 3). Of Harriot's work—all buried in these famous manuscripts—Newton was surely wholly ignorant. In the *Optical Lectures* he assigned the sine-law unequivocally to Descartes; by the time the *Principia mathematica* were on the stocks, he knew that Snel had discovered the constancy of the secants of the angles (which is correct), equivalent to the law of sines, adding "as Descartes explained", which is perhaps only scant justice (*Principia* (1687), p. 231; Shapiro 1984, p. 169).

To explain the rainbow, Descartes considers an arbitrary circular section through a raindrop. Using the sine-law, he calculates the overall angle of refraction between the incident ray EF and the emergent ray NP, supposing refractions at F and N and a single reflection at K; he also makes the alternative calculation with two internal reflections for the secondary bow (Fig. 2). The extremely ingenious (and laborious) operation that he now undertook was to compute, for a number of parallel rays of sunlight falling upon the quarter-circle AD—that is, rays normal to AB—their angles of emergence from the drop. The computation showed that when the incident rays EF were at a distance of between eight-tenths and nine-tenths of the radius (AB) from the centre-line AC, they emerged nearly parallel to one

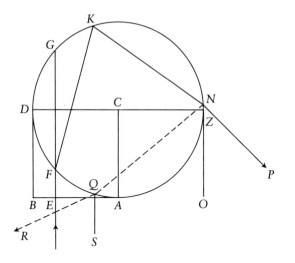

Fig. 2. Descartes's treatment of refractions and reflection within a single raindrop. After Descartes (1672), p. 221. At N some light is refracted to P, other light reflected to Q and there refracted to R.

another at N at an angle of about 40° to the original direction. Likewise, after two internal reflections, they emerged parallel at an angle of about 54°. Descartes plausibly deduced that these strong concentrations of rays produced the bands of the rainbows, having these same angular diameters:

we see that the greatest angle ONP can be only 41½° and the minimum SQR 51° 54′ , to which we add or from which we subtract about 17′ for the solar diameter, thus finding 41° 47′ for the greatest diameter of the inner rainbow and 51° 37′ for the least diameter of the interior bow (Descartes 1672, pp. 222, 224).

As Newton never read French from choice, we may be sure that he read the *Météores* (and also *La Geométrie* and *La Dioptrique*) in one of the Latin collected editions of Descartes's writings, one of which was in his library. Thus he was well acquainted with Descartes's physical theory of the cause of the rainbow colours, which (like his medieval precursors) he justified by analogy with prismatic colours (*Météores*, Cap. VIII, Sections 4 to 8).

Descartes's concept of light

Descartes experimented with a prism in a way that seems strange to post-Newtonians. He let sunlight fall full on one face of an acute-angled prism, while another face was obstructed by an opaque sheet or layer through which one very small hole allowed the light to pass (Fig. 3). Leaving this second face of the prism, the beam of light thus formed shone upon a white

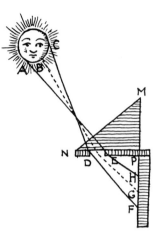

Fig. 3. Descartes's prismatic experiment. After Descartes (1672), p. 224. *NM* is the face of the prism, *DE* the small hole in the opaque layer *NP* through which a beam passes to form the partial spectrum *HGF*.

paper at *PF*, showing red at *F* and blue or violet at *H*, with all the colours of the rainbow between (Descartes affirms). This image was bounded by the shadow cast by the opaque layer; as Descartes pointed out, if the hole in it were too large no spectrum would be seen. The spectral colours cannot appear without a dark border: 'a shadow or boundary to the light is necessary' (Descartes 1672, p. 216).

Now Descartes taught that light is 'a certain motion, or prompt and vivid action, in the luminous body' (*Dioptrique*, Ch. I, Section 3) transmitted instantaneously through the optical aether and penetrating all transparent bodies until it reaches the eye (it is like a quick blow transmitted down a rigid stick from one end to the other). The aether consists of very small, perfectly spherical particles, which rotate as they move. Colour is not in objects, but in the peculiar rotations of the particles of aether, which are changed by their contacts with bodies (ibid., Section 4). *Les Météores*, Chapter VIII, adds more detail to this theory. The particles in the beam of light which we may imagine as travelling through the hole in the opaque layer (though really they do not, according the Descartes; it is a pulse that travels) accordingly brush against inactive, stationary particles in the dark area surrounding the beam. The friction causes them to lose or gain rotary motion, or spin; if they move more rapidly than usual they cause the sensation of redness, if more slowly the sensation of blueness. Since Descartes's arrangement did not form a well-delineated spectrum, though he was aware that its range of colours corresponded to that of the rainbow, he remained ignorant of the asymmetry of the spectrum, which so powerfully impressed Newton as a great oddity when he first examined the phenomena—as he told the Royal Society in February 1672.

Newton's particle theory of light

Descartes's theory was unsatisfactory to Newton's mind for a number of reasons. He did not believe that an aetherial pulse would propagate in straight lines, as light does; he was at first doubtful that light moves instantaneously, then later certain that it does not; his own experiments taught him that coloured light is not a modified form of white light, obvious though this notion might seem from our experience of pigments, dyes, and coloured glass windows; and he satisfied himself that the shadow bounding a beam of light has nothing to do with the coloration of the beam. In *Opticks* as in earlier papers on optics Newton was to refute Descartes on all these points; though his great predecessor is not mentioned by name— nor indeed was he alone in putting forward the notions that Newton challenged—it is obvious that Descartes was the major established authority to be overcome. Particularly Newton was to insist on the atomicity (as we may call it) of the rays of light, a notion incompatible with any kind of aetherical motion. It seemed to Newton that the rectilinearity of light required it to be a radiation of *matter*, not of pressure or vibratory motion; a streaming out of projectile-like particles. Just as atoms combine into bodies, so these particles combine into a beam of light; and as atoms retain their identity no matter what compounds they form, so these particles retain theirs though they seem to be lost in the heterogeneous mixture which is white light. For (Newton came to believe) we chiefly recognize the identity of the light-particles as colour (itself of course, a product of our physiological system). A homogeneous coloured beam is a stream of identical particles, though in what original property their identity lay Newton could never positively determine. When we mix two such beams of different colours, say red and blue, two streams of identical particles, each differing from those of the other stream, combine to form a new impression upon the eye, in this case purple. On the basis of this theory of the atomicity of the light-particles, groups of which can be combined or separated without the identity of a single particle ever being altered, Newton was able to account for the ordinary colours of objects seen in white light as well as the spectral colours, a feat beyond Descartes.

Since its 'colour' (whatever the physical property may be that we recognize as such) is a characteristic feature of each light-particle correlated with its refrangibility, it follows that on the gross scale colours can be changed by the addition or subtraction of particles, but not by altering the immutable particles themselves in any way. Nor can the compound beam be modified (save by addition and subtraction of light), for example by its proximity to the shadow, since its constituents are as immutable as atoms.

Newton usually speaks of these particles or atoms of light as 'rays', an ambiguous word. In geometrical optics a ray of light was represented as a continuous straight line, that is, as finite in length but infinitely small in thickness. Some early followers of Newton define 'ray' in this manner (for example, Smith 1738, p. 2) but Newton was careful in *Opticks* to define 'ray' as *discontinuous* or successive in time (Definition 1, p. 1) and when in the late Queries concluding the book his last thoughts were disclosed more plainly, it became clear that a light-ray had dimensions, can exert force, and can be in contact with another ray. The 'ray' is in fact a physical entity, perhaps a particle, not a geometrical figment.

Newton always insisted that his mathematical and experimental demonstrations of the properties of light did not depend in the least upon physical hypotheses about the nature of light. Thus he insisted that the compound nature of white light and the varied refrangibility of its component coloured rays were experimentally demonstrated facts, not inferences from some hypothesis of light. Thus his rejection of Cartesian affirmations—such as the impossibility of spectral colours' being formed without the assistance of the bounding shadow—was (he asserted) founded directly upon experimental evidence, not upon any difference in his own concept of light from that of Descartes.

The eye and vision

As the starting-point of Newton's investigation of refraction and subsequently of colour more generally may be found in Descartes's *Dioptrique* and *Météores*, so the former work provided his basic knowledge of the eye and the processes of vision. In turn, Descartes had drawn upon Kepler's optical writings, and so transmitted to Newton, with modifications, salient points from *Ad Vitellionem Paralipomena* (1604) and *Dioptrice* (1611), books little (if at all) studied by Newton himself, at least in his younger years. (Only a 1682 edition of *Dioptrice* was present in his library at his death.) Descartes had made a thorough anatomical study of the eye and its nervous connection to the brain, a topic to which Newton added little. The fundamental idea of vision as understood in the seventeenth century was that the lens near the front of the eye focuses an image of the outside world upon the back wall of the eye, where it falls upon the retina, which is a specialized development of the optic nerve. Or in Newton's words, the light entering the eye paints

the Picture of the Object upon that skin (called the *Tunica Retina*) with which the bottom of the Eye is covered. For Anatomists, when they have taken off from the bottom of the Eye that outward and most thick Coat called the *Dura Mater*, can then see through the thinner Coats, the Pictures of Objects lively painted thereon (1952, p. 15).

The transmission of the "Pictures" by motion along the fibres of the nerves to the brain (or sensorium, where they enter our consciousness) is, Newton explained much later, by an aetherial vibration. Of course Newton never supposed that the light-particles striking the eye penetrated to the sensorium. In Newton's physiology fibres from the right sides of both eyes join to reach the right side of the brain together, while other fibres from the left sides of both eyes join to reach the left side of the brain together, so that the two eyes make the same picture in the sensorium. Newton did not consider stereoscopic vision (pp. 346–7).

Behind the few sentences devoted by Newton to this topic lies a long tradition of enquiry and anatomical dissection; before Descartes, we need only note here Kepler's development of the concept of the eye as a kind of *camera obscura* in which pictures are painted (the comparison is specifically made by Newton) in *Ad Vitellionem Paralipomena*, and Felix Plater's observation that the retina is the structure in the eye that receives and transmits the image (1583). For Newton, Descartes provided a sufficient knowledge of this matter (see Crombie 1967).

Robert Boyle and Isaac Newton

Besides the French philosopher, two English authorities exercised a power-ful formative influence upon Newton during the mid-1660s. It is curious that although Newton at the end of his life owned 23 works by the first of them, Robert Boyle (1627–91), he did not own a copy of that most relevant to optics, *Experiments and Considerations touching Colours* (1664). Most of Boyle's books in Newton's library were published after their personal acquaintance began in the 1670s, many of them being presentation copies, yet Newton did own *New Experiments Physico-Mechanicall* (1660) and *New Experiments . . . touching Cold* (1665). But that Newton in youth read Boyle on colours very carefully is certain from his annotations. Boyle and Newton never had any common ground in mathematical science, but with relation to natural philosophy in the broadest sense and experimental method in particular they shared similar ideas. In so far as Newton thought science should be built up as a mosaic of carefully planned experiments, scrupulously performed, repeated, and recorded he had Boyle before him as a model. But more than this, Boyle had demonstrated how a deliberate programme of experiments could be used to test, explore, and extend a set of theoretical ideas; experimentation was not to be a random eliciting of new facts nor on the other hand a selective confirmation of preconceived ideas. For all Boyle's pose of noble amateurishness and the loose construc-tion of his treatises, they are in fact the result of careful preparation and forethought, as well as of skilled laboratory work; each constitutes an ingeniously articulated web of precise experimental reporting and theor-etical analysis. In this broad structural sense Boyle's books provided a model for *Opticks*, but Newton was also influenced by the mathematical, axiomatic type of structure which Boyle did not exemplify.

Boyle on colours

The central theme of Boyle's book is not optics in any conventional sense, but rather the relationship of the structure of matter to its optical properties, including colour. Sunlight Boyle is not much concerned with. Newton might have learned from him, however, the idea that the surface colours of bodies depend upon the physical characteristics of the surfaces, which facilitate the absorption or the reflection of light. Investigating the difference between blackness and whiteness Boyle satisfied himself that the former is an effect of high absorption, the latter of high reflectivity. This relationship he was able to illustrate by an experiment with a clay tile. Part was left its natural red, part of it was painted black, and part painted white. Exposed to the heat and light of the sun, 'whilst the whited part of the Tile remained Cool enough, the Black'd part of the same Tile was grown not only Sensibl[y], but very Hot' (pp. 126–7), while the red was of an intermediate temperature. (Such a variation of heat absorption with colour had been observed long before by Benedetto Castelli.)

After reviewing six different notions ancient and modern about the nature of colour, Boyle reiterated three statements that seemed to him well-founded:

1. The colours of bodies are not qualities (in Aristotle's sense) of the bodies themselves, but are characteristics of the light reflected from or refracted by the bodies to the eye. Newton was to agree with this.

2. Coloured light—light bearing this sense of colour to the eye—is white light modified in some way. Newton was to reject the idea that the physical nature of light can be modified.

3. The modification, whatever it may be, is effected by a 'Quality residing in the body that is said to be Colour'd'.

In Boyle's meaning this 'Quality' is wholly mechanical: it is

a certain disposition, whereby they [bodies] do so trouble the Light that comes from them to our Eye, as that it there makes that distinct Impression, upon whose Account we say, that the Seen body is either White or Black, or Red or Yellow . . . (p. 21).

He imagined it as a more or less rough or complex surface texture. Boyle admitted that this hypothesis

concerning the differing forms of Asperity in Bodies, by which Differences the incident Light either comes to be Reflected with more or less of Shade . . . or else happens to be otherwise Modify'd or Troubl'd, is but Conjectural . . .

but he hoped that with more perfect microscopes such as 'I fear are more to be wish'd than hop'd for' men might actually see the particles forming the surface structures of bodies and their various effects upon incident light (p. 40). Newton expressed the same hope.

Boyle's is thus a two-factor theory: one factor, inherent in the nature of light, interacts with a second factor, inherent in the structure of bodies (in transparent materials the factor is obviously not limited to the surface). As we shall see, Newton's theory of the natural colours of bodies is also a two-factor theory of a similar kind, but each of Newton's two factors is differently conceived from Boyle's.

As regards the modification of white light that (in his view) causes it to appear coloured Boyle felt it unnecessary for his purposes to propose a definite model. The limitations of his endeavour are expressed in a manner presaging Newton's analogous declarations later:

But whether I think this Modification of the Light to be perform'd by Mixing it with Shades, or by Varying the Proportion of the Progress and Rotation of the *Cartesian Globuli Coelestes*, or by some other way which I am not now to mention, I pretend not here to Declare. Much less do I pretend to Determine, or scarce so much as to Hope to know all that were requisite to be Known, to give . . . a perfect account of the Theory of Vision and Colours, for in order to such an undertaking I would first Know what Light is, . . . Then I would Know the Nature of Refraction, which I take to be one of the Abstrusest things (not to explicate Plausibly, but to explicate Satisfactorily) that I have met with in Physicks; I would further Know what Kind and what Degree of Commixture of Darkness or Shades is made by Refractions or Reflections, or both, in the Superficial particles of those Bodies, that being Shin'd upon, constantly exhibit the one, for Instance, a Blew, the other a Yellow . . . These, and perhaps other things I should think requisite to be Known, before I should judge my Self to have fully Comprehended the True and Whole Nature of Colours . . . (pp. 90–2).

I make no apology for this long quotation, because one can almost imagine the twenty-two year old Newton, full of unacknowledged ambition, finding in it a programme for his own future investigations.

Newton's reading of Boyle's Colours

His surviving annotations upon Boyle's *Colours* in his notebooks are, it must be confessed, of a more humdrum character; for example:

Lignum Nephriticum sliced & . . . infused . . . reflects blew rays & transmits yellow ones.

The flat peices of some kinds of Glase will exhibit the same Phaenomena with Lignum Nephriticum (Hall 1955, p. 28).

The former passage is based on Boyle's book, Part III, Experiment 10 (pp. 199–212), the second on Experiment 11 (pp. 216–19). Humdrum: but Newton never forgot this curious (and sometimes beautiful) property of certain materials to appear differently coloured by transmitted and reflected light (like the well-known Roman 'Lycurgus' Cup); it re-appears in *Opticks*, Book II, Part III, Proposition 5 (p. 252). Newton found, following Hooke's lead, as we shall see, that a certain thickness of glass will reflect (say) blue while transmitting the remaining reddish light; at a different thickness the converse will be seen. So the particles in the solution of the pharmaceutical wood must be of such a size as to be like thin layers of glass, transmitting the yellow/red end of the spectrum while reflecting the blue/green.

Mamiani has pointed out that Boyle gave Newton far more precise stimulus than this (1976, pp. 83–5; 1986, pp. 17 ff). In Part III, Experiment 4 of *Colours* Boyle embarks on trials with a prism:

And this we thought might be Best done, not (as is usual) in an ordinary Inlightn'd Room, where (by reason of the Difficulty of doing otherwise) ev'n the Curious have left Particulars Unheeded, which may in a convenient place be easily taken notice of; but in a Darken'd Room, where by placing the Glass in a convenient Posture, the Various Reflections and Refractions may be Distinctly observ'd; and where it may appear *what* Beams are Unting'd, and *which* they are, that upon the Bodyes that terminate them, do Paint either the Primary or Secondary Iris (pp. 191–2).

Boyle's language is rather strange, and he set his prism in perhaps the worst possible position; nevertheless he furnished Newton with an experimental plan very different from Descartes's. Like Newton later, though far less fruitfully, Boyle examined the spectrum formed by a narrow beam of light and also subjected the beam refracted through the prism to further reflections and refractions, finding 'that Refraction did as little Destroy those Colours as Reflection' (p. 193), a conclusion that Newton was to develop with great precision.

At the theoretical level, however, Newton's departure from Boyle's admittedly indefinite notion that light is 'troubled' or 'modified' by contact with matter was fundamental, though if we give Boyle the benefit of the doubt with regard to the significance of 'shades' the transition from his ideas about the colours of bodies to Newton's is quite easy. One point should be clear: in any ordinary sense of the word, light is *modified* when shone through a filter, or diffracted, or dispersed by refraction, or partially absorbed in reflection. If the light were wholly unmodified it would remain white, not become coloured. To make the distinction between different concepts turn upon *this* word was and is erroneous. The real difference between the concepts of Descartes, Boyle, and Hooke on the one hand, and of Newton on the other, is that according to the former colour is a quality made by the filter (etc.) while according to the latter it is a basic entity revealed. The essence of the Newtonian theory of colour (and hence of light) is that true colours always exist, just as atoms always exist, and cannot by any process be created (except by the creation of white light). The rays are the colours and the colours are the rays, or to be more physically exact the property of the ray that we perceive as colour is indissolubly part of it and cannot be altered. True, if we combine blue and yellow we make a green, but this is not the homogeneous green of the spectrum since it yields to analysis by the prism or other means. The atomic character of a true green ray renders it incapable of change. Therefore we might better term the so-called 'modification' theories, theories of *labile colour* and Newton's theory, a theory of *real colour*. Of the latter Boyle had no inkling. But his hypothesis that the structure of bodies acts upon light, causing colours to appear, is valid, whether the colours are considered to be factitious or real.

Hooke: the colours of thin plates

Robert Hooke (1635–1703) had constructed the air-pump with which Boyle experimented at Oxford during the late 1650s, and for his own use made a compound microscope with which he began to prepare the magnificent plates of insects and other small objects published in *Micrographia* (1665). Boyle had proposed the examination of the colours in mother-of-pearl with the microscope (p. 40); Hooke used his instrument to examine 'Muscovy glass' or talc, a fissile transparent mineral (Observation 9). Looking at a thin flake of it he saw white specks or flaws

and others diversely coloured with all the Colours of the *Rainbow*; and with the *Microscope* I could perceive, that these Colours were ranged in rings that incompassed the white speck or flaw, and were round or irregular, according to the shape of the spot which they terminated; and the position of Colours, in respect of one another, was the very same as in the *Rainbow* (Hooke 1665, p. 48).

A succession of as many as ten sets of rings might be seen, each in the order blue, purple, scarlet, yellow, green, with sometimes a bright spot of one colour at the centre. He also observed that a fairly large area of one flake might be tinged with colour, another with another colour, and that by superposition of these patches of colour a third colour might be formed, 'As perhaps a *faint yellow* and a *blew* may produce a very *deep purple*' (p. 49).

Hooke at once perceived that the colour seen was in some way a function of the thickness of the talc, and further found that if two pieces of dry polished glass were pressed together, 'that when they approach each other very near, there will appear several *Irises* or coloured Lines, in the same manner almost as in the *Muscovy-glass*'. Or liquids could be put between the plates; and very thin blown glass, and soap-bubbles, manifested the same colours; Hooke supposed the colours of hot metals and of such natural objects as mother-of-pearl or organic films to have the same origin (p. 53).

Hooke's theory of optical pulses

These phenomena 'of thin plates' led Hooke into a long essay upon colour, in order to explain them, beginning inevitably with Descartes, whom Hooke follows closely in geometry though not in physics. The new colours he had found did not have a shadow boundary to spin Descartes's optical globuli, nor result from refraction. What is Light? asks Hooke: it is a *short vibrating motion* in the luminous body (which may be cold, like phosphorescent matter). This vibration spreads out symmetrically through the uniform transparent medium (or aether) surrounding the luminous source in the form of pulses, each of an expanding spherical shape. A beam of light arises when the spherical expansion of the pulses is obstructed, save where an aperture permits them to pass through in a straight line; the pulses are equally spaced, identical, and at right angles to the beam. But should this beam fall upon an interface bounding a second transparent medium, the pulses will travel more or less quickly than in the first, as with the Cartesian globuli. In consequence, as Hooke explains in detail, the pulse becomes distorted: it is no longer normal to the beam, and the leading edge is blunted by attrition. This distortion of the pulses constitutes colour; the distinction between colours is in the asymmetry of the refracted beam (Fig. 4a):

Blue is an impression on the Retina of an oblique and confus'd pulse of light, whose weakest part precedes, and whose strongest follows . . . Red is an impression on the Retina of an oblique and confus'd pulse of light, whose strongest part precedes, and whose weakest follows.

Descartes's account of rainbow colours had been refuted, in Hooke's view.

On the basis of these notions, Hooke's explanation of the thin-plate colours he had first described is highly ingenious and indeed prescient. He recognized that light would be reflected back to the eye by both the upper and the lower surfaces of the plate, and the light reflected from the lower surface he assumed to be weaker than the other (Fig. 4b). The combined beam of light reaching the eye would accordingly contain two streams of pulses, one stream weaker than the other. The two sets of pulses would be out-of-phase with each other by rather more than twice the thickness of the plate. Four patterns of the combined sets of pulses are possible: strong closely followed by weak, or weak closely followed by strong; and the same pairs with the spacing nearly equal. In Hooke's theory the former case was appropriate to red and the second to blue; the other cases would give intermediate colours.

The chief elements in Hooke's theory to be later rejected by Newton are: (1) Light is a motion in the aether; Newton did not believe such a motion could possess either the atomicity or the rectilinearity of light. (2) Colours in light are labile qualities made by distorting the physical state of white light, so that if (for instance) we could restore a red ray to its pristine

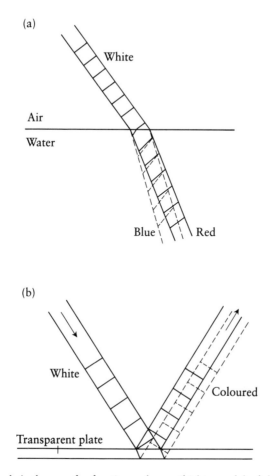

Fig. 4. (a) Hooke's theory of refraction colours; (b) his model of the formation of the colours of thin plates. After *Micrographia*, Scheme V, figs. 1, 2, and 6.

condition by an inverse refraction, it would then be white. Newton believed that true colours are real; they are changed only by the subtraction or addition of immutable rays. (3) 'the *Phantasm* of Colour is caus'd by the sensation of the *oblique* or uneven pulse of Light which is capable of no more varieties than two that arise from the two sides of the *oblique* pulse though each of these be capable of infinite gradations or degrees' (p. 67). Hooke meant that the colour-making physical change in light is dualistic and that all colours other than the two polar colours blue and red (or yellow; for Hooke could not decide whether red or yellow is the polar opposite of blue) are diluted or mixed forms of these two. Newton believed that the range of coloured rays filling the spectrum between violet and red is infinite, but that there are seven principal primary colours. (4) Data from experiments on pigments can be used in the construction of a theory about the spectral colours. Newton believed that this only caused confusion and error. (5) The dispersion of the refracted ray does not need to be accounted for; like Descartes, Hooke seems tacitly to suppose that the refracted ray diverges—such divergence is shown in his diagrams and is entailed by his theory—only because the sun is not a point source of light.

I shall consider Hooke's positive influences upon Newton in a moment.

Newton's annotations upon *Micrographia* exist, but they are naturally undated. Assuming that he had no access to such a new scientific book at his home in Lincolnshire, he might have read it at Cambridge during the first six months of 1665, or during the spring of 1666, but not after that before April 1667. We have no reason to exclude the first possibility. Newton's annotations are extensive—14 pages in the edition of Hall and Hall (1962). They cover pages 4 to 234 of *Micrographia*. The optical material (relating to pages 48 to 83 of the book) occupies nearly three pages of the notes. Almost all Newton's comments are hostile, for example:

[page] 60 Though Descartes may bee mistaken so is Mr Hook in confuting his 10 Sec. 38 Cap. Meteorum . . .

[page] 56. 62. Light is a vibration of the Aether. Why then may not light deflect from streight lines as well as sound &c? How doth the formost weake pulse keepe pace with the following stronger & can it bee then sufficiently weaker.

[page] 73 [Upon Hooke's contention that colours are changed by dilution] Object[ion]: The thickness of some liquors varys not their colours only makes them more or lesse strong. nor are all redds diluted to yellow by more water nor can yellow layd upon yellow make a red.

Except with regard to colours, Newton seems to have accepted *Micrographia* as a source of reliable information and sound ideas. He so far admired Hooke as an experimenter that he twice referred to Hooke, not Robert Boyle, as having proved Boyle's Law—called by Newton "Mr Towneley's Hypothesis" (Hall and Hall 1962, pp. 223, 399).

Since Newton recorded in these *Micrographia* notes (ibid., p. 403) as his own observation dilation of the coloured circles when the eye is held obliquely, it is possible that Newton's earliest optical experiments had been initiated before he read that book, and that he had seen "the colours of thin plates" already. We must, however, assign to Hooke the first perception that the rings of colours imply a periodicity in light, in his case expressed in the periodicity of the pulses. When Newton for the first time (in 1666?) experimented upon Newton's rings (as we may now, however unfairly, call them) he too recognized the physical evidence of periodicity, and indeed wrote of the "pulses" having a "thickness" that varied with the colour of the ring. Precisely what functions the pulses were to perform is not at all clear, nor does it become clear in the later and more experimentally exact paper (*c*.1670?) on "Coloured Circles betwixt two contiguous Glasses" first published in Westfall (1965). It is inconceivable that Newton ever took the pulses to be light, as Hooke did. By 1672 at latest, as we shall see, Newton had simplified Hooke's complex pulse model to an elegant wave-theory in which the wave-lengths are correlated with colour, but for Newton these waves are *not* light. Light is a stream of particles; but in the 1672 theory the interaction of the particles with matter is modulated by aether-waves which are disturbances in the aether caused by the light-particles passing through it. This theory was in turn revised into the theory of 'fits' in *Opticks*, which we may take as the final evidence of Hooke's influence upon Newtonian concepts of light and colour.

Marcus Marci on the rainbow

Incongruous as it may seem, for the sake of completeness a few words must be said about a book Newton could not have read: *Thaumantias: liber de arcu coelestis deque colorum apparentium natura, ortu & causis* (1648). Its author, Marcus Marci (1595–1667), a Bohemian, professor of medicine at Prague University, was the most active scientific investigator in Bohemia at this period, though in England his name was known only indirectly as that of a speculative philosopher (Marek 1968).

The intellectual context of Marci's work on the rainbow was very unlike that of Newton's and their fundamental concepts were far different. Marci seems to have known no writer on optics after Kepler. He rejected the idea that colour is dependent upon a mixture of light and shade, but he does find its cause in a qualitative change in light: 'Condensation changes colour both in kind and degree' (p. 6). This assertion is justified by references to dyes and pigments. Marci devoted an unnumbered chapter of *Thaumantias* to the *Iris trigonia*, the prismatic rainbow, containing 36 theorems (pp. 94–131). His account suffers from ignorance of Snel's Law and Descartes's *Dioptrique* (see Theorem XI) and like Boyle he turned his prism so that its vertex pointed to the sun. He explained that the colours could only be seen in a darkened room and (curiously) defined only four of them: red, green, blue, and purple (p. 95). These colours in the beams of light emerging from the prism are, he supposed, caused by variations in the condensation of light as it shines through varying thickness of the prism (p. 88: 'Cum itaque condensatio lucis mutet colores tam in specie, quam in gradu per Theorem 2: diversae lucis refractiones causabunt colores diversos'). Marci certainly had no idea that homogeneous coloured rays are the constitutents of white light. Theorem XVIII asserts that the same colour cannot [arise] from a different refraction, nor can several colours [arise] from the same [refraction]; Marci means that all things being equal (I presume with the prism set in its fixed position), a greater refraction causes a greater condensation of the light and so a different colour, and vice versa, and therefore a particular colour corresponds to each refraction. (Note that Marci speaks always of *refractions* and never of *refrangibility*.) He seems here to be making a logical rather than an experimental point; the same cause (that is, refraction) must always produce the same effect (that is, colour). Theorem XX provided the closest anticipation of Newton's results: when a coloured ray submits to a second refraction it does not alter the nature of its colour ('Refractio superveniens radio colorato non mutat speciem coloris'—p. 100). One experiment in proof of this proposition is as follows: 'Place a globe of glass between the eye and a prism; you will see the light of a candle with its colours, inverted.' Although the image has been inverted by the globe, its refraction has not changed the colours.

Thus, to a limited extent, Marci enunciated propositions reminiscent of Newton's in their language, but carrying very different overtones of meaning and especially lacking all the particular theoretical force that Newton was to bring out in his Optical Lectures and short first communication of 1672. Marci was no Newtonian *avant la lettre* and his ideas of light and colour in no way anticipated Newton's; as Lohne writes: 'his books abound in incoherent and often contradictory *ad hoc* explanations' (Lohne 1968, p. 175). Unfortunately for him, Marci lived far outside the post-Keplerian circulation of optical discoveries and ideas in Europe, and therefore his investigation could find no place within it.

Isaac Barrow's lectures upon optics

There can hardly be a greater contrast than that between *Thaumantias* and the last book to be mentioned here, Isaac Barrow's *Lectiones XVIII . . . in quibus opticorum phaenomenon genuinae rationes investigantur, ac exponuntur* (1669). It is a book very largely devoted to the geometry of image-location. Its 'principal achievement was to determine the location of the image after any reflection or refraction in plane and spherical surfaces', looking back to the earlier work of Kepler (Shapiro 1990, p. 105). Barrow repeated the old distinction between *lux* (that which reaches the eye directly from the luminous source) and *lumen* (the light reflected, scattered, or otherwise affected by interaction with bodies before it reaches the eye) but explicitly disclaimed any intention of entering into physical optics by discussing the nature of light (Whewell 1860, II, pp. 14–15). Subsequently, Barrow specified the properties of rays so that the diffusion of light could be treated geometrically (ibid., pp. 18–29). There was originality in the geometry of the book that won Newton's admiration, but there were no experiments and Barrow's remarks on colour 'were scarcely less shadowy than the Cartesian hypothesis . . . they were meant to supplant' (Whiteside 1969, p. 438). They indicate a concept not dissimilar from Boyle's: coloured light is white light modified by interaction with the corpuscular surfaces of bodies, which weaken, thicken, or dilute it; the chief colours are red and blue, green is akin to blue (*'Discrimen* explorent sagaciores . . .'!), yellow a weak red, purple a mixture (Whewell 1860, II, pp. 107–8). Barrow, twelve years older than Newton and sixteen years his senior in Trinity College, Cambridge (of which he was appointed Master in 1673) combined strong abilities in both mathematics and theology with a conservative temperament that imposed a self-exile from England during the Cromwellian years and an utter conformity in Church and State. As a man, he was very unlike Newton; as a scholar, he perceived and encouraged his brilliant if eccentric 'pupil' (which, formally, Newton never was).

§3. The birth of physical optics

The development of the telescope

It might be argued that the fundamental event in the development of geometrical optics during the seventeenth century was a practical discovery of 1608, that of the 'Dutch' or 'Galilean' telescope (Van Helden 1977). For two generations men had sought a way to combine lenses, or lenses and mirrors, so that a sharp, magnified image of a distant object would be formed on the eye, just as a single convex lens would form such an image of a nearby object. Theory had not been of much use to the seekers; after success had been attained, it was for the geometers to find out how to explain it. This was a more real and fertile problem than such teasers as Alhazen's Problem (given a mirror of any regular geometrical form, for example a cylinder, to find on the mirror the places at which light is reflected from one of two arbitrarily fixed points to the other), by no means neglected in the seventeenth century (Hall and Hall 1965–86, x, *passim*). The telescope presented other problems besides those of image-formation: how could its aperture and magnification be increased, how could the quality of its image be improved? To such questions Newton gave his own startling answers, his preference for the reflecting telescope (soundly grounded in his theory) being in a sense vindicated by the supremacy of that form in the largest astronomical telescopes from the time of William Herschel onwards.

New phenomena of light

Since Newton actually constructed the first reflecting telescope—giving it a configuration of his own invention though he did not invent the principle of magnification by reflection—we may consider this as much a practical invention as was (say) the Huygenian eyepiece. But whereas Huygens was, like Isaac Barrow, Newton's predecessor in the Lucasian Professorship of Mathematics at Cambridge, a man profoundly interested in geometrical optics, Newton was not. True, his complete mastery of this specialized field of applied mathematics is unquestionable (Whiteside 1969, pp. 435–542), and his assistance to Barrow in seeing his Lucasian *Lectiones XVIII opticorum* into print is well known, but Newton's real enthusiasm was for experimental and philosophical enquiries in optics. It is a truism that Newton created the science of physical optics. As geometrical optics was promoted by the invention of the refracting telescope, so of course physical optics was promoted by serendipitous discoveries, such as Ole Rømer's of the finite velocity of light (1676), to which we might add phosphorescence and (much later) electroluminescence. The most important new phenomena of light were, however, those elicited by men deliberately engaged in such work: Robert Hooke's observation of thin-plate colours (1665), Erasmus Bartholin's of birefringence (1669), Newton's of the elongated spectrum (1672). The most puzzling, if not as yet the most significant, of all these was diffraction, discovered by Francesco Maria Grimaldi (1665), because diffraction demonstrated an interaction between light and ordinary opaque matter. Nor was this the only new observation tending to show that the interactions between matter and light were far from straightforward, ranging beyond the anciently-known effects of reflection and refraction. Boyle and Newton clarified the concept of absorption—that whatever the physical nature of light, it must somehow incorporate itself with matter. On the other hand, recently established ideas about the celestial spaces and the structure of matter suggested that ordinary matter was not needed for the transmission of light, a suggestion confirmed by experiments with the air-pump. Observation also taught that the absorption of light—not yet distinguished from radiant heat—varied with the *colour* of the absorbing surface. Such things hinted that light should not be considered only as a metaphysical, or physiological or psychological entity, but that it was an entity having a definable physical nature, and that its associated phenomena, above all those of colour, also possessed an objective physical existence of some kind.

Mechanical models of light

In the philosophical and methodological context of the seventeenth century such hints could only be realized in terms of the mechanical philosophy of nature; simply put, the physical nature of light had to be expressed in the mechanical model. It was one of the weaknesses of the ancient atomism recently revived by Gassendi (and others before him) that it could not yield such a model for light of any credibility. However, two good mechanical models were available: one was the material, emission, or projectile theory; the other, the undulatory, pulse, or motion theory. The former was closer to the ancient atomic tradition; it matched the cognate idea of 'heat atoms'; it could account for the interactions of light and matter such as absorption.

The second exploited the fertile analogy between light and sound, so well developed by Newton himself, dogmatic enemy of the wave-hypothesis as he was. This analogy, treacherous in several ways yet one of the great new concepts of seventeenth-century science, was given mathematical intelligibility by Christiaan Huygens. (Newton's study of wave-motion and acoustics is highly important too, but it has nothing to do with light.) In spite of Huygens, Newton was to claim that the wave-theory failed because it could not be reconciled with the rectilinear propagation of light; if we set aside this possibly biased objection, the chief conceptual difficulty in it was that it entailed filling all the space and matter of the universe with a light-bearing aether, either too thin to offer resistance to planets and comets or capable of transporting them in their orbits. On the other hand, light-particles constantly radiated into and traversing the immense vacuities of space equally strained the physicists' credulity, since they must be virtually massless, swift, and paradoxical in their interactions with matter. Indeed, the problem of light strained beyond its capacities the duality of matter and motion as interpreted in seventeenth-century mechanical philosophy, because light required its principles to be extended to apparent voids. Light seemed to be an incredibly swift motion without a material agent (in the air-pump receiver, for example), but this was inconceivable. Therefore it was necessary to postulate either a space-filling aether to support vibrations or particles to shoot across it.

It is well known that the mathematical physics of optical wave-motion had to await elucidation, after the sound beginnings of Huygens's *Traité de la Lumière* (1690), from Young and Fresnel. It was Newton, rather than Hooke or Huygens, who pointed out that colour-differences might be hypothetically interpreted as sensations arising from real differences in the wave-lengths of the rays. But he adhered always to the view that the ray is a stream of particles, which possessed the great advantage that (after 1684) Newton knew how to calculate the trajectories of projectiles under the action of forces. His concept of optical force, introduced in the *Principia mathematica* (1687), imperfect as it was, at least made a plausible micro-physics of light possible and yielded the first general theory of the inter-actions between light and matter. It permitted one of the greatest of Newton's achievements in theoretical optics, the unification of reflection and refraction as physical processes. The greater speed of light in a denser medium is the rational consequence of the medium's stronger optical force. In principle, at least—for, as we shall see, grave difficulties obstructed Newton's realization of his dynamical dreams—the mechanics of optical force could account for every variety of curvature in the trajectories of the optical particles, the appearance of colours by the dispersion of light, and (more shakily) the effects arising from the absorption of light by matter.

But alas! dynamics alone could not resolve all the problems of light. The manifest periodicity of light—Hooke's terrible vengeance upon

Newton—could not be an intrinsic feature of an emission theory. Newton could not avoid grafting upon his dynamics a secondary theory, the theory of "fits of easy transmission and easy reflection", which plays an important role in the latter part of *Opticks*, coping not only with the colours of thin plates but with the complex phenomena occurring at the critical angle and the reflected colours of opaque bodies. The strange quasi-medical term "fits" (*vices* in Latin, 'alternations') can hardly disguise the fact that these are waves modulating the behaviour of each ray. The theory of "fits" has to be either purely arbitrary (that is, unintelligible) or else it demands the existence of an aether. A theory involving both particles and "fits", it seems, must be (in seventeenth-century terms) one that chooses the worst of all possible worlds, but Newton could find no escape. Indeed, in the course of long life he proposed three or more aetherial hypotheses.

Newton's methodology in Opticks

If Newton had meant to make *Opticks* a treatise strictly parallel to the *Principia mathematica*, setting out a dynamical theory of the emission of light-particles from luminous bodies, he would (as modern analyses show) certainly have failed. 'Newton had no real success in this goal for physical optics, in the sense that is true of his work on the motion of mass points under the action of central forces' (Cohen 1980, p. 136). Twenty years before *Opticks* assumed a coherent form he knew that emission alone could not account for Newton's rings; this was long before there was any systematic Newtonian mechanics. Accordingly, the main text of *Opticks* was set in a different mould: Newton analysed experiments, showed how mathematical regularities might be detected in them, and used these regularities to establish quantitative physical generalizations. These were then used to explain phenomena. So (in brief) by experiments on refraction in Book I he established the fixed identities of the rays of light; in Book II from the investigation of Newton's rings he established the sizes of the 'Fits'. Together, these theories accounted quantitatively for all manifestations of colour, save for those of diffraction, by which Newton was defeated in Book III.

There is no single 'Newtonian method' for composing an original work of science according to a formula. It has always been recognized that *Opticks* is a book of a very different stamp from the *Principia mathematica*. The latter contains some important experiments and many astronomical measurements, but no one would claim that these are essential to the development and structure of the exposition, as its experiments are essential to *Opticks*. This point is not affected by the fact that Newton in several places deliberately omitted from *Opticks* geometrical demonstrations that he had provided in his Optical Lectures, for if the Lectures could hardly be described as 'a book of experiments in a popular style', neither are they 'an illustration of the method of elaboration by mathematical techniques of the properties of imaginative [? imaginary] constructs' (Cohen 1980, p. xiv). The description of experiments is used to establish a detailed, organized picture of phenomena: so the whole content of Book II, Part I of *Opticks* is the reporting of 24 "Observations concerning the Reflexions, Refractions, and Colours of thin transparent Bodies". The quantitative analysis and interpretation of these follow in Part II. But Newton also used experiment inversely to confirm a prediction; then he employs "The Proof by Experiments". An especially interesting case occurs in Book I, Part I, Proposition 6. Newton sought to prove that just as the mean 'white' refracted ray obeys Snel's Law, so do the individual coloured rays, whose sines therefore are each in a constant proportion to the sine of the mean ray, and so to each other. (This implies, obviously, that the dispersion is a constant function of the refraction.) In Experiment 15, using glass prisms with different included angles, Newton showed that the positions of the various spectra cast—the sun meanwhile standing still, it seems!—were consistent with this constant proportionality of the sines of the refracted constituent rays. "So then the Proposition holds true in every Ray apart, so far as appears by Experiment" (*Opticks* 1952, p. 79). Now, Newton went on, it may also be demonstrated mathematically that this result is true, provided it is first granted "That Bodies refract Light by acting upon its Rays in Lines perpendicular to their Surfaces."

This is, of course, the very same assumption made by Descartes in *La Dioptrique* in order to demonstrate Snel's Law. But whereas Descartes could offer no valid reason for the acceleration of the light-ray as it enters a denser medium, and vice versa, Newton attributed the change of velocity to the greater or less optical force in the second medium. Pursuing this dynamic argument, he demonstrated that "The Sine of Incidence of every Ray [in a beam of white light] considered apart, is to its Sine of Refraction in a given Ratio", or to put this otherwise, Snel's Law holds for each individual coloured ray (though, since there is dispersion of the rays, the refractive index for each colour varies slightly). Upon this formal demonstration Newton comments:

And this Demonstration being general, without determining what Light is, or by what kind of force it is refracted, or assuming any thing farther than that the refracting Body acts upon the Rays in Lines perpendicular to its Surface; I take it to be a very convincing Argument of the full Truth of this Proposition.

So then, if the *ratio* of the Sines of Incidence and Refraction of any sort [that is, colour] of Rays be found in any one case, 'tis given in all cases; . . . (pp. 81–2).

Newton means, I presume, all cases of refraction between two specified mediums. 'Here then' remarks I. Bernard Cohen, 'is a single isolated instance of the working out, in the *Opticks*, of the method which I have characterized as being the essence of the science of the *Principia* and hence the source of the Newtonian revolution in science' (Cohen 1980, p. 136).

Nothing like this, certainly, is to be found in the Optical Lectures from which derives so much of Book I of *Opticks*, and indeed the sense of this proposition is no exception. In Lectures 14 and 15 of the manuscript version, or Lecture 8 of the printed version ["Oct 1670"] Newton investigated refraction at an interface very generally, of course by geometry: he considered light passing through one or more interfaces, into mediums of varying optical densities, at various angles of incidence, the interface being plane or curved. He proved, for example, that the dispersion varied with changes in these factors. He gave the purport of Proposition 6 of *Opticks* in rational form, unbuttressed by experiments or dynamical considerations such as the existence of an optical force, relying only upon Snel's Law. Presumably in 'October 1670' he did not have experimental evidence to hand in confirmation of his theorems, and certainly the dynamical treatment of refraction by Newton was still far in the future. It is not surprising that Proposition 6 should recall the method of the *Principia mathematica*, since it is based upon the very theory that was first exposed there (Book I, Section 14; Whiteside 1974, pp. 422–34).

Rational and dynamical reasoning

Thus we can readily identify two kinds of mathematical reasoning used by Newton. The first, frequently exemplified in the Optical Lectures, we may call *rational*, since it makes slight use of physical presuppositions, and these are cast in an idealistic geometrical form: rays of light are rectilinear, refraction follows Snel's Law of sines; in fact, this is a developed form of geometrical optics. The second, in Proposition 6 of *Opticks* and generally in the *Principia mathematica*, makes use of such dynamical entities as force and mass-points; it has been carefully analysed by Professor Cohen (1980). To me, it seems that the demonstration of the rainbow in Book I, Part II, Proposition 9 is also close to the *Principia* type of reasoning, though of course it is not dynamical. If we would seek justification for Newton's repeated contention that he had rendered the science of colours mathematical, for example in lines omitted from the printed version of his "New Theory about Light and Colours" (March 1672):

A naturalist would scearce expect to see the science of [colours] become mathematicall, & yet I dare affirm that there is as much certainty in it as in any other part of Opticks (Turnbull 1959, p. 96)

we should first look into the Optical Lectures, rather than the experimentally-weighted *Opticks*. In another passage also unprinted in Newton's lifetime (ibid, pp. 187–8) he told Robert Hooke that if the physical principles of optics be such that on them a Mathematician may determin all the Phaenomena of colours that can be caused by refractions, & that by computing or demonstrating after what manner & how much those refractions doe separate or mingle the rays in which severall colours are originally inherent; I suppose the *Science of Colours* will be granted *Mathematicall* & as certain as any part of *Opticks*. And that this may be done I have good reason to beleive, because ever since I became first acquainted with these Principles, I have with constant successe in the events made use of them for this purpose.

The restriction to refraction colours in the above passage is obviously significant. I read it as Newton's claim that he had rendered catoptrics and dioptrics, formerly monochromatic, fully polychromatic as is Nature herself.* The principles of which he wrote were the fixed identity of the rays, the immutable association of refrangibility with colour, and so on; by introducing these he had created a new polychromatic geometrical optics, which is to be found in the Optical Lectures (to which appeal is not infrequently made in *Opticks*). By this new geometrical optics he could, for example, compute how much more scattered the divergent coloured rays are at the focus of a lens, than are the white rays at the focus of a spherical mirror. In this restricted claim Newton was amply justified by his writings; this limited science of colour was fully mathematical in the first sense stated above.

Twenty years or so after addressing those lines to Hooke, Newton in *Opticks* restated virtually the same position rather more elaborately:

these Theorems [on the refraction and dispersion of light] being admitted into Opticks, there would be scope enough of handling that Science voluminously after a new manner, not only by teaching those things which tend to the perfection of Vision, but also by determining mathematically all kinds of Phaenomena of Colours which could be produced by Refractions. For to do this, there is nothing else requisite than to find out the Separations of heterogeneous Rays, and their various Mixtures and Proportions in every Mixture (Book I, Part II, p. 131).

A little later in the Book, Newton emphasized how essential an understanding of the composition of sunlight is for an understanding of the true theory of colours:

For if the Sun's Light is mix'd of several sorts of Rays, each of which have originally their several Refrangibilities and colorific Qualities, and notwithstanding their Refractions and Reflexions, and their various Separations or Mixtures, keep those their original Properties perpetually the same without alteration; then all the Colours in the World must be such as constantly ought to arise from the original

---

* So far as Newton was concerned, this distinction was one of tradition and convenience only. From a physical point of view, he maintained (Book II, Part III, Proposition 9, p. 269), bodies "reflect and refract Light by one and the same power, variously exercised in various Circumstances". In *Opticks* this identity of reflection and refraction is justified experimentally; in *Principia mathematica* Book I, Section 14, it is demonstrated dynamically.

colorific qualities of the Rays whereof the Lights consist by which those Colours are seen. And therefore if the reason of any Colour whatever be required, we have nothing else to do than to consider how the Rays in the Sun's Light have by Reflexions or Refractions, or other causes, been parted from one another or mixed together; or otherwise to find out what sort of Rays are in the Light by which that Colour is made, and in what Proportion (p. 160).

From the close connection in wording between this passage and the one quoted just before it is certain that Newton thought of the analysis and synthesis of sunlight he described as being a mathematically calculable, as well as an experimentally demonstrable process. And while he still laid the chief stress on polychromatic catoptrics and dioptrics, Newton now envisaged that the rays in sunlight might be separated by "other causes", of which more in a moment. The reader is also by now able to form a richer picture of the properties to be attributed to the particles (or "Rays") of Light: indestructibility, immutable refrangibility, and linked "colorific Quality" deriving from unknown features of physical structure, submission to the optical force of matter, ability to combine with matter but also to be ejected by matter, power to affect the nervous systems of living things . . . altogether a long (and still incomplete) list that (in my view) makes Newton's "Rays"—which moreover certainly possess dynamical properties— as much 'imaginary constructs' as any entity in Newtonian mechanics.

The theory of "fits"

As Newton embarked in Book II on quite new ground, not previously convered in his Optical Lectures, where factors other than ordinary reflection and refraction begin to dominate the phenomena, Newton's handling of them seems to become less confident. Book II, Part I contains some of his finest experimental work, upon Newton's rings. In Part II the reader is again assured that "all these things follow from the properties of Light by a mathematical way of reasoning" (p. 240), but it proved impossible to make them follow from the characters of the rays already defined; instead, in order to relate the succession of transmissions and reflections of light through thin plates to the various thicknesses of the plates or layers, Newton had to introduce a new quasi-mathematical property, at first called a "Disposition":

And what is said of their [the "several Rays"] Refrangibility may be also understood of their Reflexibility, that is, of their Dispositions to be reflected, some at a greater and some at a less thickness of thin Plates or Bubbles; namely, that those Dispositions are also connate with the Rays, and immutable; . . . (pp. 242–3).

Nevertheless, Newton *was* confident that the new phenomena confirmed the association between reflexibility, refrangibility, and colour established in Book I, and therefore he could still affirm that the colorifick Dispositions of Rays are also connate with them, and immutable; and by consequence, that all the Productions and Appearances of Colours in the World are derived, not from any physical Change caused in Light by Refraction or Reflexion, but only from the various Mixtures or Separations of Rays, by virtue of their different Refrangibility or Reflexibility. And in this respect the Science of Colours becomes a speculation as truly mathematical as any other part of Opticks (p. 244).

Another nail driven into Hooke's coffin!

Note that the alternating "colorifick Dispositions of Rays" to be transmitted or reflected are *not* the same as the connate "colorific Qualities" (p. 160) which identify the various rays when each is separated from white light. In the following Book III, Proposition 12 these "Dispositions" are renamed "fits", and the theory of "fits" in its relation to the colours of thin and thick plates and of the surface particles of bodies is developed in propositions subsequent to that. The "Dispositions" or "fits"—Newton continued to use the former term—are defined as

a certain transient constitution or State, which in the progress of the Ray returns at equal Intervals, and disposes the Ray at every return to be easily transmitted through the next refracting Surface, and between the returns to be easily reflected by it (p. 278).

Roughly speaking, the experimentally-measured thicknesses associated with successive rings of colour in Book II, Part I, have now been 'translated' into a series of regular states or alternations, transmission of a particular colour always coinciding with the presence of the 'peaks' at 0, 2, 4, 6, . . . and its reflection coinciding with the 'troughs' at 1, 3, 5, 7, ... Newton refused to give a considered physical meaning to this alternating state travelling along the ray (or stream of rays):

What kind of action or disposition this is; Whether it consists in a circulating or vibrating motion of the Ray, or of the Medium, or something else, I do not here enquire (p. 280).

Thus Newton left his readers with a purely phenomenalistic theory, admittedly of a quasi-mathematical character, which defied dynamical interpretation and of which he could offer no definite physical model.

The failure of mathematization

The final sixty pages or so of *Opticks* and the optical portions of the Queries that follow do not extend the great achievements of the preceding, more extensive part of the book, though they do contain accounts of excellent descriptive work. The theory of "fits" was left incomplete; Newton equally failed with birefringence and diffraction, at least he failed to relate these phenomena to any theory of the interactions between light and matter. The deep inconsistencies of his dynamical model could never be overcome either:

A rigorous and mathematical treatment of it would have demonstrated that the model violated one of the main rules for model construction, a rule which, as I have suggested, NEWTON had introduced into the methodology of theoretical science, namely, that only those features may be admitted into the atomic model which may be found to exist in the observable world (Bechler 1973, p. 35).

For all his magnificent development of polychromatic geometrical optics in Book I, including his precise determinations of the ratios between the breadths of the spectral colours and, even more remarkable, his very exact measures of 'Newton's Rings' in Book II, much of the hoped-for mathematization of the theory of colours was to remain no more than an 'idle dream' in so far as there was no fundamental mathematical–physical structure upon which it could rest, comparable to the theory of mechanics in the *Principia*. Hence one may agree with Bernard Cohen that Newton did not in *Opticks*

succeed in speaking in the same mathematical language of nature that he had employed in the *Principia* . . . the *Opticks* represents a level of inquiry far removed from that of the *Principia* and displays the enquiring mind of an experimental natural philosopher rather than that of a mathematical physicist (Cohen 1980, p. 141).

For example, there is nothing in the *Principia* like Newton's rather forced, repeated identification of spectral and musical intervals (*Opticks* 1952, pp. 126, 154; P. Gouk in Fauvel *et al.* 1988, pp. 101–24). But if, with our present highly mathematical view of the proper content of science we were tempted to conclude that the experimental natural philosopher is in some sense subservient to the mathematical physicist who formulates our most general ideas of Nature, we should be at odds with many of the eighteenth-century Newtonians, and their successors also. In Newton's lifetime non-mathematicians like John Locke, Stephen Hales, J. T. Desaguliers, and Denis Diderot delighted in the experimental method of *Opticks*, as Cohen emphasized in an earlier study (Cohen 1956, e.g. pp. 121–5, 159 ff.). Some early Newtonians seem to suggest that *Opticks* might be more fruitful for natural philosophy than the *Principia mathematica* would be for astronomy and mechanics. Though such expectations were not to be verified by posterity, Professor Cohen has opined that the speculations of the Queries did give a great impetus to such new branches of experimental physics as electricity, and Henry Guerlac has linked them with eighteenth-century chemistry. As we shall see, *Opticks* had the greater appeal for translators and popularizers, notably Algarotti and Voltaire. However, the high popularity of a book may indicate an almost excessively happy suitability to its environment; that *Opticks* was very much a book of its time and nation, while the *Principia mathematica* is a work of timeless immortality belonging to all of numerate mankind, few will doubt.

TWO

Preparations: experiment and polemic

§1. Early optical experiments, 1664–1666

First readings in science

Isaac Newton's early reading, first at school in Grantham then at the University of Cambridge, is surprisingly well known to us. Apart from the work necessitated by the usual courses of academic study, we know (for example) that as a boy he bought and read John Bates's *Mysteries of Nature and Art* (1634), from which he learned about ingenious mechanical contrivances of various types, and that three or four years later he studied Walter Charleton's *Physiologia Epicuro-Gassendo-Charltoniana* (1654) attentively. This latter book, confused as it is, either gave Newton his lifelong attachment to the atomistic philosophy or confirmed him in it. It was the first work of 'modern' natural philosophy that Newton read, so far as we know, and though Newton was to reject at once (or very soon) many of Charleton's detailed theories, including his treatment of light and colours, the influence of *Physiologia* on the young Newton was profound. After Charleton Newton went on to more original and more recent authors: Robert Boyle—whose *Experimental History of Colours* (1664) was critically important for its influence upon Newton in the present context, Robert Hooke's *Micrographia* (1665) which was no less influential upon Newton's optics, Henry More's *Immortality of the Soul* (1659), of lasting metaphysical significance, and not least the *Principia philosophiae* (1644) of René Descartes, to which Newton devoted great attention. Besides these he was reading mathematical authors like William Oughtred, John Wallis, and (again of great importance) Descartes, *La Géometrie* in the large edition of van Schooten. He probably attended Isaac Barrow's courses of mathematical lectures in Cambridge from March 1664 onwards. We know of this detailed preparation for a life's work because Newton in boyhood began to take notes of the books he read, a practice he continued for at least forty years, and these notes were carefully preserved by his heirs. Unfortunately, as dates are seldom met with among the notes, the absolute dating and even the temporal order of the various records is far from certain.

He begins optics

Besides the annotations from books, Newton's early notebooks (about 1661–6) record his own early thoughts about his reading: from the perpetual motion machines of his childhood to the physical theories of his university days. It is likely that Newton wrote down his first ideas about light and colours when he had read nothing more than Charleton's *Physiologia* (Hendry 1980). Its influence may be seen in the following note, for example:

Colours arise either from shadows intermixed with light, or stronger & weaker reflection, or parts of the body mixed with & carried away by light.

Later in his comments Newton found reason to reject both Descartes's interpretation of light as an aetherial pressure, and Hooke's theory of the propagation of a pulse in the aether:

Light cannot be by pression for then wee should see in the night as well or better than in the day . . . Why may not light deflect from streight lines as well as sounds . . . ?

Even thus early there are signs of a mechanical theory:

That darke colours seeme further of than light ones may be from hence that the beames loose little of their force in reflecting from a white body because they are powerfully assisted thereby but a darke body by reason of the looseness of its parts give[s] some admission to the light & reflects it but weakly . . . (Hall 1948, p. 246; Hendry 1980, pp. 231–3).

Although, as these notes indicate, optics was the first physical science pursued to any depth by Newton, the development of his experiments and theories to maturity occupied several years. His early annotations range widely—into physiology, for example—and his intense creative attention seems to have been first stimulated by pure mathematics, in which he ranged far outside any university requirements. Having plunged into mathematics with great success, owing to the sudden and rich flow of his original ideas, he turned next to its natural correlative, mechanics. Long afterwards Newton recollected this progress of his mental activity:

In the beginning of the year 1665 I found the Method of approximating series & the Rule for reducing any dignity of any Binomial into such a series. The same year in May I found the method of Tangents of Gregory & Slusius, & in November had the direct method of fluxions & the next year in January had the Theory of Colours & in May following I had entrance into the inverse method of fluxions. And the same year I began to think of gravity extending to the orb of the Moon . . . (ibid., p. 241).

According to this, then, Newton developed his "Theory of Colours" in January 1666, while in his very first publication Newton also reported:

in the beginning of the year 1666 (at which time I applied myself to the grinding of Optick glasses of other figures than *Spherical*,) I procured me a Triangular glass-Prisme, to try therewith the celebrated *Phenomena* of *Colours* (Letter 40, p. 92).

Provided we are willing to allow Newton no more than a few weeks for his initial experiments with the prism, and the first perception of his "Theory of Colours", the later account is consistent with this previous (1672) statement in print, as of course Newton intended.

However, as with other men, Newton's autobiographical assertions are not to be trusted without verification. It is evident that not only was Newton's memory fallible, but (in drafting the printed statement of 1672) he had a rhetorical purpose. He wished to emphasize that his new theory of light and colour—which he was about to outline—sprang immediately from his observations of the elongation of the prismatic spectrum. He had no wish to retread at this point the actual, more tortuous route by which he had taught himself that differently coloured rays of light have different susceptibilities to refraction. He therefore suppressed, in this first printed paper, any allusion to his earliest optical experiments, with the object of making that discovery which he had described as "being in my Judgement the oddest if not the most considerable detection which hath hitherto beene made in the operations of Nature" stand out directly and starkly as flowing from a single experimental fact (Letter 35, p. 83).

Cambridge influences

It is quite possible that Newton's interest in optics was aroused in 1664, the year of his first mathematical accomplishments. At this time Newton was still an undergraduate at Trinity College, Cambridge University, and may not yet have passed his twenty-second birthday. Surviving evidence indicates that though he was elected first a Scholar, and later a Fellow, of his College, Newton displayed no extraordinary brilliance in going through the by now rather old-fashioned curriculum of studies; the brilliance appears only in his private notes. He was just possibly, in this time of his early development, already acquainted with Isaac Barrow, Fellow of his own College and Lucasian Professor of Mathematics, and with Henry More, Fellow of Christ's College. These two men were both luminaries in a University not remarkable for creative talent. Barrow had no formal responsibility for Newton's education, but it was Barrow who first introduced Newton's name into London mathematical circles (1669) and it was Barrow whose *Lectiones XVIII opticorum*, printed in the same year, acknowledged Newton's assistance. Henry More was a man of a very different stamp from the hard-headed Barrow. He was a metaphysical philosopher and theologian. Newton had been born only a few miles from More's home town of Grantham; they had attended the same school there, and had common acquaintances. Newton was deeply impressed by More's book on *The Immortality of the Soul* (1659), from which he derived a lifelong conviction of the reality of atoms. It is possible that one or both of these senior scholars urged Newton to the study of the writings of René Descartes, which he certainly undertook at this time; More's had been the leading influence in making them known in England, and in Cambridge particularly.

Descartes, Boyle: first experiments with a prism

It was Descartes, indeed, who in his *Dioptrique* (1637) had advised that optical instruments should incorporate lenses with aspherical curvatures, in order to correct the baneful effects of spherical aberration, which he had himself revealed. Therefore Newton must have read Descartes before he began (early in 1666, or perhaps before then) his own attemps to grind "Optic glasses of other figures then Spherical", following Descartes's own mechanical methods. Newton's notes and sketches relating to this topic exist in a notebook on pages headed "Of Refractions", the same notebook also containing mathematical material dating to the years between 1663 and 1665 (Hall 1955). Other notebooks indicate the even earlier formative influence of Robert Boyle's *Experiments and Considerations touching Colour* (dated 1664, but probably on sale before the close of 1663). It is likely that Newton read this book fairly soon after its publication. From it he derived much material about the colours of bodies and the chemistry of colour, incoporated into his long compilation 'Quaestiones quaedam Philosophiae' ('Some Problems in Philosophy'). These notes and reflections are very wide-ranging; the section of "Of Colours" forms a large part of the whole and draws heavily upon Boyle's book. Newton noted: "no colours arise out of the mixture of pure black and white" then proposed to himself the experiment "try if two prisms the one casting blew upon the other's red doe not produce a white" (Hall 1948, p. 247; McGuire and Tamny 1983). It then becomes evident that Newton already possessed at least one prism, and that with this he did actually try the effect of shining a single colour from a prism upon a coloured surface: "Blue from a prism falling upon red gives green."

No doubt Newton also looked at objects through the prism, placing it upon a printed page, for example. If he placed the prism upon some such material as coloured woven fabric, he might have noticed that straight lines parallel to the axis of the prism no longer appeared straight and continuous. This suggested the following experiment (Fig. 5):

If one halfe of the thred *abc* be blew & the other red & a shade or black body be put behind it then looking on the thred through a prism one halfe of the thred shall appear higher than the other, not both in one direct line, by reason of the unequal refraction in the differing colours (Hall 1948, pp. 247–8).

Newton had discovered that "the rays which make blew are refracted more than the rays which make red". Thus early appears Newton's fundamental discovery, unbeknownst to him already stated in 1648 by Marcus Marci of Prague, and of course implied by Descartes's theory of the rainbow. In "Some

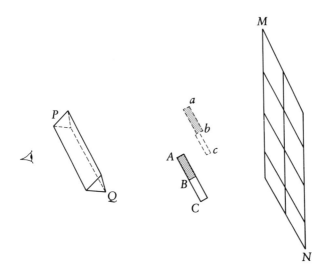

Fig. 5. Newton discovers that blue light is more refracted than red. *ABC* the "thread" (or slip of paper) half (*AB*), blue, half red, seen normally. *abc* the raised image of the 'thread' as seen through the prism (PQ), the blue (*ab*) more refracted than the red (*bc*). After *Opticks*, p. 22, and Hall (1955), p. 28.

Problems in Philosophy" Newton not only described other experiments on colours seen through the prism, and on mixtures of colours, but speculated on the reasons for the unequal refrangibility of rays of different colours. He clearly imagined the rays to be composed of a physical body (or bodies) travelling from the source to the eye, and hypothesized that the significant factor modified by refraction is the velocity of the ray, for "slowly moved rays are refracted more than swift ones". Now the experiments showed that rays which make blue are more refracted than those that make red, implying that the red rays are the more swift. The middle colours of the spectrum are of mean velocity.

Hence redness, yellowness &c are made in bodys by stoping the slowly moved rays without much hindering of the motion of the swifter rays, & blew, greene & purple by diminishing the motion of the swifter rays & not of the slower (ibid., p. 248).

Here Newton proposed a mechanism of velocity-selection whereby either refraction in transparent bodies, or reflection in opaque ones, might alter the balance between the variously coloured rays confused in white light, so that the resultant beam would seem coloured. Though the slower blue rays would be more bent or absorbed than the faster red ones, the nature of the rays themselves was not changed. The idea that the surfaces of bodies appear of a certain colour because they reflect it preferentially was expressed earlier by Boyle.

To us, it seems obvious that Newton's hypotheses imply the notion that the colours made manifest by refraction or reflection are contained in white light. If a body appears red because the blue rays have been "stoped" and the red reflected without much hindering of their motion, it must be the case that the incident white light already was composed of the blue, red, and other rays. Such indeed was Newton's meaning. And he could similarly speculate that light might (alternatively) consist of a variety of corpuscles of different sizes, all moving at the same speed; neither refraction nor reflection could be supposed to alter the *sizes* of the corpuscles, but these processes might (somehow) selectively separate one size (and colour) from another.

However, Newton's earliest optical notes (as it seems) make no mention of such a heterogeneity in white light, nor of the passage of a beam of sunlight through a prism to form a spectrum. When Newton returned to optical experiments, presumably after reading Descartes's *Dioptrique* and *Météores*, having now a better understanding of refraction and of Descartes's colour-theory, his new set of notes again begins with a summary of Boyle's work, and then he repeats the experiment of colours seen through a prism:

On a black peice of paper I drew a line *opq* whereof one halfe *op* was a good blew the other *pq* a good deepe red . . . And looking on it through the Prisme *adf*, it appeared broken in two betwixt the colours, as at *rst*, the blew parte *rs* being nearer the vertex *ab* of the Prisme than the red parte *st*. Soe that blew rays suffer a greater refraction than red ones (Hall 1955, p. 28).

In a slightly modified form this experiment, omitted from Newton's first optical paper (1672), re-appeared in *Opticks*, Book I, Part 1, Experiment 1. The following Experiment 2 of *Opticks* is also foreshadowed in the notebook as "the same experiment may be tryed with a thred of two colours held against the darke", which is also the same as that quoted from "Some Problems in Philosophy" above. In *Opticks* Newton used these two experiments to demonstrate his first theorem: "Lights which differ in Colour differ also in Degrees of Refrangibility", recording his first discovery. The continuity of the record is complete.

A beam shone through a prism

However, in these later notes Newton soon turned to the passage of a beam of light through a prism (Fig. 6):

Taking a Prisme, (whose angle *fbd* was about 60 gr) into a darke roome into which the sun shone only at one little round hole *k* and laying it close to the hole *k* in such manner that the rays, being equally refracted at (*n* & *h*) their going in & out of it cast colours *rstv* on the opposite wall. The colours should have beene in a round circle were all the rays alike refracted, but their forme was oblong terminated at their

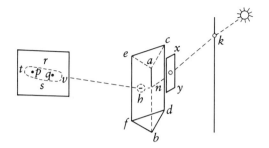

Fig. 6. Forming the spectrum by shining a beam of light through a prism. Newton sketched the second form of this experiment with the diaphragm *xy* added. After Hall (1955), p. 28.

sides *r* & *s* with streight lines; their bredth *rs* being 2⅓ inches, theire length *tv* about 7 or eight inches, & the centers of the red & blew, (*q* & *p*) being distant about 2¾ or 3 inches. The distance of the wall *trsv* from the Prisme being 260 inches (ibid.).

Having established that while the breadth of the spectrum corresponded to the sun's angular diameter of 31 minutes of arc, its length corresponded to a divergence between the limiting rays of about 1° 40′, Newton made a second experiment to measure the difference between the refractions of the blue and red rays more exactly: he placed a diaphragm pierced by a small hole at some (unspecified) distance from the round hole in the window-shutter, and then positioned his prism adjacent to the diaphragm. When the beam entering the prism was thus made almost parallel-sided, the spectrum was much reduced in size, but the ratio of length to breadth was greatly increased. Newton did not use this experiment in print, but the diaphragm idea was used again in the well-known 'crucial experiment'.

Obviously Newton employed several prisms. Included angles of 60°, 62½°, 63° 12′, 63½°, and 64° are mentioned (not requiring as many different prisms, of course) and some experiments are described as using as many as three at once. More than one place of experiment may be indicated by the various distances over which the spectrum was formed: 22 feet in the notes and first optical paper (1672), 18¼ feet in *Opticks*. In England, optical experiments for which sunlight is necessary have usually to be carried out in the summer, and because the sun and its image are constantly in motion some of the manipulations described by Newton must have been difficult to perform. Occasionally he mentions the use of an assistant (compare Mills 1981).

Simon Schaffer has emphasized Newton's transformation of the prism from being little more than an unusual toy (sold at Stourbridge fair!) to being a scientific instrument of precision from which scientific information of great theoretical import could be obtained (Schaffer 1989, 67 ff.) To the eighteenth century Newton was the author of universal gravitation, but he was also the man of the prism (see Chapter 4, §4). His precise and exhaustive experimentation upon the spectrum, and careful measurement of other refractive effects produced by the prism, gave him a wealth of ammunition with which to overwhelm critics of his own ideas about light and colours. As we shall see further below, the full richness of Newton's technique emerged only slowly, and to some extent the problems encountered by these critics in his narration of his results were exacerbated by their misunderstanding of his technique, as well as of his methodological position. A further difficulty impeding the repetition of Newton's optical experiments was the limited availability of glass of even fair optical quality: in Italy—and perhaps elsewhere—suitable prisms were not easy to obtain.

Optical experiments after the plague of 1665–1666

As Henry Guerlac has pointed out, Newton's mention of an assistant implies Cambridge—doubtless Newton's 'chamberfellow' and (later) amanuensis, John Wickins, would have served—rather than Newton's home at Woolsthorpe in Lincolnshire (Guerlac 1983, p. 75). The change from one notebook to another, the return to Boyle's book preceding the sequence of experiments just quoted, as well as the complexity and detail of the experiments themselves suggest a considerable break between the earlier series of experiments, which we may attribute to Cambridge *before* the outbreak of plague in the summer of 1665, and the later series using as many as three prisms, which we may attribute to Cambridge *after* the plague. In his first optical paper Newton related that his thoughts about the implications of his new notions about colour for the design of optical instruments were interrupted when he "was forced from *Cambridge* by the Intervening Plague, and it was more than two years before I proceeded further" (Letter 40, pp. 95–6). We know that Newton was absent from Cambridge from June or July 1665 to March 1666, when he returned for about three months; he was again absent until April 1667. Six months later he became a Minor Fellow of Trinity College and went on to spend most of the next thirty years of his life residing in College, with few absences. He went home for a long Christmas holiday (4 December 1667 to 12 February 1668) and next, for reasons now unknown, spent the greater part of August and September 1668 in London (Brewster 1855, pp. 32–3).

There were thus two long periods (April to December 1667 and February to August 1668) during which Newton was working steadily in Cambridge, when we cannot positively define his occupations. (It is certain that during the earlier Lincolnshire sojourns Newton advanced his mathematics with great energy.) In the course of 1667 he bought a number of tools, 'glass bubbles', and a magnet; probably after 16 March 1668 he bought three prisms and 'putty' for polishing optical surfaces. (I do not follow Guerlac's guess that these purchases were made during Newton's stay in London, when he *did* buy chemicals and chemical apparatus.).

He probably could not have made optical experiments at Cambridge in the autumn of 1668 and was soon thereafter involved in academic concerns and chemistry. On balance it seems likely that Newton carried out intensive optical experimentation during the summer days of May to August 1668 which is reflected in the long sequence of notes we have just considered. Other evidence witnesses to the importance of this time. In Letter 151 (10 January 1676) Newton assured Oldenburg that he had followed the same method of experimenting with the spectrum for seven years. The remark suggests that while he had examined spectra before January 1668, his definitive method of investigating their properties was established during the twelvemonth following that date. And Newton's silence about his own optical ideas when assisting Isaac Barrow in the preparation of the latter's *Lectiones XVIII opticorum* is explained if we imagine (as is just chronologically feasible) that Newton's series of conclusive experiments was still incomplete at the time (Guerlac 1983, pp. 79–80).

Perhaps the most important of the second series of experimental records is the following:

Refracting the rays through a Prisme into a darke roome (as in the 7th Experiment) And holding another Prisme about 5 or 6 yards from the former to refract the rays again I found First that the blew rays did suffer a greater Refraction by the second Prisme than the Red ones.

And secondly that the purely Red rays refracted by the second Prisme made noe other colours but Red & the purely blew ones noe other colours but blew ones (Hall 1955, p. 35).

There are no further details of an experiment very like the *experimentum crucis* of the "New Theory", nor any diagram. Nevertheless, this was clearly a carefully planned test, whose result had been correctly anticipated by Newton. However, the notes still lack explicit statement of the heterogeneity of white light and the homogeneity of the pure coloured ray.

If we may suppose that all the notes quoted in the last pages and some others were made before the end of 1668, then I think we may conclude that the illuminating discovery that Newton called the "Theory of Colour", completed in the summer of 1668, may be summarized in three statements:

1. A pure coloured ray of light is homogeneous and elemental.

2. To each pure colour belongs a specific degree of refrangibility,

3. White light is a mixture of such rays.

(1) is a basic theoretical proposition. (2) is the basis of the mathematical theory of colour, and Newton attached immense importance to it. (3) is a basic proposition about the natural world, essential to any physical theory of the nature of light. All the evidence now available suggests and all

scholars agree that Newton began to grasp these ideas some three years before their perfection. The "New Theory of Light and Colours" was not framed at a stroke nor as the response to a single experiment, however 'crucial'. Its evolution had taken time.

Newton believed that he was the first to introduce mathematics into the discussion of colour, and that by doing so he had rendered "the Science of Colours . . . as certain as any other part of Optiques" (Letter 40, p. 96; Letter 67, p. 187), whereas previously it had been qualitative and indeed speculative. He was of course aware that statement (3) is also a physiological proposition: we cannot know that sunlight appears 'white' to any visual system other than our own. But that it is a mixture is a physical truth.

Newton reads Micrographia

Long before this time, though the book had no positive bearing upon Newton's "Theory of Colour", he had read Robert Hooke's *Micrographia*, which was in the bookshops before the end of 1664. Newton's annotations upon this book survive (Chapter I). He took down little (and that with adverse comments) from the many pages about light and colour, and the greater part of what interested him in this part of Hooke's book concerned the reflected colours of bodies. He discounted Hooke's hypothesis that light is (in Newton's words): "a vibration of the Aether, which pulse is made oblique by refraction & the motion of the precedent part of the pulse being deaded by the adjacent quiet medium makes blew . . ." with the objection to which he adhered all his life: "Why then may not light deflect from streight lines as well as sounds &c?"

He also objected against a purported experiment of Hooke's on colour-mixing that coloured solutions do not change their colour by dilution. Most important is the fact that Newton now read of Hooke's discovery of interference colours, and his hypothesis of their causation:

Thin flakes of Muscovy glasse [mica], aire, water, metalline scumme doe exhibit divers colours according to their thicknesse, if the midst be thinnest there will be a broad spot of one colour and perhaps coloured rings about it (outward in this order . . .) (Hall and Hall 1962, p. 403).

'Newton's rings'

Newton himself first produced interference colours in a rather odd way, possibly before his reading of *Micrographia*, when tying two glass prisms firmly together to make a parallelopipedon (a shape he used to investigate the passage of a ray through a thick piece of glass; cf. *Opticks*, p. 57, Expt. 10). Colours formed in the thin layer of air between the two prisms varied as the pressure altered its thickness. As the notebook records

In the 27th Experiment when the colour white or red was trajected on B, there would appear several circles of colours about the white spot at B . . . (Hall 1955, pp. 30–2).

Having counted the alternations of these coloured rings, and also proved that when formed by monochromatic light (from a third prism) they reappeared as rings of the same colour, Newton went far beyond Hooke when he began to form the coloured rings by pressing "a sphericall object glass of a Prospective (telescope)" upon a flat glass plate "so as to make the said spot with the circles of colours appeare" (ibid., p. 33). Knowing the focal length of the convex lens and hence its radius of curvature Newton could compute the thickness of the air-space between the two glasses associated with any particular ring. Despite his own objection to a wave-theory of light, Newton (like Hooke before him) found himself compelled to interpret the regular periodicity of the rings as arising from some periodic effect that was linked with light reflected and refracted in a narrow space. His measurements allowed him to infer the lengths of the alternations or pulses, on the assumption that when (at high pressure) a black spot appeared in the centre the glasses were in actual contact. It is evident that the notebook contains close anticipations of material in *Opticks*, Book II (see below).

The reflecting telescope

One further optical achievement of Newton's before his appointment (as successor to Barrow) to the Lucasian Chair of Mathematics at Cambridge on 29 October 1669 remains to be mentioned. This was his construction of a miniature reflecting telescope, the event first bringing him fame. Perhaps, besides the 'putty', the furnaces he bought in 1668 were intended to make its metal specula—naturally using a white cuprous alloy of Newton's own devising. This might have been the task that he took up after his return from London at the end of September 1668. One of Newton's oldest extant letters confirms this date; it was written in February 1669 and speaks of the telescope as recently completed (Letter 3).

Spherical and chromatic aberration

Newton had (in our terms) complemented Descartes's discovery of spherical aberration in lenses with the discovery of chromatic aberration, caused by the dispersion of white light. It is a curious fact that as Descartes missed the practical means of remedying the former defect, so Newton missed—or half missed—the practical means to correct the latter. He understood that not all transparent substances possess the same refractive index, but did not energetically pursue the production of compound achromatic lenses. Success in this direction came only a century later. Realizing that a single lens must always yield coloured and diffuse images, Newton determined to attempt magnification by means of a concave mirror—still needing an eye-lens—as indeed others had done before, without anyone's attaining practical success. Newton himself was only marginally more fortunate: the two miniature reflectors he constructed with his own hands worked well for their size (at least until the polished metal mirrors became tarnished); for tradesmen to reproduce them on a larger, more serviceable scale was another matter altogether. The reflecting telescope did not become a serious astronomical instrument in Newton's lifetime, and William Herschel was perhaps the first astronomer to make a discovery with it.

Both these miniature telescopes (the second constructed in the autumn of 1671) have now vanished (Mills and Turvey 1979). It was the second that introduced Newton to the London world of science, for the mathematician John Collins—to whom Isaac Barrow had imparted Newton's early work in mathematics—had done little to make Newton's name among the Fellows of the Royal Society. The amazing toy that was not a toy aroused great interest, even at the flippant Court of Charles II, after Barrow, once more acting as Newton's friend, carried it to London for examination by the Royal Society (Hall and Hall 1965–86, VIII, p. 525). Soon came the opportunity to lay before the same public the experimental trials and theoretical ideas from which that telescope had sprung: Newton wrote to the Society on 6 February 1672 the letter that was to become his first printed paper. It appeared in the *Philosophical Transactions* dated 19 February.

A revolutionary concept of light explained

Newton's "New Theory of Colours" astounded his contemporaries; some of the best qualified judges among them, including Robert Hooke, were unable to accept or even comprehend it. A major feature baffling them was Newton's insistence that whiteness is a mixture of all colours. If white sunlight is not pure and elemental, as all men believed, why could it not equally well be the result of combining two elemental colours only (on the universal principle of dichotomy)? Newton dealt with this matter in a succession of letters written in the months following the publication of his first paper, confessing that "this assertion [the production of whiteness by mixtures] above the rest appears *Paradoxicall*, & is with most difficulty admitted" (Letter 67, p. 183).

His amplification in these letters shows, as do the earlier Optical Lectures, how much experimental work was done by Newton in the years between 1666 and 1670 which is unrecorded in his notebooks. For example, Newton now writes, in a letter to Henry Oldenburg (the Secretary of the Royal Society) dated 11 June 1672 (ibid., p. 182), of the 'spoked wheel' or comb (interruptor) by means of which, in the arrangement given in the figure, he showed that if all the colours dispersed by a prism are

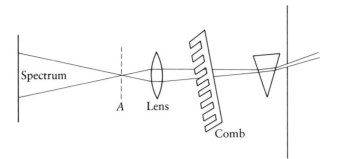

Fig. 7. Experiments on the recombination of the spectral rays by means of a lens; a white circle is seen upon the screen *A* placed at its focus. The 'comb interruptor' blocks particular coloured rays in the refracted beam. After *Opticks*, p. 137. In the Optical Lectures a toothed wheel was used instead of a comb.

reunited by a lens, the bright spot at the focus of the lens is white (Fig. 7); if one or more colours is blocked by the interruptor, however, the spot is tinged by those that pass; but if the interruptor is passed quickly through the beam so that each colour is blocked only for an instant, the spot is again perceived as white (because of the eye's persistence of vision, in modern terms). This rather elaborate experiment, not indicated in Newton's notes, must have been made in the years between 1666 and 1670. It is indeed found in one manuscript of the Optical Lectures (Shapiro 1984, pp. 31, 487).

It is therefore certain that all the material and most of the thought of Book I of *Opticks* became known to Newton, if not exactly in "the prime of his age for invention" (1655–6) then shortly thereafter. As Westfall has remarked, it is trivial to dispute over a year or two when such momentous matters are at stake, and the full assimilation into science of Newton's optical work was (in any case) to be deferred for a generation and more.

The study of the colours seen in films and thin plates, the 'Newton's rings' of *Opticks*, Book II, was clearly subsequent to the great progress he had made with refraction. He did not treat it in his Optical Lectures. Nevertheless, as we shall see, it too is firmly recorded in his early notebooks and drafts.

§2. The Optical Lectures, 1670–1672

Newton becomes Lucasian Professor

On the twenty-ninth of October, 1669, Isaac Newton, while still retaining his Fellowship at Trinity College, became Lucasian Professor of Mathematics in the University of Cambridge. In this office he succeeded Isaac

Barrow, in a few years to be Master of the College, whom we may
tentatively identify as Newton's patron. Barrow had lectured once a week
during a single one of three academic terms in each year. Newton followed
his example, or at any rate deposited eight lectures for each year (to 1687)
in the University Library, as was required of him. Each lecture lasted half
an hour. In this respect Newton was exceptionally dutiful; many professors
lectured not at all (as Newton did not from 1687 to 1701) and some did
not even reside in the University (as Newton did not from 1696 to 1701,
only in the last year paying William Whiston as his deputy). One who had
known Newton well wrote that 'so few went to Hear him, & fewer that
understood him, that oft times he did in a manner, for want of Hearers,
read to the Walls' (Westfall 1980, p. 209). Hardly any names of those who
heard Newton lecture are recorded. However, he was no more abstruse
than his learned predecessor.

Even in seventeenth-century Cambridge it was possible to win golden
opinions, if not by good preaching, then by good teaching, as the naturalist
John Ray had done in Newton's own College. Newton certainly made the
effort to satisfy his patron and colleagues, even to the extent (like Barrow
just before) of preparing his lectures for the press.

Again, Newton decided to follow Barrow's example in taking optics as
the subject of his first course of lectures. It apparently extended over three
years. Barrow's course on geometrical optics was published as *Lectiones
XVIII opticorum* (1669) and Newton received Barrow's thanks in the book
as 'a truly outstanding man of genius and remarkable knowledge' who had
'revised one copy, advising us of some points to be corrected and, with no
little pains, suggesting some things which you may here and there discover
annexed . . .' (Hall 1960, p. 39). In return, Newton opened his own course
with a generous allusion to his predecessor:

> since the lectures that you heard here not so long ago brought together such a
> great variety of topics and a vast quantity of discoveries with their very accurate
> demonstrations, it might perhaps seem a vain endeavour and futile effort for me to
> undertake to treat this science again.

Newton then explained why his labour was not superfluous: the refraction
of light had been wholly misunderstood by geometers [such as Barrow!] and
so it was necessary to "subject the principles of this science" to a new
and strict examination performed by means of experiments (Shapiro 1984,
pp. 47, 281).

Newton's Optical Lectures

We cannot be sure precisely what words Newton read to his auditors.
The official set of his lectures, deposited in the University Library by
Newton himself in 1674 and posthumously printed in 1729, contains 31

lectures bearing a series of dates. This manuscript was probably prepared in the autumn of 1671 and the winter of 1671–2. A shorter set, of only 18 lectures with different dates attached to the matter, remained among Newton's own papers; this was first printed in 1973 (Whiteside 1973). This shorter, unfinished manuscript—it breaks off abruptly—was probably abandoned in 1671. Newton evidently decided to change the order of his exposition in a new draft, but why he also decided to rewrite it upon a larger scale is not known with certainty. Increasing length is a characteristic of Newton's process of generating successive drafts. Moreover, as Alan Shapiro has argued, the longer text may reflect the critical reaction to Newton's first optical letter (the "New Theory of Light and Colours") which was printed in March 1672. For in it Newton presented experimental evidence against the notion that refraction brings about a "diffusion" or "splitting" of the light beam, a notion favoured by such critics as Robert Hooke and Father Pardies. The *experiments* themselves are in the early version of the lectures, but not this use of them (Shapiro 1975, pp. 209–10).

Two conclusions follow from this argument. Firstly, this portion of the second, longer version may not have been written before Newton was aware of the 'diffusionist' criticism of the views expressed in his letter, that is, before March 1672. Secondly, it is unlikely that Newton would really have presented this material to his Cambridge audience, as he would have passed this point in the course before the later winter of 1672.

However, if the 31 lectures are too long to be the spoken course, the 18 lectures seem too short. The former are nearly half as large in bulk again as the latter, and include a number of additional topics essential to Newton's purpose, and indeed to his earlier promises, such as optical in-strumentation, the colours of the rainbow, the colours of bodies seen through a prism, and the colours of natural bodies. Nothing casts doubt upon Shapiro's inference that Newton did in fact treat all these additional topics in the lectures as actually delivered, as well as those in the first draft of 18 lectures. The evidence does not support the otherwise plausible guess that Newton gave the shorter course in the first years of his teaching, and the longer course in later years, for we have no reason to suppose that he covered the same ground more than once. About four-fifths of the material in the short version was transferred to the revise without significant change.

A plan for printing the Lectures

Though Newton's pains in preparing these successive texts for the press were to prove useless, it is certain that they were intended for publication. Newton himself noted, long after, that he was preparing for the press a "tract" concerning optics in 1671, and news of this work came from Isaac Barrow to John Collins in London. To Collins it was of particular interest that Newton planned to print some of his pure mathematical investigations with his optics (Letter 57, p. 146). Barely, however, had this good news reached London about Christmas 1671 than the contrary information came that Newton had decided not to proceed. There can be little doubt that it was the hostile reception accorded to his first optical paper that caused Newton to change his mind. In May 1672 he wrote to John Collins:

Your Kindnesse to me in profering to promote the edition of my Lectures which Dr. Barrow told you of, I reccon amongst the greatest, considering the multitude of businesse in which you are involved. But I have now determined otherwise of them; finding already by that little use I have made of the Presse, that I shall not enjoy my former serene liberty till I have done with it; which I hope will be as soon as I have made good what is already extant on my account. Yet I may possibly complete the discourse of resolving Problemes by infinite series of which I wrote the better half the last christmas with intension that it should accompany my Lectures but it proves larger than I expected & is not yet finished (Letter 63, p. 161).

So far as the optical lectures are concerned, this was the end of the matter in Newton's lifetime. The first large account of Newton's work on re-fraction and the theory of colours was to be given to the public in *Opticks* a generation later. Not that Newton failed entirely to communicate his work and ideas to the public, as we shall see, nor indeed that he did not at times entertain designs for publishing a different book on optics from the lectures; but these latter schemes also came to nothing. As the years went by Newton's embroilment in controversy increased rather than diminished, and his dislike of this trouble in even greater proportion.

The Lectures compared with Opticks

So far as I know no one has yet attempted a detailed comparison between *Opticks* and the Optical Lectures (1729), or attempted to assess the degree of innovation introduced by Newton into the former work. Shapiro remarks that 'though the essential elements of the theory of colour and its supporting experiments are substantially the same in the two works, the structure of the theory itself and its demonstrations differ in many fundamental ways' (Shapiro 1984, p. 23). Notably, in *Opticks*, Newton devoted a more detailed exposition and experimental demonstration to the unequal refrangibility of the coloured rays composing white light, the very point that had been most severely questioned and misunderstood after the appearance of his first paper in 1672. On the other hand, both forms of the optical lectures contain a great deal more mathematics: the massive review of geometrical optics (Part I, Lectures 4 to 15 in the text printed in 1728, corresponding to Lectures 9 to 18 in the manuscript) is only represented quite sketchily in *Opticks* (ibid., pp. 311–429 and 179–269). In the same spirit the latter work, though opening in the traditional way with series of Definitions and Axioms, is written in a less didactic, discursive style befitting the vernacular tongue. Further—to state the obvious—the study of colours in thin and thick transparent plates (*Opticks*, Book II) is not found in the lectures. Inevitably the lectures lack any reference to Bartholin's discovery of double refraction and Roemer's of the velocity of light, both treated in *Opticks*, since neither discovery was known to Newton at the time of writing the lectures.

All historians are agreed that the lectures provided a rich source from which Newton could draw in preparing his first printed paper, and later in writing *Opticks*. Alan E. Shapiro has given clear summaries and English translations of both the short and the long versions of the lectures; here I shall only illustrate some contrasts and comparisons with *Opticks*, taking into consideration the shorter, manuscript version as being the earliest text that we have.

Newton opens with a firm insistence upon Descartes's mistake in supposing that spherical aberration was the unique source of error in the images formed by lenses, for he has discovered a hitherto unsuspected property of light which demands a reconstruction of the theory of microscopes and telescopes. All light rays are not, as formerly was supposed, equally refrangible, since the rays generating a red colour are refracted less by a prism or lens than those generating blue or purple. This is at once demonstrated by the common experiment of forming a varicoloured spectrum with a glass prism: geometry shows that at a certain orientation of the prism the sun's image projected upon a screen should be circular (the demonstration of this is omitted from *Opticks*). But in experience, Newton affirms, the spectrum cannot be made less than four times as long as broad, and examination shows that the spectrum is bounded by two semicircular ends joined by parallel straight sides. It is in fact composed of innumerable overlapping circular images of the sun, each formed by light of slightly different refrangibility from that forming adjacent circles (this argument, with a figure, is in *Opticks*, pp. 38–9). Newton then shows that the spectrum formed by a brilliant point-source of light such as the planet Venus is linear; the dispersion of the now minute circles has become almost infinitely greater than the diameter of each circle. Newton lays more stress on this experiment, not noted in *Opticks*, than on what he was later to call his "crucial experiment". He finishes Lecture 2 with a refutation of the notion that the extension of the spectrum might be merely adventitious.

The modification theory refuted

With Lecture 3 (in the manuscript) Newton embarks upon a discussion of colour in general, starting from chromatic aberration (as we call it) and the impossibility of correcting this defect of instruments by elaborate figuring of single lenses. (Repetitions early in each lecture seem to indicate breaks between lectures as actually delivered.) Summarizing his rejection of all philosophical ideas of colour in the assertion that they are not qualities of bodies, Newton continues:

I find that the modification of [white] light whereby colours originate is connate to light and arises neither from reflection nor from refraction nor from the qualities or any modes whatsoever of bodies, and it cannot be destroyed or changed in any way by them (Shapiro 1984, pp. 85, 437).

This topic is discussed at much greater length in *Opticks*, Book I, Part 2, where Newton denies that colours are caused by new modifications of light. It is obvious that Newton is these various passages uses the word 'modification' in different senses. In Lecture 3 he says that if incident white light is modified (that is, segregated) by a reflecting surface that tends to absorb the blue–green rays, the reflected light will be reddish in colour, since it now lacks some of the rays that it contained when white; the reflected light is *less* than the incident light. In *Opticks* (and elsewhere) Newton denies that light can be modified (altered in its physical nature) so that, for example, the *whole* of a white beam becomes red, in the same way that a cylindrical rod can be made of square section by passing it through a die.

And white light is not split

Newton is insistent in the lectures as in *Opticks* that white light is never forcibly split into components not previously existing within it, nor is it ever re-formed from a bundle of coloured rays into a white beam by a process of fusion or homologization. Rather, white light is a mixture of infinitely many constituents, each having a physical identity of its own, constituents which are segregated by their various responses to a refracting or reflecting surface; conversely, when the segregated constituents are again simply commingled, as by a reversed prism or a converging lens, white is restored. It is often imagined that Newton supposed the number of constituent elements in white to be small, largely because of his division of the spectrum into seven primary colours, and his comparison of these seven intervals with those of the octave in music. But the occurrence of a whole tone at (say) 256 c.p.s. and the next whole tone at (say) 292 c.p.s. does not exclude sounds having frequencies of 257, 258 . . . etc. c.p.s., and similarly with light; it is essential to Newton's system that although the eye perceives a green patch in the spectrum, not all the rays seen as green have the same refrangibility. If they did the patch would be infinitely narrow. Newton understood that the number of coloured rays in white is infinitely great, and that our division of them by colours is physiological rather than physical. Hence he stresses the need for caution when the experimenter attempts to produce a pure coloured ray, for it is quite easy to single out a red that on passing through a second prism yields yellow, or a green that yields blue.

It was through lack of scrupulous care in this respect that Edmé Mariotte (1681) thought he had convicted Newton of error (Guerlac 1981, pp. 98–9).

Each ray denoted by its refrangibility

This infinity of the diverging rays becomes the more obvious when Newton emphasizes that the fundamental identity of each ray is mathematically established by its refrangibility, not by its colour-appearance to our eyes. The science of colours (he writes) is properly a mathematical science in the same way that geography and mechanics are mathematical sciences. Fore-shadowing his own future, Newton asserts (without false modesty):

since an exact science of them [colours] seems to be one of the most recalcitrant things that is lacking in Philosophy, I hope to show—as it were by my example—how valuable mathematics is in natural philosophy; and on that basis I can exhort geometers to investigate nature more rigorously, and those who are desirous of understanding nature to take up geometry first . . . So that, by the efforts of philosophical geometers and of philosophers employing geometry, we may bring to birth a natural science confirmed by the strongest of evidence, in place of the conjectures and probabilities that are everywhere bandied about (Shapiro 1984, pp. 87, 439).

The same point is made in *Opticks* and in many other places in Newton's writings, but not always with so much vigour and methodological precision.

The degree of Newton's success in placing the science of colours upon a sound mathematical and evidential foundation, in pursuit of his own de-claration, was debated by readers of his first optical paper (1672). As we shall see later, his critics argued that Newton, whether or not he had dis-covered a new phenomenon of light, had accounted for it in terms of a hypothesis of light favoured by himself and so was no less a probabilist than those whose opinions he was seeking to supplant. They could not see that Newton had positively demonstrated—rather than *inferred*—the existence of innumerable colours in white light, and some modern critics have agreed with them, at least so far as the first optical paper is concerned (Sabra 1967, Ch. 11). It can scarcely be doubted that Newton did frame (though not 'feign') hypotheses, of which the Queries in *Opticks* provide several ex-amples; it is no less certain that Newton pursued, with all his immense intellectual powers, the goal of creating a natural science "confirmed by the strongest evidence", that is, evidence obtained from sound experiments and accurate measurements, or at least (as with the optical – musical equivalence) the best testimony of observers. Arguments based upon such evidence, especially if fitted into a coherent mathematical structure, Newton distinguished from speculative or conjectural propositions, such as the 'optical' theorems in Book I, Section XIV of the *Principia*. At least, this was the ideal; but it must be admitted that Newton sometimes strove too hard to match real experimental results with his ideal principles and mathematical models (Westfall 1973).

White light compounded of coloured rays

Newton next proceeded in his lectures to build up the body of experimental evidence demonstrating that the rays (composing white light) of equal incidence form variously refracted rays of various colours, the rays being "more and more refracted as they produce the successive colours in this order: red, yellow, green, blue and purple, *together with all their intermediate gradations*" (my italics; Shapiro 1984, pp. 89, 441). The most important experiment is that in which two prisms, fixed with their axes at right angles, receive the beam of light successively: the result is not a spectrum spread out into a square, but the spectrum as before rotated through 45° (see Fig. 10 in the next Section and *Opticks*, p. 34). Newton then demonstrates the re-compounding of white light from the totality of coloured rays by letting the spectra of two or three prisms fall upon one another (*Opticks*, p. 147) or by bringing the dispersed rays together at the focus of a convex lens (*Opticks*, p. 116; Shapiro 1984, pp. 99, 115, 463, 477). This last experiment is particularly cogent because it is evident that "the disposition of dissimilar rays to produce diverse colours is not destroyed by mixing them, since they paint the same colours when they are separated as they painted before they were mixed" (Shapiro, ibid., pp. 117, 479). (Newton does not remark that this fact proves that the 'white' at the focus in this experiment is not the same as the white of ordinary sunlight brought to a focus, since this will not, when diverging again beyond the focus, paint colours.) Perhaps for this reason, he omitted this deduction from *Opticks*, instead drawing the conclusion from the experiment that "one and the same part of the Light in one and the same place, according to the various Inclinations of the [white screen] appeared in one case white, in another yellow or red, in the other blue" (p. 116). In *Opticks* the emphasis is heavily upon the non-transformation of light by refraction, and the irrelevance of the shadow-edge to the colour (a matter also treated in the lectures, of course). But Newton's revised conclusion also has its problems, since (unless the focused spot be infinitely small) the inclination of the screen to the line of the refracted beam must alter the distance of any observed point within the focal image (except its centre) from both the prism and the centre of the image.

In *Opticks* also Newton experiments at some length with a coarse 'comb', using its 'teeth' so that different coloured rays either pass between them or are impeded by them (Fig. 7, p. 45). He examines the phenomena when the light is re-compounded by a lens. These experiments are not recounted in the optical lectures, but Newton there employs a toothed wheel to similar effect; he knew that if coloured rays are rapidly interrupted the re-constituted light at the focus will still appear white to the eye. He also describes there the use of a concave mirror to unite dispersed light into a white focus (Shapiro 1984, pp. 125, 487).

The core of Newton's theory of light was the assertion that light is compounded of rays of all colours not only as it leaves the prism and is not yet separated into those colours, but also when it has not yet reached the prism and prior to any refraction (ibid., pp. 129, 491).

That is to say, the structure of light is not modified by refraction: it is merely 'unmixed', and the same is true, Newton now adds, of reflected light. (This matter is treated at an earlier point in the exposition of *Opticks*, in Experiment 9 of Book I, Part I, p. 54). The argument is essentially the same in both texts. In the arrangement shown (Fig. 8), the rays reflected from the base of the prism, undergoing no refraction, produce a round, white image at *P*. Rays refracted at the base form a spectrum at *T*. If the prism is rotated about its axis it is possible to make the blue rays in the incoming white light be reflected to *P*, while the red and yellow rays are still refracted to *T*; with further rotation all the rays are internally reflected to *P*. "This in no way could have occurred" writes Newton (perhaps too confidently) "unless it be conceded that the difference is present in the rays just as they come from the sun", adding that it is because the red and yellow rays from the sun penetrate the base of the prism more vigorously than the blue and purple rays do, and so suffer a smaller refraction, that they are able to go on to *T*, while the less vigorous blue–purple rays, more sharply curved,

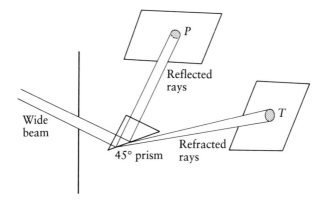

Fig. 8. The differential separation of colours at the critical angle. Turning the prism slowly upon its axis the spectrum of colours at *T* begins 'to vanish and to be reflected to *P*: first purple, then blue, green and yellow, and last red'. After Shapiro (1984), pp. 129, 131, 492.

become reflected to *P* (ibid., pp. 131, 493). This estimation of the relative vigour of the rays was not repeated in *Opticks*, where Newton declares:

the Beam of Light reflected by the Base of the Prism, being augmented first by the more refrangible [blue] rays, and afterwards by the less refrangible ones, is compounded of rays differently refrangible. And that all such reflected Light is of the same Nature with the Sun's Light before its incidence on the Base of the Prism, no Man ever doubted; it being generally allowed, that Light by such Reflexions suffers no Alteration in its Modifications and Properties (p. 55).

We may agree that so long as a white patch at P is produced by light totally reflected at the base of the prism it is pure reflected sunlight; but when the light at P is tinged with colour it is because partial refraction and reflection has occurred at the basal surface. In other words, difference in reflexibility with respect to colour may be considered a consequence of a difference of refrangibility, as Newton had explained in the lectures and was to explain dynamically in Section XIV of Book I of the *Principia*. It is clear that no colour can be seen at P without refraction at the base, and therefore the question of whether colours existed before refraction, or are produced by it, remains in the same state as before.

Colour connate with the ray

Newton concludes Lecture 6 with his strongest affirmation so far:

. . . since the inherent dispositions or forms of the rays whereby they are fitted to exhibit some colour cannot be destroyed nor in any way changed by the power of reflection or refraction, what else can be concluded but that those dispositions are innate to the rays from their origin and, as I may say, are connate to them, although they cannot exhibit their own colours before the heterogeneous rays are separated from one another by the power of refractions (Shapiro 1984, pp. 143–5, 505).

In *Opticks* this position is confirmed (in Book I, Part I, Prop. 2: 1952, p. 46) by the celebrated experiment which Newton had called in his first optical paper (1672) his *experimentum crucis*. This best-known of all Newton's experimental processes (Fig. 9) does not precisely appear in the optical lectures, though it is drawn on the last leaf of the earlier version (MS. 4002, fo. 128a). Something close to it is found in a late notebook entry, and different experiments, similar in their arrangements of prisms and diaphragms, are described in the lectures. In one rays of monochromatic light are formed in order to study the dependence of the critical angle upon refrangibility or colour (Hall 1955, p. 35; Shapiro 1984, pp. 135, 497).

Lecture 7 is devoted to the formation of colours by mixing spectral elemental colours, and to the effect of shadow upon coloration; these topics are discussed more elaborately in the revised lectures and briefly in *Opticks*. In the revise Newton reverts at this point to some of his earliest experiments

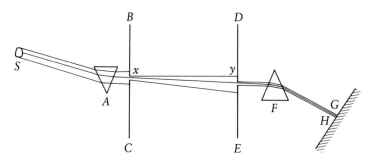

Fig. 9. The "crucial experiment", 1672. *A*, the first prism, *F* the second prism. *BC* the first diaphragm pierced at *x*; *DE* the second diaphragm pierced at *y*, about 12 feet from the former. *S* the hole in the shutter admitting the beam. As *A* is slowly turned axially, a succession of pure colours appears at different points on the screen *GH* [about twenty feet from *S*] such as red at *G*, violet at *H*, others in turn falling between. From Newton to Oldenburg for Pardies, 11 June 1672; *Philosophical Transactions* no. 85, 15 July 1672, p. 5016.

on colours seen by the eye through a prism, which in *Opticks* are placed at the opening of the book (pp. 20–6; Hall 1948, p. 247). In both versions of the lectures Newton notes that because the spectrum can be cut short at any point by blocking the light, without any change in colour where the cut is made, there cannot be any colour-forming interaction between the edge of the ray and the surrounding medium as Descartes and Hooke had supposed (Shapiro 1984, pp. 161, 533). Such an interaction must seem less likely to one taking light to consist of bodies projected through an aether or vacuum, than if it is taken to be a wave- or pulse-motion in the aether. Newton concludes Lecture 8 by describing an optical bench more than 8 feet long consisting of two prisms and a lens; using this, with a third free prism, the experimental lessons he has in mind can be learned (ibid., pp. 165, 519; *Opticks*, pp. 186–91).

Geometrical optics

From the opening of Lecture 9 to the end of the first version of the lectures Newton was concerned with geometrical optics, founded upon the sine-law of refraction here attributed to Descartes; the treatment is mathematical, inevitably, not experimental. In the longer, revised version of the lectures Newton transferred all this material to an earlier position, starting with Lecture 4; it largely constitutes Part I of that text. The same material is very much compressed and simplified in the first twenty pages of *Opticks*, and therefore need not be considered in detail here.

The analogy between spectrum and octave

However, it is worth while to review one or two examples of topics that are found in the revised text of the lectures and again in *Opticks*, though not found in the shorter manuscript. In the revise, for instance, after proving that prismatic colours are not affected by the shadow-edge (as above), Newton added pages on the measurement of the spectrum and the various coloured bands seen within it, which include the suggestion that

the parts of the image occupied by the colours were proportional to [the divisions of] a [resonant] string divided so that it would cause the individual notes of the octave to be sounded (Shapiro 1984, p. 543; *Opticks*, pp. 125–9).

To establish the analogy, he divided the spectrum into seven "homogeneal" colours, adding indigo (a semitone) at the extremity of blue before violet; orange was the other semitone, the remaining five colours (red, yellow, green, blue, violet) occupying whole tones. There is, however, some discrepancy between both the music and the numerical statements about the refracted bands in the two texts. Only in the revise did Newton point out that a string "divided geometrically" so as to sound the fundamental, the octave above, and six notes between would differ insensibly from a string divided in the conventional manner of musicians, declaring that he preferred the latter because

it agrees with the phenomena very well, [and] because it perhaps involves something about the harmonies of colours (such as painters are not altogether unacquainted with, but which I myself have not yet sufficiently studied) perhaps analogous to the concordances of sounds. To render it more probable, consider that the affinity between the extreme purple and the extreme red, at the limits of the colours, is like that between the limits of the octave, which we can take to be in unison (Shapiro 1984, p. 545).

We can hardly be far astray if we interpret this passage as indicating Newton's unspecific awareness of a common periodicity in the phenomena of music and colour, an awareness that was to find a more explicit expression in 1675, and (especially) at various levels in *Opticks* (see Chapter 3, §2 below).

The rainbow

The explanation of the colours of the rainbow is dealt with by Newton in two places in the revised lectures. Lecture 15 contains an exact geometrical determination of the radii of the primary and the secondary bows; *Opticks* (Book I, Part II, Prop. 9, pp. 169–71) relies on these demonstrations, of which Newton recapitulates the results without detailing the argument. Then in Lecture 16 he accounts for the bands of colours in the two bows, reversed in the secondary as compared with the primary bow. The principles of the explanation in *Opticks* (pp. 171–8) are the same as in the lectures, but there are many differerences of detail. For example, in the lectures Newton computed the least and greatest radii of the primary bow as 41° and 43° 6′ and those of the secondary as 49° 2′ and 52° 51′. In the *Opticks*, having changed his values for the indices of refraction, these numbers are modified to 40° 17′ / 42° 2′ and 50° 57′ / 54° 7′. Such a preoccupation with the rather over-precise determination of quantities and the achievement of a literal agreement between predicated and measured values, if necessary by a little quiet 'fudging', is typical of Newton's mature style of mathematico-physical argument (Westfall 1973). It is perhaps less easy to understand why Newton, when describing the formation of colours in the raindrops, should in the lectures have mistakenly written that the inside of the primary bow is red, a mistake corrected in the printed text as in *Opticks*. Another difference is that in *Opticks* Newton carefully specifies that the lines from the observer's eye to the raindrops forming colours describe "conical Superficies" in the atmosphere, though we commonly perceive the bows as circular arcs; in the lectures he does not make this much concession to the reader's interest in the apparent locus of the bow in the sky.

A curious change introduced into *Opticks* between about 1692 and 1698 was that whereby Newton removed from Descartes the honour of being his own chief precursor in the explanation of the rainbow. In the text of *Opticks* as printed, though not in the oldest manuscript, Newton gave the chief credit to Antonio de Dominis, author of *De radiis visus et lucis in vitris perspectivis et iride tractatus* (Venice 1611), adding only 'The same Explication *Des-Cartes* hath pursued in his Meteors, and mended that of the exterior Bow'. As Shapiro has pointed out, Newton's revision was vastly unfair to Descartes, who (in particular) was the first to show how the quantity of light refracted at specific angles causes the bands to form (Shapiro 1984, p. 593 note 1).

The style of the Lectures *differs from that of* Opticks

What may be gathered from all this as to the relationship between the optical lectures and the book *Opticks* written some twenty years later? Only in a very general way can it be said that Book I of *Opticks* is derived from the lectures, for though the ground covered is the same and the arguments are often transferred from one to the other, the exposition is very different. In rhetorical or literary terms the two texts have little in common. Newton completely reworked his material, and some parts of his semi-popular argument could not have stood mathematically without reference to the lectures (in the posthumous editions of *Opticks* such cross-references were inserted, the Optical Lectures being by then accessible in print). There is a tight, precise, scientific quality about the lectures, written when much of the experimental work was still very fresh in Newton's mind, which the *Opticks* seems to lack, for all its far greater readability and, on many points, greater clarity. It is not altogether our hindsight that presents the lectures to us as the taut and enthusiastic work of an eager young man, setting his experimental discoveries and new conceptions before his audience with as much vigour as the academic circumstances allowed, while *Opticks* reads like the emotion of discovery recollected in tranquillity; it is the book of a middle-aged man who has pondered long and deeply on his topic and is not very unhappy to skate lightly over certain difficult passages. Nevertheless we can admire the vitality in Newton's recollections of former triumphs, and the strength of intellect that enabled him to recapture and reconstruct for his readers the investigations that he had made so long before.

Part of the interest of the optical lectures is that they allow us to reconstruct the *Opticks* that Newton might have written about 1670 or 1671. When he came to go over this material again about twenty years later Newton knew much more about light than before. He had perfected his study of interference colours, 'Newton's Rings'; he now knew of diffraction (treated in the *Principia*) and also of double refraction as seen in Icelandic spar (calcite). As we shall see shortly, Newton was forced at some time in the early 1670s to cope with the necessity of incorporating periodicity into his discussion of light and colour, if it was to be other than very limited, indeed artificial. No simple theory, no model of the light-beam as a stream of extremely swift, extremely minute particles, could accommodate interference (in our language). Although Newton still presented such a model of the beam in the *Principia* (Book I, Section XIV), in order to give a dynamical analysis of the reflection–refraction transition in the interaction of light with bodies, the utility of the model and the analysis was limited to a single surface and could not be extended to embrace the phenomena of two surfaces in thin plates or layers (interference). At the close of the last of his optical lectures (in the revised text) Newton recognized the incompleteness of his exposition to that point:

Besides the phenomena of colours which we have discussed, there remain not a few others (especially concerning the colours of very thin transparent plates such as the globes of soap-bubbles and air compressed between two pieces of glass and the very thin skins of many bodies) of which the dimensions and causes cannot be determined without mathematical reasoning; but I seem to have been too long [immersed] in these matters and so I have decided to direct myself now to the more abstract parts of mathematics (Shapiro 1984, p. 602).

While it is true that in his research into the colours of thin plates (made within a year or so of the above quotation) Newton performed feats of precise measurement, and made some use of calculation, this part of his

work contained nothing of the geometrical complexity of his study of refraction. And the 'determination of causes' now required an extra concept,
of which the optical lectures gave no hint.

The nature of light still uncertain

Although Newton criticized Descartes for the inadequacy of his physical
conception of light (as a substance, whose moving spheres variously rotating impress our senses as colours), and although he enormously enriched
our physico-mathematical understanding of light and colour in his optical
lectures, he left the physical concept of light no more intelligible than before. We must reconsider this point later: what is significant here is that we
may consider the lectures as representing Newton (as it were) in a state of
innocence, when he could still consider a simple emission theory as essentially sufficient to account for the principle phenomena of light. It was
different twenty years later when he composed *Opticks*. It is obvious, of
course, that in order to cover the ground of his lectures—or Book I of
Opticks—Newton did not need to follow Descartes's example in first establishing a theory of the physical nature of light. His experimental and
mathematical method allowed him to adopt a more positivist position.
Therefore he did not have to cope with the problem of proposing a theory
that could also be made to embrace all those other phenomena of light
which—as he confessed—he had not considered. On reaching the end of the
optical lectures, however, a reader might reasonably wonder whether
Newton could succeed, following the same scientific methodology, in also
treating these other phenomena of light with equal success, and without
creating an internal inconsistency. As we shall see later, some contemporary
readers of Newton's first optical paper were unwilling to set aside these
manifestations of light as Newton had done (at least temporarily) or to fall
in with his positivist approach. And the question of consistency was not to
be resolved with entire success.

§3. First publication, first disputes, 1672

Though two or three Fellows of the Royal Society were aware of Newton
as a promising young professor of mathematics at Cambridge during the
first years of his tenure, it was the arrival in London (by Barrow's hands)
of his six-inch-long reflecting telescope that brought sudden fame to him
just before Christmas 1671. John Wallis at Oxford had been writing mathematical books for thirty years without ever stirring up the excitement
aroused by this seeming toy capable of showing the moons of Jupiter.
Hardly had the world taken it in when Henry Oldenburg, the Secretary of
the Royal Society, received from Newton a proposal that he submit an account showing how the design of the new instrument had sprung from a

deep theory and a fundamental discovery. Strictly, such an account was
redundant in the sense that the reflecting telescope had been proposed before, on the obvious (though fallacious) ground that it must be easier to
polish a large, cast mirror of metal than to grind large lenses, for large
pieces of glass of optical quality were practically unobtainable. Moreover—as Newton knew—his success with the miniature reflector owed
nothing to his theory, and could not render the theory more convincing. But
Newton, reticent and withdrawn by nature as he was, and hesitant to publish, was nevertheless receptive of applause, and a little applause urged him
to seek more. The new telescope was a little thing; his "New Theory of Light
and Colours" was a great thing which went far beyond what Barrow had
done, and it was a true philosophical discovery, not the result of some lucky
experimental trick.

So Newton wrote to Oldenburg on 18 January 1672 to ask if the Royal
Society still continued its weekly meetings

because if they continue them for any time I am purposing them, to be considered
of & examined, an accompt of a Philosophicall discovery which induced mee to the
making of the said Telescope, & which I doubt not will prove much more gratefull
then the communication of that instrument, being in my Judgment the oddest if not
the most considerable detection which hath hitherto beene made in the operations
of Nature (Letter 35).

Oldenburg replied two days later. At Cambridge Newton must at once have
put pen to paper, dating his composition 6 February 1672. It came to the
secretary's hands on the day of the Royal Society's meeting, the 8th, and he
at once read it to the assembled company.

If we imagine that Newton's intention was to report the 'philosophical
discovery' from which his conviction of the inherent superiority of the reflecting telesope ensued, then what he had to explain were the properties
of the dispersion of light, or chromatic aberration of lenses, arising from its
refraction, or (in his own terms) the unequal refrangibility of the differently
coloured rays that refraction brings to view. He did not need to account for
the fact that refraction creates the colours of the rainbow or the spectrum
formed by a prism; it is enough for his subsequent argument that they are
so formed. Newton might also (perhaps) have been expected to look into
the question whether, although it is certain that a single refraction (in a
raindrop, a prism, or a lens) gives rise to colours, some more complex
process of refraction—involving, say, two or more transparent materials—
might not avoid this complication; but this possibility, eminently of practical
relevance as it is in the manufacture of optical instruments, never seems
to have attracted Newton's interest strongly. Newton proceeded as though
satisfied that chromatic aberration could not be corrected by any practical
method.

Given that dispersion or chromatic aberration could be asserted as a fact, Newton did not need to consider the eye and its vision of colour, nor the physical nature of light, nor the relationship of white light to coloured light, nor many other such issues less easy to establish than that matter of fact. Newton himself felt, however, that something more than such a narrow approach was necessary. He saw it as an essential part of his task, indeed as an essential element in his philosophical discovery, to make it clear that the dispersion of the coloured rays associated with refraction was not some sort of accident or casual circumstance associated with refraction, but was unavoidable in the physical nature of things because each coloured ray— forming a band in the rainbow, for example—is not only always identified by its own peculiar degree of refrangibility but always exists as a distinct entity, an element of white light. The coloured rays are the elements, white light a compound. This was the odd, and indeed truly paradoxical discovery.

The "New Theory about Light and Colours"

Newton was not the last and perhaps was not the first scientist to augment his readers' problems in assimilating his work by first propounding it in too brief and terse a form. Perhaps, had the readers of the first optical paper that Newton addressed to Henry Oldenburg (which the latter printed in his *Philosophical Transactions* on 19 February) been able to work through the rather forbidding pages of the optical lectures, they would have perceived that Newton was no lightweight paradoxer and better comprehended the points that he was making.

The paper or letter begins straightforwardly enough. In the first few pages Newton describes his surprise at the elongation of the spectrum formed by shining a beam of light through a glass prism in a darkened room, in the direction normal to the axis of the prism; and relates how he was drawn on to the "crucial experiment" wherein he refracted the separated coloured rays through a second prism parallel to the first (Fig. 9, p. 55) and then measured, one by one, their unlike refractions.

And so the true cause of the length of that Image [spectrum] was detected to be no other, then that *Light* consists of *Rays differently refrangible*, which, without any respect to a difference in their incidence, were, according to their degrees of re-frangibility, transmitted towards divers parts of the wall (Letter 40, p. 95).

Newton's terse and polished narrative was a highly artificial reconstruction of what actually happened, and therefore some writers (like Lohne) have been inclined to infer that Newton's most famous experiment may have been as imaginary as it was crucial, at least in its precise details. But even if the experiment was a heuristic device, it was a concise representation of much solid experience. Among his contemporaries, Newton's real difficulties began with the next paragraph of the paper in which, without further justification of his inference, Newton boldly declared that "Light it self is a *Heterogeneous mixture of differently refrangible Rays* (ibid.)."

This, his second philosophical discovery, and surely in his own mind that of deeper significance, in a rather curious way Newton failed to examine in detail in the paper. Instead he argued (correctly) for the greater significance of chromatic aberration as compared with spherical aberration as an imperfection in lenses, and then laid down a "doctrine" of colours:

not an Hypothesis but most rigid consequence, not conjectured by barely inferring 'tis thus because not otherwise or because it satisfies all phenomena (the Philosophers universall Topick,) but evinced by the mediation of experiments concluding directly & without any suspicion of doubt (ibid., p. 97).

Briefly, the "doctrine" embraces the following propositions:

1. A specific refrangibility is in one-to-one correspondence with each colour: so the science of colours is mathematical (in relation to refraction).

2. This correspondence is fixed and unalterable.

3. Primary colours are constant, homogeneous, and unchangeable; compounded colours may be formed from them, and again resolved into their elements by refraction.

4. Refraction analyses heterogeneous white light into its homogeneous coloured constituents, separated as distinct rays.

5. Reflection also analyses white light, reflecting surfaces returning one or more constituents more copiously and then appearing of the appropriate colour.

It will be noted that Newton here suppresed his belief that the variety of refrangible rays is infinite (though the shading of colour perceived by the eye is not); the borders of the orange band in the spectrum, for example, must have diverged through refraction, or the band would appear infinitely narrow.

Newton concluded with notes on the precautions to be observed in repeating his experiments, if they were to reveal the same phenomena that he had detected. He added the experiment in which refracted light was reunited by a large lens (see Fig. 7, p. 45), describing the effect of blocking a colour so that its light does not reach the lens.

Reactions to the "New Theory"

Discussion of Newton's "New Theory" lasted until 1678. Relatively little of this was concerned with the original discovery of divergence (chromatic aberration), and this part—in principle at least—was easy to dispose of. For example, the Jesuit Father Pardies's objections that the elongation of the spectrum could (contrary to Newton) be reconciled with the ordinary geometry of refraction was answered by Newton's pointing out that he had been careful to ensure equality of the incident and emergent angles of the beam of light at the faces of the prism (Ziggelaar 1971); in this condition, a small angular disparity between the incident rays (corresponding to the sun's diameter of half a degree) can only cause a very slightly larger disparity among the emergent rays, not the excess of more than two degrees found in Newton's observation. So with much else of a straightforward character (Letter 55, pp. 140–1).

On the other hand, the reiterated preference of the two great practical opticians in the Royal Society, Christiaan Huygens and Robert Hooke, for the established refracting telescope was harder to overcome. Neither man could accept at first Newton's argument that the scattering of rays due to chromatic aberration was greater than that due to spherical aberration; and Hooke pointed out that the image formed by a mirror is as much impaired by the latter effect, as the image formed by a lens. (Mistakenly, he supposed that it would be harder to parabolize a mirror than to make a hyperbolic lens, such as Descartes had suggested for the correction of spherical aberration.) Hooke and Huygens were justified in their scepticism so far as late-seventeenth-century astronomical practice was concerned, for the refracting telescope continued to be that used by astronomers (including Newton himself). Nevertheless (and quite correctly) Newton was to prove in 15 pages of *Opticks*, as formerly in his replies to his critics printed in the *Philosophical Transactions*, that "it is not the spherical Figures of Glasses, but the different refrangibility of the Rays which hinders the perfection of Telescopes" (*Opticks*, p 100). It is at this place (Book I, Part I, Prop. 7) that Newton speaks of a compound lens, not for the correction of chromatic aberration, but rather to correct the *spherical* error:

by this means might Telescopes be brought to sufficient perfection, were it not for the different Refrangibility of [the] several sorts of Rays. But by reason of this different Refrangibility, I do not yet see any other means of improving Telescopes by Refractions alone, than that of increasing their lengths . . . (p. 102).

Hooke's rejection of the "New Theory"

Far more troublesome, and far more of an impediment to the acceptance of Newton's ideas about light and colour (on the Continent in particular) was the inability of qualified commentators to perceive that these ideas necessarily flowed from his experiments. Robert Hooke, for example, in his report to the Royal Society on Newton's first optical paper, simply restated his own conception of light: that it is 'a pulse or motion, propagated through an homogeneous, uniform and transparent medium'. Refraction, occurring at the interface between two different transparent mediums—for reasons believed by Hooke to be adequately explained in his own *Micrographia* (1665)—caused a splitting or rarefaction of the incident beam and a modification of its pulse, so that the 'two colours' (that is, red and blue) appeared at the edges of the beam, and others between 'by the dilutings and intermixture of those two'. In Hooke's view, a second refraction in the opposite sense to the first simply restored the 'simple and uniform pulse as it was at first'. Apart from Hooke's failure to understand Newton's experiments (which he did not attempt to fault) in a precise and literal sense, it is obvious that while Newton held throughout his life to a notion of light based upon the phenomenon of refraction, Hooke equally held always to a notion based on interference phenomena (as we call them).

Hooke exceedingly annoyed Newton by referring to Newton's 'hypothesis of solving the phenomena of colours' and his assertion that Hooke's own 'hypothesis'—or indeed other ideas altogether—would account for the experiments just as well, 'without any manner of difficulty or straining' (Letter 44, pp. 110–14). Newton's object, as the optical lectures make abundantly clear, had throughout been not to propose a plausible hypothesis for the nature of light but to propound certain precise, if incomplete, conclusions that he regarded as irrefutable. As Alan Shapiro has well argued, Newton was no probabilist, but rather in true Baconian fashion a seeker after definite truths solidly established by experiment and mathematical reasoning. For Hooke to maintain that 'splitting of the homogeneous' was as good an account of what Newton had seen in his experiments as 'separation of the heterogeneous' appeared to Newton to display not only a lack of discrimination in the meaning of concepts and a prejudiced adherence to Hooke's own notions, but a flagrant disregard of the evidence. How could a pure prismatic green be a product of blue and red when as green it survived a second refraction? How could there not be an infinity of coloured rays forming the spectrum when each part of it is illuminated by a ray following a uniquely refracted path?

The incomprehension of Huygens

Huygens too, whose basic work in optics lay already (like Hooke's) in the past, though its publication was still far in the future, could not understand why variations and combinations of two colours only—in his case yellow and blue—should not suffice to produce all the others, and white. It would be easier, Huygens thought, to find a mechanical hypothesis, an 'hypothesis of motion', to account for just two colours than for an infinite variety. Until Newton

hath found this *Hypothesis*, he hath not taught us, what it is wherein consists the nature and difference of Colours, but only this accident (which certainly is very considerable,) of their *different Refrangibility* (Letter 99; Cohen 1958a, p. 136).

Huygens evidently had not considered that Newton had made no claim to explore the physical nature of light and colours, and his limitation of theory to two colours seemed as strange to Newton as it does to us. Hooke had offered against Newton the ingenious analogy that there is no more necessity

that all those motions, or whatever else it be that makes colours, should originally be in the simple rays of light, . . . than that all those sounds must be in the air of the bellows, which are afterwards to issue from the organ-pipes (Letter 44, p. 111);

turning the same analogy against Huygens, it might have been urged that we do not imagine all sounds to be variations and combinations of two fundamental notes.

These long debates, filling the greater part of the first volume of Newton's printed *Correspondence*, neither sprang from nor engendered true meetings of minds. Newton's experimental study of refraction and its associated colour-phenomena, already codified in the optical lectures, not to say the precision of his geometrical treatment, was so far beyond anything known to his contemporaries that their criticisms were largely beside the point. Hooke did, however, correctly identify Newton's preference for a corpuscular or emission theory of light as a substance over a pulse or wave theory of light as a mode of motion, preferred by Huygens and himself. These two men can hardly have failed to perceive that in a corpuscular theory the light-bodies could be infinitely varied in their velocity of movement, their magnitude, or their rotation (as Decartes had imagined). Curiously, both men formulated their own notions of light in such a way as to deny such infinite variation—hence their preference for the dichotomous hypothesis. It was left to Newton himself to point out that waves of constant velocity can vary infinitely in length (or frequency), for in his reply to Hooke's report (11 June 1672) Newton told him that the most natural form of the wave-theory was to suppose that the "agitated parts of [luminous] bodies . . . do excite Vibrations in the *aether* of various depths or bignesses, which being promiscuously propagated through that *Medium* to our Eyes, effect in us a Sensation of Light of a *White* colour". Whiteness, then, is the perceived mixture of all the vibrations, as naturally propagated by extremely hot bodies. By "depth or bigness" Newton might mean the amplitude of vibrations (or we may perhaps say, waves in the aether) but far more probably wavelength; the relation $c = f.\lambda$ was of course obvious to him. Then, he goes on to argue that the colour red will be associated with the uniformly longer of these diverse vibrations, blue with the uniformly shorter ones, with other colours falling between these limits. He draws the obvious analogy with sound (Letter 67, p. 175). The longer vibrations are also stronger, and "are best able to overcome the resistance of a Refracting superficies, and so break through it with least Refraction . . .", a property causing the dispersion of light in the spectrum.

Difficulties for Newton in establishing his position

It was thus quite unnecessary that the preference for a wave or pulse hypothesis entertained by Hooke or Huygens should have prevented their treating seriously Newton's discovery of the infinite range of rays within the
limits of the visible spectrum—which was to prove the first step towards the
later series of discoveries of the extent of the electro-magnetic spectrum as
a whole. That Newton's letter on his "New Theory of Light and Colours"
contained substantial discoveries was certainly appreciated by members of
the Royal Society (Barrow among them), who were disconcerted by
Hooke's swift and biting criticisms of them, and by such men as Richard
Towneley, who suggested that the letter ought to be given a wide circulation
in a Latin translation. But the well-known technical difficulties of repeating
Newton's "crucial experiment" precisely, and the difficulty also of demonstrating the pre-existence of the colours seen in the spectrum in seemingly
undifferentiated white light before its refraction for a long time impeded the
general acceptance of Newton's "New Theory" and the experiments upon
which it was based.

Newton's efforts, in the face of objections, to vindicate his theory of the
heterogeneity of white light against its various critics are not altogether easy
to understand, especially as he opened his defence (against Hooke) by refuting a different point, that colours might arise from "irregularities" in the
rays. Newton says that two refractions, the second opposite to the first,
revealed no such "irregularities". Then,

amongst other irregularities, if the first Prism had spread & dissipated every ray into
an indefinite number of diverging parts, the second should in like manner have
spread and dissipated every one of those parts into a further indefinite number,
whereby the Image would have been still more dilated; contrary to the event (ibid.,
p. 178).

Since everything that happens in refraction is related to the geometry of
the refracting body, it is inconceivable that Hooke (or anyone else) would
suppose that a second refraction, by a prism placed in the opposite sense
to the first prism, would increase the effect of the first refraction; if, however, the second refraction be made in a second prism placed in the same
sense as the first, then Hooke or another would have been correct in claiming that thereby 'the Image is still more dilated' by the second refraction.
It would be inconsistent with Newton's own ideas of refraction to suppose
otherwise. In the nineteenth century many spectroscopes were made with
trains of prisms placed in the same sense purposely to 'dilate the Image' and
so separate the spectral lines. It is hard to see the fault that Newton found
in Hooke.

The experiment with crossed prisms

Newton's most telling evidence against Hooke's view of refraction was the experiment with crossed prisms (Fig. 10—to be distinguished from the "crucial experiment" with parallel prisms, as in Fig. 9). Here, instead of the refracted beam's being stretched transversely into a square by the second prism—which must be roughly identical with the first—the resultant spectrum is of the same shape and size as that produced by the first prism alone, but is now inclined at an angle of 45° to the axes of the crossed prisms. This event is readily explained by Newton's view that the usual spectrum consists of innumerable overlapping images of the solar disk, each formed by light of a particular, mathematically-defined refrangibility. If each cone of light forming an image is bent first one way, and then equally another way normal to the first, a 45° displacement of the spectrum must result. Hooke's hypothesis of a 'splitting' of the beam could be accommodated to explain this experimental finding by the supposition that the initial splitting created cones of light exactly like those which Newton supposed to have pre-existed in the incident white beam.

It will be noted that Newton's theory attends *exactly* to the geometry of the formation of the spectrum in a way which Hooke's had not done, and perhaps could not do. Moreover, the further a 'Hooke' concept of refraction is stretched to accommodate Newtonian experimental results, the more arbitrary and the less defensible it must seem.

It is not surprising that in *Opticks* (Book I, Part I, Prop. 2, Experiment 5, pp. 34–45) Newton dwelt at some length on this experiment of the crossed prisms and the twisted spectrum, and its elaborations. It had not been mentioned in the first paper on the "New Theory of Light and Colours" and in both versions of the optical lectures it had served a different purpose,

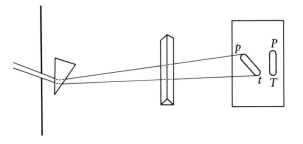

Fig. 10. The experiment with crossed prisms, showing that the spectrum is neither split nor dilated, but displaced as a whole by the second prism; *PT* is the normal spectrum, *pt* the displaced spectrum. After *Opticks*, p. 36; the same in Shapiro (1984), p. 440.

that of demonstrating simply the fact of the varying refraction of the coloured rays (Shapiro 1984, pp. 89, 441). The use of the experiment to prove that a spectrum cannot be stretched laterally (or dilated) by a second refraction, because a second refraction normal to the first can only shift the axis of the spectrum askew, seems to have occurred to Newton only when he needed to defend his concept of the heterogeneity of light, to the exposition of which the whole of Book I, Part I, Prop. 2 is devoted. Here is a major example of the way in which the polemic following the publication of the "New Theory" caused Newton both to amplify and to modify his former exposition.

The colours of thin plates again

With some show of reluctance, Newton allowed his replies to Hooke and other critics to be published in the *Philosophical Transactions* during the year 1672. As he prepared these *ad hominem* replies, Newton's mind turned to a fuller account of his ideas and experiments concerning light and colour, going beyond the material already written out in the optical lectures, which he surely felt by now did not meet the situation developing after the publication of the "New Theory". Negatively, he would have to dispose in advance of the various difficulties already raised by his critics; positively, he needed to bring within the scope of his own theory optical phenomena of colours not known to him in the 1660s, such as the phenomena of thin plates (Hooke) and of diffraction (Grimaldi). The former had been barely alluded to in the optical lectures. Accordingly, he indicated to Henry Oldenburg in May 1672 that he had meant his reply to Hooke to be accompanied by a "discourse" on

the Phaenomena of Plated Bodies, concerning which I shall by experiments first show how according to their several thicknesses they reflect or transmit the rays indued with severall colours, and then consider the relation which these thin transparent Plates have to the parts of other naturall Bodies, in order to a fuller understanding of the causes of their colours also (Letter 62, p. 160).

Characteristically, Newton added that the purport of this discourse was to declare the different *reflectibility* of the several sorts of rays, as it had been that of the "New Theory" to declare their different refrangibility. In the event, Newton realized that he could not make Pardies and Hooke wait for their answers while he composed such a paper, which would in any case be irrelevant to the matters at issue with them; he therefore dispatched separate replies to Oldenburg, and the discourse sank from sight for a further two and a half years. Nevertheless, it is certain that Newton was already preparing the material that was in due time to be published as Book II of *Opticks*.

Others besides Hooke and Huygens disputed either Newton's experimental descriptions or his interpretations. Though it may be doubted whether Fr. Ignace Gaston Pardies or the Jesuits of Liège presented so formidable a challenge to Newton or raised questions of such deep scientific interest, their doubts do invoke issues concerning authority and confirmation in the acceptance of scientific research. Fr. Pardies, a capable mathematician, withdrew his objections upon receiving further enlightenment from Newton. The Jesuits, on the other hand, carried on a long and to Newton a tiresome battle. They refused to accept Newton's 'geometrical idealization' of the prismatic spectrum, which T. S. Kuhn thought 'symptomatic of the intellectual extrapolations that mark his contributions to science' (Cohen 1958*a*, p. 35); and they found with their prism that the spectrum was less elongated, in proportion to its breadth, than Newton had claimed. From this discrepancy it might have been gathered that all glasses do not possess equal powers of dispersion; but such an idea did not pass through Newton's mind (ibid., pp. 169–75).

§4. The "Discourse of Observations", 1675

Newton measures the 'rings'

In *Micrographia* (1665) Robert Hooke noted the (interference) colours occurring in thin transparent plates or layers, like those of mica, and explained them as produced by the interaction between light reflected directly to the eye from the upper surface of the plate, and other light reflected upwards from the lower, internal surface, and therefore twice refracted through the upper surface (*Micrographia*, p. 66). His explanation accounted for the critically small interval between the two surfaces bounding the plate. We have no certain means of knowing whether Newton's first notes upon colours of this kind followed or preceded his reading of *Micrographia*—his annotations upon this book barely record Hooke's account. Nor is the absolute date of Newton's first experiments upon the colours of thin plates any more certain. Westfall has attributed them to 1666 (1965, p. 182), but nothing dictates that they were not made after his return to Cambridge from Lincolnshire in 1667.

What is clear is that Newton's experiments began very differently from Hooke's: nothing like mica figured in them. Newton had been studying, with prisms, the transition from refraction to reflection and vice versa at the critical angle. In some configurations (as shown in *Opticks*, Book, I, Part I, Prop. 2, Experiment 10, p. 29) he used two prisms tied together to make a glass parallelopiped. He noticed dark or white spots appearing in the centre of the contiguous surfaces, and "severall circles of colours" surrounding them. Sometimes as many as 25 alternations of red and blue could be detected; in monochromatic light cast by a prism they were all of the chosen hue. Newton then took a step Hooke had not taken. He created a precisely shaped air-space between two glass surfaces by pressing a convex lens of 25 inches radius hard upon a flat glass plate. Assuming actual contact at the centre, he could calculate the thickness of the air-layer at each distance from the centre (or spot) where a coloured ring appeared. Finding by measurement that the fifth ring or circle of colour was 6¼ hundredths of an inch in diameter, Newton calculated that the air-thickness between the lens and the plate at the first circle was 1/64 000 inch; he supposed this thickness to double, treble, etc. for successive circles. (Later, more correctly, Newton supposed these thicknesses to increase, at equal distances from the centre, as the series of odd numbers.)

In a subsequent series of experiments—certainly made before 1672, when Newton had a paper on this topic ready for the Royal Society—he used a lens of 50 feet radius, making considerably larger circles, as recorded both in the notebook and in a more theoretical essay "On coloured circles twixt two contiguous Glasses" (printed in Westfall, 1965). By now, if not before, he was convinced that the minimum interval of 1/64 000 (which he tended to diminish to 1/83 000, in *Opticks* to 1/89 000) represented "the space of a pulse of the vibrating medium": he would explain later that these vibrations in the aether were caused by the passage through it of the light-particles. Filling the space between the glasses with water rather than air, "the thickness of a vibration was 1/100,000 inch, or 3/4 of its former dimensions, viz. as the densitys of the interjected mediums". Since like Descartes and Hooke, Newton supposed the refraction of a light beam at the interface between two media to be caused by a change in its velocity, this observation suggested that the same velocity variation was a factor affecting the diameters of the coloured circles. For

If the rays were incident obliquely, the circles increased so that their diameters are as the secants of the rays obliquity within the film of air, or reciprocally as their celerity within the said film.

And the thicknesse belonging to each vibration is as the squares of these secants of celeritys. And the lengths of the rays belonging to each vibration as their cubes.

Just as Newton had formerly measured the relative refrangibilities of the red and violet rays in the prismatic spectrum, so now starting from the actual measurement of the diameters of circles he established the relative lengths of the pulses associated with red and violet: "The thicknesse of a pulse of extreme rubiform rays to that of purpuriform ones perpendicularly incident is greater than 3 to 2 & lesse than 5 to 3. viz. as 9 to 14 or 13 to 20." Then, extending the same technique, he established a series of ratios:

the thicknesse belonging to each colour is 13, 14, 14½, 15½, 16½, 17½, 18½ 19 for extreame purple, intense purple, Indico, blew, green, the terminus of green & yellow, yellow, orang, red, extream red (Hall 1955, p. 35).

Thus the periodicity of the coloured circles, perceived by Hooke, and hence of the physical mechanism by which they are produced, was quantitatively established by Newton's measurements.

That the circles broaden as the light falls on the glass more and more obliquely is also noted in Newton's annotations upon *Micrographia*, perhaps indicating his prior knowledge of these colours. Newton appreciated that the obliquity of the ray increased the path-length between the glass surfaces, and so broadened the circles, but in *Opticks* (1952, p. 298) he also remarked that if the incident light became so oblique as to reach the critical angle (though he does not use this term) the formation of the coloured circles would again be modified.

The manuscripts make it clear that Newton's early investigations of interference-colours were in their experimental detail and precision of quite a different order from Hooke's. It is hardly surprising that he reacted angrily (in two letters) to Hooke's sneer that the sum of what Newton had sent to the Royal Society was to be found in his own *Micrographia*. In a letter to Oldenburg (21 December 1675) Newton acknowledged that the observation of "plated bodies exhibiting colours [was] a Phaenomenon for the notice of which I thank him", but, Newton went on

he left me to find out & make such experiments about it as might inform me of the manner of production of those colours to ground an Hypothesis on; he having given no further insight into it then this that the colour depended on some certain thickness of the plate: though what that thickness was at every colour he confesses in his *Micrographia* he had attempted in vain to learn & therefore seeing I was left to measure it my self I suppose he will allow me to make use of what I tooke the pains to find out (Letter 150, p. 406).

Despite an apologetic letter from Hooke (who sought to put the blame for misunderstanding on Oldenburg) his position in Newton's esteem could never be restored.

The published form of Newton's investigation of the coloured rings formed in thin transparent bodies, in *Opticks* Book II, was based upon a "Discourse of Observations" sent by him to the Royal Society on 7 December 1675. Before sending it, he had written to Oldenburg (on 13 November):

I have one discourse by me of that subject [optics] written when I sent my first letters to you about colours & of which I then gave you notice. This you may command when you think it will be convenient . . . (Letter 143, p. 358).

Here indicated was the letter of 21 May 1672, quoted at the close of the last chapter, in which Newton had indeed promised a discourse about the optics of "Plated Bodies". Oldenburg naturally found it convenient to receive as soon as possible this long-deferred communication. Newton, obligingly submitting the paper at once, never permitted Oldenburg to print it.

To fill the gap between the notebook entries of the late 1660s and this "Discourse" of mid-1672 there is the manuscript headed "Of the coloured

circles twixt two continguous glasses" discovered by Richard S. Westfall and
by him assigned to 1670. It records all that we know of Newton's study of
this subject before the "Discourse", and marks the end of his long involvement with optical experiments. Still to follow were two isolated episodes:
the investigation of the colours of *thick* plates (?1681) and of diffraction
(?*c*. 1691). This 1670 sketch derived from the notebooks and was to be in
turn the source of the "Discourse". Notably in it Newton derived the ratio
14:9 or 20:13 as that of the lengths of the pulses of purple and red light,
from which ratio he in turn derived the relative sizes of the particles constituting the surface of opaque bodies, upon which sizes their colours (as we
see them) depend (cf. *Opticks*, p. 210; Westfall 1980, pp. 216, 221).

The first two parts of Book II of *Opticks* and the first six propositions
of Part 3 (to p. 262), making some 69 printed pages in all, follow the "Discourse" almost word for word. Newton did add some new material, and he
changed many of the numbers; but the essence and the greater part of the
detail in the two texts is the same. Not all the diagrams of the printed book
are to be found in the "Discourse", however, at least as it was printed for
the first time by Thomas Birch in 1756. Sometimes in his work of revision
Newton nodded over trifles. For example, he reworked the numbers in the
Table (p. 233) giving the thicknesses of plates of various materials at which
colours of the various successive rings were seen. Later, relating these
dimensions to those of the corpuscles of bodies he correctly in *Opticks*
(p. 255) inserted his revised numerator of the fraction, 16¼, in place of
17½, but incorrectly wrote the denominator as 10 000, instead of 1 000 000
as rightly given in the "Discourse".

When, in the revision, he came to the end of the third section of the
"Discourse" Newton added for *Opticks* a long section on the impossibility
of light's being reflected by the solid particles of bodies: light striking these
is probably "stifled and lost". Rather, Newton holds, "Reflection of a Ray
is effected not be a single point of the reflecting Body [such as a corpuscle]
but by some power of the Body which is evenly diffused all over its Surface,
and by which it acts upon the Ray without immediate contact. For that the
parts of Bodies do act upon Light at a distance shall be shown hereafter"
(p. 266). Newton had, in fact, already made this point in a more speculative
way in the *Principia* (Book I, Section XIV) and gives substance to it by his
diffraction experiments reported later in *Opticks*. Ultimately, he was to
assert the existence of both an attractive and a repulsive force.

'Matter' is largely vacuity

We need not review all Newton's arguments here, but may mention one
because it led him at this point in *Opticks* to introduce a short essay on a
favourite topic: his contention that the solid parts (corpuscles or atoms) of
bodies form only a minute proportion of their volume, the greater part of

the whole bulk even of gold consisting of the spaces between the particles—whether vacuous or filled by aether. It is clearly inconsistent with this contention that most of the incident light should be reflected or refracted by the surfaces of the solid particles, since most of the light must pass between the atoms and only a rare ray will strike one directly. Hence (paradoxically enough) it must be the case that most of the light leaving the body must have been reflected or refracted by the spaces between the particles.

Through the earlier sections of Book II Newton develops his theory of the colours arising in thin plates (involving the segregation of the coloured rays in white light both by refraction and by reflection) and so acquires quantitative information about the association between colour and the sizes of the corpuscles that seem to the eye to possess these colours. Having established this association he can then explain why bodies appear coloured, still maintaining that "Bodies reflect and refract Light by one and the same power, variously expressed in various Circumstances" (Opticks, p. 269). What these 'circumstances' are Newton then goes on to explain by elaborating his theory of alternate "fits" of easy transmission and easy reflection.

These pages of Opticks draw no less heavily upon material first submitted to the Royal Society in December 1675, under the title of "An Hypothesis explaining the Properties of Light discoursed of in my severall Papers", sent to London with the "Discourse of Observations" just discussed. The "Hypothesis" was in fact read and debated by the Society before the "Discourse".

The "Hypothesis of Light"

Newton had hitherto no more explained how coloured rings are actually caused to appear in thin plates, than he had explained how the prism segregates the coloured rays in white light to form the spectrum. It was of course obvious to him that the rings must be produced by a similar segregation of the coloured rays in white light, but the physical mechanism of the two phenomena could not be the same, if only because the rings are markedly periodic and are functionally related (as Hooke had discovered) to the thickness of the layer causing them. Newton was also aware of the fact that while in the 'Newton's rings' experiment some rays are reflected back to the eye, counterpart rays are transmitted through the layer forming the rings to become visible on the far side of the plate (Opticks, p. 206, Observation 9). Now whatever may be said for or against Hooke's theory of the pulse nature of light, it is evident that he had succeeded (if with some strain upon the imagination) in linking the colours of ordinary refraction with those of thin plates. Now Newton had to do as much: the segregation of the bands of colours in the spectrum had to be shown to be functionally linked with the segregation of colours into rings. There was, in fact, no adequate experimental or mathematical approach accessible to Newton (or anyone else) by which he could link the two phenomena. Therefore he could only propose a hypothesis about the nature of this process of segregation, which in turn required a hypothesis about the nature of light.

Newton's scientific fantasy

Once released from a self-imposed restriction to tell only what he firmly and for sound experimental reasons believed to be true, and after prudently declaring that he would not be held to account positively for anything contained in the "Hypothesis", Newton launched with extraordinary speculative freedom into a scientific fantasy which has few parallels in his writings; among them are the well-known and closely-connected letter to Robert Boyle of 28 February 1679, the strange alchemical paper on 'The Vegetation of Metals' (Burndy MS 16, still unpublished; see Westfall 1980, pp. 305–6)—if this was really composed by Newton, and some passages in the Queries appended to *Opticks*. (Only these last were printed in Newton's lifetime.) Here, Newton seems to be saying, is a picture of the inner, secret workings of Nature as we can best imagine them. It is a picture so unlike that yielded by the established mechanical philosophies of Descartes and Gassendi, so far beyond the confines of mathematical science as practised by Galileo, Huygens, and Wallis, so much influenced by the reading of chemical and alchemical authors that Newton had undertaken during the previous six years (at least) that some have seen here the intrusion of occult traditions into Newton's scientific outlook. We find Newton expatiating on not only capillary attraction and the conservation of heat in the Sun, but muscular physiology and the action of the nerves, electrical effluvia excited by friction and their attractive and repulsive effects, and the sociability of metals one with another, all by way of expounding an aetherial hypothesis of light. As Westfall has remarked, Newton's powerful philosophical imagination, hitherto pent up, suddenly burst forth in an inspired rhapsody. This was no routine essay: 'No amount of feigned indifference and [Newton's] hard words about insignificant disputes could obscure the significance the enterprise held for him' (Westfall 1980, p. 270).

De Aere et Aethere

Newton may already, before composing the "Hypothesis", have begun "Upon Air and Aether", which he soon abandoned. In this he attributed a number of phenomena to a repulsion of air-particles from solid matter, which repulsion he may have intended to explain by the action of a universal aether (Hall and Hall 1962, pp. 214–20). At any rate, in the "Hypothesis" he made the aether the active agent in Nature. It is "much of the same constitution with air, but far rarer, subtiler & more strongly Elastic;" perhaps matter itself may be only this aether "condensed by a fermental principle". Perhaps the aether causes a pendulum to come to rest quite quickly even within a vessel exhausted of air. It is probably involved in electrical effluvia, penetrates glass and other solids, and may be the cause of gravity. Nature "is a perpetuall circulatory worker, generating fluids out of solids, and solids out of fluids" and a sort of circulation of aether by the "vast body of the Earth, which may be everywhere to the very center in perpetuall working" is possibly an important factor in its economy. This aether (Newton wrote) is repelled by matter and so, becoming denser in empty spaces, it causes adhesion and cohesion in matter and the activity of animal muscles in animals. It may also be the 'animal spirits' of the physicians, controlled by the soul, which react in various ways with the solid substances of the animal body. And so on . . . at some length (Letter 146). The continuity of ideas so characteristic of Newton's intellect is indicated by his resurrection of such notions in the final lines added to the second edition of the *Principia* (1713):

Some things might now be added about a certain most subtle spirit pervading gross bodies and lying unperceived in them, by whose force and actions the particles of bodies at the least distances attract one another mutually and when they become contiguous cohere; and electric bodies act at greater distances, both repelling and attracting light objects; and light is emitted, reflected, refracted, diffracted and heats bodies; and all sensation is stimulated and the limbs of animals are moved at will, that is, by the vibrations of this spirit propagated from the external organs of sensation to the brain and from the brain to the muscles, through the solid filaments of the nerves.

Refraction and reflection reconciled

The optical theory of the "Hypothesis" is one whereby Newton is enabled to reach his goal of uniting optical reflection and refraction in a single physical mechanism: as he explained in the "Discourse of Observations" (and later in *Opticks*) the "disposition" in the ray to be reflected or refracted is connate in the ray, and immutable, and of course associated with colour. "Light", Newton wrote, "is neither this Aether nor its vibrating motion, but something of a different kind propagated from lucid bodies . . . let every man here take his fancy" (Letter 146, p. 370). Whatever it is, light must possess a heterogeneous character, and, further, its motion must be such that it creates vibrations in the aether. Newton argues that these vibrations are not themselves light because (1) the sharpness of shadows requires strictly rectilinear propagation, and (2) the colours of thin plates require a dual factor; for, the periodicity of the rings

argues that it depends upon the number of vibrations between the two superficies of the plate whether the ray shall be reflected or transmitted; yet I cannot see, how the number should vary the case, be it greater or less, whole or broken, unless Light be supposed something else then these vibrations (ibid., p. 371).

Now where there is a boundary between two transparent bodies of different refractive index, the aether will be less dense on the one side than on the other (the density varying through a small distance) and this change of density causes a curvature in the ray passing through the boundary. If this bending is fairly small it is, in effect, refraction according to the sine-law, as Descartes had shown; but if the curvature is extreme the ray bends right back and is, in effect, reflected (as in *Principia*, Book I, Section XIV). The greater the difference in aether-density the greater the curvature of the ray, which perhaps (Newton says) accounts for the high reflectivity of metals. But why is it that when parallel rays in air strike transparent bodies (glass, water) "they may be at the same time some reflected, other refracted"? The answer, wrote Newton, is that the impact of the light-ray upon the denser medium causes vibrations in it, much like sound-waves, which spread through both media and heat both:

Aetherial vibrations are therefore the best means by which such a Subtile Agent as Light can shake the gross particles of Solid bodyes to heat them (Letter 146, p. 374).

The vibrations or waves in the aether rarefy and condense it alternately; where the aether is condensed it will have a stronger tendency to reflect the light-ray—conversely, to refract it where the aether is rarefied.

Aether-waves

Moreover, Newton suggests, the aether-waves are as various as the light-rays to which they correspond: the longest waves associate with the red rays, the shortest with the purple. It is these waves (rather than the rays directly) that affect the human nervous system, enabling us to perceive colours "And possibly colour may be distinguisht into its principall Degrees, Red, Orange, Yellow, Green, Blew, Indigo and deep Violett, on the same ground, that Sound within an eighth [octave] is graduated into tones" (ibid., p. 376). For the first time since the lectures, Newton here explains his curious speculation about the harmonic division of the spectrum (see §3 above).

So far Newton has spoken of an unspecified differentiation in the rays themselves, to which corresponds the wavelength differentiation in the vibrations that the rays create in the aether. Now he makes the assertion that the differentiation in the rays is one of "bigness" or "strength" in some way:

the biggest or strongest rays must penetrate the refracting superficies [boundary] more freely & easily then the weaker, & so be less turned awry by it, that is, less refracted; . . . (ibid., p. 377).

This was, as we have seen, an old 'projectile' idea of Newton's. Schematically, we have

Colour	Ray	Aether wave	Refrangibility	Reflexibility
Red	Strong	Long	Slight	Slight
Violet	Weak	Short	Great	Great

(Here, "Refrangibililty" and "Reflexibility" signify the ease or difficulty with which the ray of any colour is refracted or reflected at an interface which it strikes near the critical angle. Both are measures of ease of deviation from the straight path, always greater in blue than in red). Newton then explains how, if the "disposition" to be transmitted or reflected is found along the length of the ray, the thickness of the plate determines the colour seen or (in the case of the lens-and-plate experiment) the succession of rings, each appearing where the interval between the boundaries is an integral multiple of the wavelength. Obviously a further hypothesis is required which Newton duly introduces: the aether-wave has to travel ahead of the ray to create the disposition at the next boundary. By implication, therefore, light is supposed to propagate at a finite speed, a point that Newton proves from astronomy (after Roemer, 1676) in *Opticks*.

The "Fits" (without waves) in Opticks

Newton modified this hypothesis in Book II of *Opticks*, where the aether and its waves disappear but the dispositions they have created in the light-rays remain, now (rather unfortunately) denominated "fits", that is alternations. In the printed book Newton was careful to put his new statement of the dispositions on a strictly phenomenalist basis, making it the twelfth proposition of Book II that

Every Ray of Light in its passage through any refracting Surface is put into a certain transient Constitution or State, which in the progress of the Ray returns at equal Intervals, and disposes the Ray at every return to be easily transmitted through the next refracting Surface, and between the returns to be easily reflected by it (*Opticks*, p. 278).

This is "manifest" by the phenomena of colours in thin plates. We do not need a hypothesis to explain this undoubted fact of the periodic dispositions in the rays, Newton goes on, but those persons who

are averse from assenting to any new Discoveries, but such as they can explain by an Hypothesis, may for the present suppose, that . . . the Rays of Light, by impinging on any refracting or reflecting Surface, excite vibrations in the refracting or reflecting Medium or Substance . . . (ibid., p. 280).

This is equivalent to the formulation on the "Hypothesis", but different from it in that there the aether was the vehicle of the vibrations.

A major conceptual advantage that Newton gains by detaching the asserted *fact* of dispositions or "fits" of easy transmission and easy reflection, repeating along the ray, from the hypothesis of aether-waves is that the aether can be dispensed with, and with it vanish awkward questions about the variations of aether-density he had postulated and the speed of waves in different aethers. The *Opticks* version was, moreover, consistent with the force-mechanics treatment of optical phenomena in the *Principia*. The major weakness of the "fits" as treated in the *Opticks* without the aetherial hypothesis, and without any clear indication of what it is that is subject to these "fits", is that it is impossible to make any model of them, just as it is impossible to make a model for Newtonian gravity. The anti-probabilistic methodology put forward by Newton in its strongest form in *Opticks* left him no choice but to affirm that the "fits" were necessarily entailed by the phenomena (just as gravity is), and therefore (like gravity) must be swallowed with whatever effort of assimilation is necessary (Shapiro 1989, p. 241). The duality or compromise of waves and particles worked adequately for a century, and the philosopher N. R. Hanson thought it needed no better justification than Newton's own: the duality was introduced 'because the data, as he knew them, *revealed themselves* as a *de facto compromise*' (Hanson 1960, p. 382). How else could the complex and indeed paradoxical phenomena of light be described?

Newton on diffraction

We have at present little or no knowledge of any manuscript background to the study by Newton (very different from the sketch in *Principia*, Book I, Section XIV) of the two types of optical phenomena with which he concluded the main text of *Opticks*. These are: the formation of coloured rays by light scattered from thick plates, and the diffraction of light by edges. The former (see below) originated from experiments made by Newton in 1681 when trying to make a large reflecting telescope. His interest in diffraction—here, the bending of light away from an object into the shadow, as discovered by F. M. Grimaldi in 1665—goes back at least to 1672. By June of that year he had learned of Grimaldi's discovery from an allusion in a letter from Fr. Pardies. But even before this, Newton may have examined Honoré Fabri's *Dialogi physici* (1669), of which John Collins had sent him a copy at the end of May 1672. The book remains to this day in Newton's library (Harrison 1978, p. 142). Fabri's first dialogue, *De Lumine*, is devoted to an analysis of Grimaldi's experiment and the reasons for preferring Fabri's explanation of the effect to Grimaldi's own. Newton must at least have scanned this dialogue, since at a meeting of the Royal Society on 18 March 1675, when Robert Hooke presented an account of his discovery of a supposedly new deflection of light in passing by a sharp edge—that is, diffraction—Newton was able to tell him that Grimaldi had preceded him, though he did not then quote Fabri's book as his authority. Having had leisure to look at the book in Cambridge, he wrote an account of Fabri's dialogue to Oldenburg (Letter 146, p. 384).

Into his "Hypothesis", then, of December 1675 Newton worked an explanation of diffraction in terms of the aether theory he had adopted, taking the phenomenon from Fabri. It is evident that he himself had as yet made no experiments bearing on the matter, and in consequence he misunderstood Fabri's far from clear account of what Grimaldi had reported. Again, in the abortive manuscript "On Air and Aether" Newton wrote of passing a very narrow beam of light of (1/20th to 1/40th of an inch wide) over "the parallel sharp edges of two or more wedges . . . you will see the image [of the sun] somewhat deflected." Since this manuscript is undated we cannot use it to establish a chronology, nor can we be sure that Newton had performed the difficult experiments of which he writes (Hall and Hall 1962, pp. 221–2). In Book I of the *Principia*, however, Newton asserted positively that

rays of light . . . in their passage near the angles of bodies, whether transparent or opaque . . . are bent and inflected round the bodies, as if they were attracted towards them. And those of these rays which in their passage approach closer to the bodies are the more curved, as though more strongly attracted, as I myself have carefully observed . . . (Newton 1687, pp. 231–2).

Despite this affirmation, these few sentences are no more precise than those devoted to diffraction by Newton in the "Hypothesis" or in "On Air and Aether", or in his speculative letter to Robert Boyle of 28 February 1679 about the aether (Letter 233). In the *Principia* passage, as in these other allusions to diffraction, Newton simply pictured diffraction as a bending of light rays round a sharp edge, so that some light reached into the geometric shadow. (This of course would make the shadow of an object placed in the beam smaller than it should be, not larger as Grimaldi, Fabri, and Hooke had all claimed.) Newton always spoke of diffraction as a "kind of refraction", and he imagined the colours of the fringes to arise by the same mechanism of segregation that he had described long before.

Diffraction in Opticks

Newton's only account of careful, indeed exemplary experiments on diffraction is in *Opticks* itself. We do not know when these experiments were made: presumably between 1685 (when Book I of the *Principia* was drafted) and the early 1690s when Newton was writing *Opticks*. As late as 1692 is likely. They are remarkable for an accuracy praised recently by Stuewer (1970), as by others before him. An accurate, if belated, view of diffraction effects must have amazed if not appalled the investigator; they were far more complex and paradoxical than he had supposed. None of his former notions could now stand, and (as we shall see) Newton was forced in Book III of *Opticks* to modify his previous ideas of the optical force. Periodic coloured circles Newton had been able to cope with by devising the theory of "fits", but periodic coloured fringes defied even his explanatory powers using the conceptual tools in his possession. The experimental work first described in the "Observations" and the theoretical scheme proposed in the "Hypothesis" provided Newton with a valuable legacy, enabling him to add a new world of optical experience to his early studies of refraction and to demonstrate still more richly the truth of his conviction that the theory of colours, of whatever origin, could be brought into a single unified scheme. But since diffraction colours occur without the light passing through an interface, and Newton understood that these are colours that are found in Nature, as in the peacock's feather, the theory of "fits" could not be further stretched to account for them, and, for all his geometrical persistence in analysing the phenomena of diffraction, Newton could not find an explanation of its colours in terms of his theoretical ideas.

§5. 'Optical Mechanics', 1685–86 (*Principia*, Book I, Section XIV, Propositions 94–96)

This section of the *Principia* is the unique portion of the book touching on light, and Newton was prudent enough to affirm only that the motions of small particles under an attractive force as studied in these propositions "are not very different from the reflections, and the refractions of light made in a given ratio of the secants, as Snell discovered, and so in a given ratio of the sines as Descartes explained" (*Principia* (1687), p. 231). The root idea of Newton's 'mechanical model' is simple: a particle moving through one medium approaches the interface separating that from a different medium. Newton treats the interface as a neutral layer of small depth (Fig. 11). At the interface the particle may be attracted normally to either medium, with a force constant at all distances. Suppose it to be attracted to the first medium, through which it has reached the interface: because the particle in passing through the interface region is effectively in a Galilean trajectory, it will describe a parabola and consequently (Newton proves) obey the sine-law in entering the second medium, the angle of emergence from the interface being greater than the angle of incidence upon the interface region from the first medium (Prop. 94). Further, the velocity of the particle is less in the second medium than in the first, also in the inverse ratio of the sines (Prop. 95). If the angle of incidence upon the interface be sufficiently large, the particle instead of penetrating into the second medium from the interface region will be attracted back into the first, and so be as it were reflected out of the interface (Prop. 96). It is clear from the ratios of the sines and the velocities in these propositions that Newton takes the first, more strongly

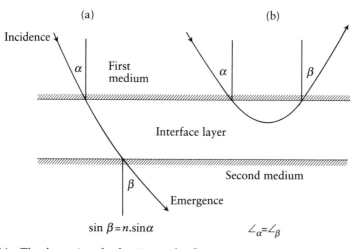

Fig. 11. The dynamics of refraction and reflection. A particle passing from a more attractive to a less attractive medium is (a) bent into a new path and slowed down or (b) turned back into the first medium. Based on *Principia* (1687), pp. 227–32.

attractive medium to be the more dense (as water or glass) and the second medium to be less dense (for example, air).

Newton had chosen his case carefully. If we treat the alternative case, disregarded in the *Principia*, where light passes from a less dense into a more dense medium, and the beam is bent towards the perpendicular to the interface, we find that the sine-law and the acceleration of the particle in the denser second medium can again be demonstrated, but Newton's argument justifying reflection cannot apply. The two cases are not symmetrical—the particle cannot reverse direction in the second medium. Perhaps this is one reason why Newton was hesitant about optical mechanics. He was aware of other problems too.

However, in support of this mechanical model, Newton noted that the velocity of light had been shown to be finite (Roemer, 1676) and that light-rays really are bent round sharp-edged obstacles: those closer to the edge are more curved than those further from it. This is the effect that Newton called 'inflection' and we call diffraction, here mentioned in print by Newton for the first time.

In subsequent propositions he demonstrated, first, that assuming light to consist of such moving particles as these, one might obtain "all those shapes [of lenses] which Descartes disclosed in his *Dioptrics* and his *Geometry* pertaining to refractions. Since Descartes made much of the [method of] discovery of these shapes and carefully concealed it, it seemed proper to explain it in this proposition" (*Principia* (1687), p. 233). Secondly, Newton demonstrated how in principle a general theory of the surfaces of biconvex lenses could be developed from the same principle.

In brief, Section XIV is the realization in the fundamental physical theory of optics—as Newton was endeavouring to formulate it—of the profound revolution in Newton's thought that had taken place in 1679–80: the revolution by which he abandoned speculations concerning the mechanical operations of quasi-Cartesian aethers, and turned instead to the postulation of forces, both attractive and repulsive, acting according to a variety of distance-laws between particles, and so causing effects visible in gross bodies. Precisely how, why, and when Newton passed through this intellectual revolution is still far from clear: his correspondence with Robert Hooke had an important share in it, while Richard S. Westfall and B. J. T. Dobbs have advanced the suggestion that Newton's alchemical lore also inspired him in this direction. It is obvious that his geometrical discovery that an elliptical orbit could be rigorously correlated with an inverse-square force-law was a powerful justification of his new concept of forces. From this origin sprang mathematical celestial mechanics: thereby Newton proved that an idea of universal gravitation could be rendered, in its consequences, demonstrable in a way that the idea of aetherial vortices and pressures could not. Partly in consequence of this, Newton's allusions to Descartes became increasingly acerbic, as in the quotation above.

Section XIV reveals the same truth in optical science. Whereas in 1675 Newton's aetherial speculations had remained vaguely qualitative, his new concept of short-range optical force (though no less speculative) was capable of mathematical expression, and so, in a general way, the action of this force could be confirmed by the consistency of propositions invoking it with well-known properties of light. Like gravitation, the optical force could be mathematized. In this way, Section XIV is Newton's greatest achievement in microphysics, that is, in the dynamics of particles. Mechanically, optical force-mechanics was a transposition into a new structure of the qualitative aetherial hypotheses of 1675 and earlier, especially in that it perpetuated Newton's ideas that optical changes of direction are curvilinear, not angular, and that in corpuscular reality the optical interface is not a geometric plane, but rather a narrow 'pseudoplanar' space, with indefinite boundaries. He saw geometrical optics as a simplified idealization of the real structure of things.

The effect of Newton's conceptual revolution upon the text of *Opticks* was negative, since this was to be a book about the experimental properties of light rather than a speculative essay on microphysics. In *Opticks* Newton largely renounced physical models. He gave no explanation of why refraction occurs, nor did he now invoke aether-waves as the causes of the "fits". There is, however, one covert allusion to Section XIV in *Opticks*, Book I, Part I where its content is emasculated to the barest geometrical postulate ("not determining what Light is, or by what kind of Force it is refracted") that "the Refracting body acts upon the Rays in Lines perpendicular to its Surface" (*Opticks* (1952), pp. 80–2). Given this postulate, Newton demonstrates the sine-law of refraction, supposing any law of force between the surface of the body and the ray of light. Passing over the two silently-made assumptions here (that the bending of the ray does not take place within the refracting body, and that this body, as it were, 'acts at a distance' upon the ray) *Opticks* appears a far more 'positivistic' text than the previous optical studies of Descartes, Hooke, and Boyle had been. And such was certainly Newton's intention.

Privately, Newton continued long to speculate about the microphysics of light, with repercussions reaching into the new Queries of 1706. These will be considered in Chapter 3. He was never able to reach a satisfactory resolution of the difficulties encountered by his concept of optical force, promising as Section XIV had seemed, and in the further Queries of the 1717 *Opticks* Newton reverted to an approximation towards the notions of an optical aether expressed in his papers of the 1670s.

THREE

The book develops

§1. The writing of *Opticks*

Newton's reluctance to publish

After the "Observations" and the "Hypothesis" had been read to the Royal Society, some years after their first drafting, they rejoined the Optical Lectures in Newton's desk drawer. In January 1676 he advised the Society:

As to the Paper of Observations which you move in the name of the Society to have printed, I cannot but return them my hearty thanks for the kind acceptance they meet with there; & know not how to deny any thing which they may desire should be done. Only I think it will be best to suspend the printing of them for a while because I have thoughts of writing such another set of Observations for determining the manner of the production of colours by the Prism, which, if done at all, ought to precede that now in your hands, & will do best to be joyned with it. But this I cannot presently do . . .

The additions that I intended, I think I must after putting you to so long expectations disappoint you in; for it puzzels me how to connect them with what I sent you . . . (Letter 150, p. 406).

Apart from the hesitation he certainly felt about giving to his most private and vulnerable speculations the permanent dignity of print, Newton was obviously aware that his pronouncements here and there about the phenomena and nature of light were far from consistent, in either intellectual or rhetorical terms. Probably he also judged that the Optical Lectures were rendered unsuitable for publication by their academic style and geometrical content, as his practice since 1671 tended increasingly to an exposition based upon the narration of experiments, though Newton was still to remind readers more than once that optics is a mathematical science.

A new book to be prepared?

Yet Newton was willing to contemplate, in principle, the preparation of a wholly new book on optics, incorporating the "Discourse of Observations" which had clearly been written for such a purpose; to this would be matched a cognate account of his discoveries and ideas concerning refraction. Probably Newton would have thought of this new book's being written in Latin for the benefit of Continental readers, much as the "Fundamentum Opticae" draft mentioned by both Whiteside and Shapiro was to be later.

(But when he came to compose this, in 1687, probably, Newton decided to revise the draft in English and continued in that tongue.) However, in 1676 and for more than a decade thereafter he was more interested in other topics (chemistry, theology, mechanics, astronomy) and the task of publishing a complete and unified account of light and colours was postponed.

Newton's friends in London went on hoping to see a book on optics from his pen. The mathematician John Collins wrote on 5 March 1677 that the engraver, David Loggan,

informs me he hath drawn your effigies in order to a sculpture [engraving] thereof to be prefixed to a book of Light Colours [&] Dioptricks which you intend to publish, of which we would be glad to have more certain notice (Letter 205).

Alas! nothing is now known of the artist's sketch or of Newton's book. Many years later, Loggan dedicated an illustration of Great St Mary's Church in Cambridge in flattering terms to Newton, who presumably paid for it. However, Newton—or someone else on Newton's behalf, and with his assistance—was certainly active with the printing-press, though no echo of this has survived in the correspondence. More than thirty years ago the late Dr D.J. Price found in the decayed binding of an old book two identical fascicules, each of eight pages numbered (9) to (16), from an unrecorded edition—or proposed edition—of Newton's "New Theory of Light and Colour" and other, related material, none of that surviving (clearly from the beginning of the pamphlet or book) being later than 1672 (Cohen 1958*b*). The most interesting feature of this curious document is that it was intended to be an annotated reprint, not a new work. Notes have been added by Newton himself; that extant, marked with the letter (c), indicating that (a) and (b) appeared in the irretrievably lost first eight pages of the printing, is a disquisition on the question whether light is a motion, a quality, or a body. It stands as an early reaction by Newton to the criticism that greeted the "New Theory".

The 'Waste Sheets', 1672

Although these 'Waste Sheets' can add nothing to our understanding of the development of *Opticks*, it is interesting to speculate on their position in the complex story of Newton's publications on light and colour. At least three major possibilities suggest themselves, two early, one later. The first is that Newton intended a separate republication of the "New Theory" followed by his own subsequent elucidations, perhaps in 1672. This possibility is favoured by the first editor of Newton's correspondence (Letter 40, p. 107, note 40); it does not seem to me to fit Newton's style of authorship, nor can I imagine that at this stage he would wish to give further publicity to his critics, as he must do in order for his replies to be intelligible. The second is that Henry Oldenburg, as proprietor and editor of the *Philosophical Transactions*, guessed at some point that there might be a sale for a reprint of some of the Newton material already published in his journal, and secured Newton's co-operation. This is quite as likely as the third possibility. This is, that after Oldenburg's death in September 1677 Newton took steps towards a reprint of the papers in the *Philosophical Transactions*, that journal ceasing for a time after its proprietor's death. Robert Hooke succeeded Oldenburg as Secretary of the Royal Society, and to him Newton wrote (December 1677) about some letters from one Anthony Lucas concerning optics that John Aubrey had sent on to Newton:

The last week I received a letter from Mr Aubrey concerning the printing of some of Mr Lucas letters. Mr Oldenburg being dead I intend God willing to take care that they be printed according to his mind, amongst some other things which are going into the Press (Letter 214).

It is of course a mere guess that Lucas's letters might have come at the end of a series beginning with the "New Theory", the publication being therefore in large part a reprint from the *Philosophical Transactions* very much 'according to Oldenburg's mind'. As so often before, nothing came of Newton's scheme, of which this fascicule may be the last relic. Westfall has suggested (1980, p. 277) that a fire in Newton's college rooms about the end of 1677 may have destroyed the papers he needed for a reprint. Many contemporaries report the story that Newton's book of light and colours, 'established upon thousands of experiments, which he had been twenty years of making, and which had cost him many a hundred pounds' was destroyed by a fire started by a candle left alight on his table while Newton went out to Chapel (or as some say, to the Bowling Green). Singed sheets do still exist among Newton's papers. While the tale was absurdly exaggerated (especially to the extent of Newton's 'running mad' in his distress) some loss of his materials certainly occurred.

At all events, it is clear that as on other occasions when he made similar angry protestations, Newton's desperate letter to Oldenburg of 18 November 1676 (Letter 195) was not to be taken literally:

I see I have made my self a slave to Philosophy, but if I get free of Mr Linus's buisiness I will resolutely bid adew to it eternally, excepting what I do for my privat satisfaction or leave to come out after me. For I see a man must either resolve to put out nothing new or to become a slave to defend it.

Opticks *begun*

To come at last to the text of *Opticks*, starting from Newton's own prefatory indication that part of the book had been written at the request of the Royal Society in 1675, while "the rest was added about twelve Years after to complete the Theory, except the Third Book, and the last Proposition of the Second, which were since put together out of scatter'd Papers." This is an astonishing utterance in two respects: first, because it obliterates all recollection of the optical lectures and their contribution to Book I of *Opticks*—indeed, only a few lines later in his preface Newton seems to dismiss these as "other Papers writ on this Subject . . . they are imperfect, and were perhaps written before I had tried all the Experiments here set down . . ."; and second because adding twelve years to 1675 brings us to 1687, the year of completion and publication of the *Principia*. In his account of reflecting telescopes in *Opticks* (p. 103) Newton also wrote: "Two of these I made about 16 years ago, and have one of them still by me." Sixteen added to 1671 again brings us to 1687, thus further discrediting the once-popular tale that Newton was mentally exhausted, indeed unhinged, by the effort of writing the *Principia*. Rather, it seems, he was stimulated to further scientific experiment and writing.

The plan of Opticks

As with the *Principia mathematica*, there were changes of plan in *Opticks*. True, both the experimental basis and much of the theoretical structure of Books I and II were already to hand and needed only some revision, with addition of afterthoughts. Even so the theory of "fits", necessary for the introduction of periodicity into the explanation of 'Newton's rings' created difficulties that were never wholly resolved: two versions of the theory leave traces in *Opticks*. The book was to have included a definitive study of diffraction, the third manifestation of the interaction between light and matter, but Newton (as he claimed, through interruption and lack of time) never completed the programme of experiments that he had planned, and the topic was left in an inconclusive state. Another plan of Newton's was to round the book off with a full dynamic treatment of light, presumably considerably richer in qualitative detail than Book I, Section XIV of the *Principia* (see above, p. 80). Among his papers is the beginning of a "Fourth book [of *Opticks*] concerning the nature of light & the power of bodies to refract & reflect it" (University Library Cambridge MS. Add. 3970.3, fo.337: Whiteside 1974, p. 424 note; Bechler 1973, pp. 20–2; Westfall 1980, pp. 520–2). Here, as on numerous other occasions, Newton endeavoured to set out in an appropriate context and full detail his faith in the consistency of Nature's mechanics. This uncompleted Fourth Book was to have begun with a series of about twenty propositions about light, followed by a group of "Hypotheses" explaining their significance, perhaps in the manner of the later Queries.

Its Hypothesis 2 draws the central analogy between the macrocosm and the microcosm, a favourite theme in many drafts written about 1690. As the great motions of the world depend upon gravity, Newton premises, "so all the little motions in the world depend upon certain kinds of forces whereby minute bodies attract or dispell one another at little distances". The theory of gravity he had already revealed in the *Principia* "to the satisfaction of my readers", and if "Nature be most simple and fully consonant to her self she observes the same method in regulating the motions of smaller bodies which she doth in regulating those of the greater". Newton then explained that while he had hinted at this idea in the Preface to the *Principia*, in Book I, Section XIV and Book II, Section V, he had not emphasized it lest this "should be accounted an extravagant freak, & so prejudice my Readers against all those things which were the main designe of the Book"; but now that the *Principia* had been approved by mathematicians he could in *Opticks* express his principle plainly.

The truth of this Hypothesis I assert not because I cannot prove it, but I think it very probable because a great part of the phaenomena of nature do easily flow from it which seem otherwise inexplicable . . .

These, as listed at some length by Newton, do indeed include the principal phenomena of physics (not least, "the reflexion & refraction of light") and of chemistry as then practised. In short, a comprehensive account of inorganic Nature might be written in terms of a dynamic microphysics analogous to the macromechanics of the *Principia* (Westfall 1971, pp. 379–80).

Some further thoughts of what this might involve had been penned by Newton in a suppressed "Conclusion" to that book. He there postulated, for example, a force of repulsion acting between gross bodies at near distances, rendering it difficult to bring them into direct contact. At less distances between the component particles of matter, however, a strong short-range attractive force caused then to cohere firmly. Later in the same text Newton combines the concept of force with that of hierarchies of particles, the series ending with matter as we perceive it:

For the matter of all things is one and the same, which is transmuted into countless forms by the operations of Nature, and more subtle and rare bodies are by fermentation and the processes of growth commonly made thicker and more condensed. By the same motion of fermentation bodies can expel certain particles, which thereupon by their repulsive forces are caused to recede from each other violently; if they are denser, they constitute vapours, exhalations and air; if on the other hand they are smaller they are transformed into light. These last [particles] undoubtedly adhere more strongly, since bodies do not shine save by a vehement heat. After they are separated they recede from bodies more violently, then in passing through other bodies sometimes they are attracted towards them, sometimes repelled; and by attraction they are certainly refracted, and sometimes reflected . . ., by repulsion they are always reflected. Bodies which reflect all incident light will shine . . . as do mercury and white metals. Others which abound in rather large translucent particles disseminated through uniform material of a different density, according to the size of the particles, more copiously reflect rays of one kind or of some other kind, whence they will appear coloured. For that the various colours of bodies arise from the various sizes of reflecting particles appears from the preceding soap-bubble experiment where the pellucid skin of the bubble reflected various colours according to variations in its thickness (Hall and Hall 1962, pp. 339–42).

From this *Principia* draft (whose purport is far from unique) it is clear how much in the writing of that work Newton's thoughts turned to optical phenomena as indicative of the secret, mathematical harmony between the microcosm and the macrocosm.

Alas! The recalcitrance of phenomena defeated Newton's high hopes of setting out a dynamical optics in more than the most general terms. He could never be satisfied with any dynamic rendering of the "fits" or of diffraction. The Fourth Book of *Opticks* was laid aside, a little of it being interjected into earlier parts of the book, and more being utilized, eventually, in the Queries, especially Query 31 (in the final numbering).

The manuscript of Opticks *takes shape*

It is hardly surprising that the text of a book put together over a period of some sixteen years should reveal a long and complex history of development. Precisely how complex a process, involving many changes of mind, was the composition of *Opticks* has very recently been demonstrated by Alan E. Shapiro in an article analysing with consummate exactitude the successive stages by which the book grew into its published form of 1704, which contains much novel information (Shapiro 1992). From his examination of the original manuscript of *Opticks*, returned to Newton after its printing, and of the watermarks of the various papers upon which it was written by Newton himself and six copyists, it is confirmed that there were two principal periods of composition: in 1687 (perhaps extending into early 1688) and in 1691–2; but the book was given its final shape only in 1703.

During most of its long gestation, according to Shapiro's researches, Book I of *Opticks* represented only Part I of the first Book as printed, while Part II appeared as Book II and the present Book II was called Book III. When written, the present Book III was Book IV (not the same as the "Fourth Book" already mentioned). The first text in English, starting life as a revised translation of the "Fundamentum Opticae" draft already mentioned (p. 84), was limited (roughly) to pages 20 to 82 and 113 to 158 of the present (1952) text. To it Newton quickly added the Definitions and Axioms, perhaps in deliberate imitation of the *Principia*'s structure, though (as Shapiro points out) he hardly troubled to work this prefixed addition into the subsequent material already written. Probably Newton went on next to rewrite from his earlier papers the concluding Propositions of Book I, Part II, bringing out the usefulness of his conception of light in explaining phenomena—the spectrum, the rainbow, the superficial colours of bodies. This, Shapiro suggests, was as far as Newton had proceeded before political events gave a temporary new course to his life; he seems to have resumed the composition of *Opticks* early in 1691, when he added to the text the largely pre-existing matter of the present Book II (without the theory of "fits") and the first state of our Book III, after which he went back to the end of Book I, Part I. To what he had already written of Proposition 6 he adjoined the quasi-Cartesian derivation of Snel's Law and the following Propositions 7 and 8 on the defects of telescopes and their rectification. (This change led to a mistake in the numbering of these Propositions in the first edition of the book.) Newton also created for himself the trouble of changing numbers in the manuscript at many points by finding it necessary at this stage to change his value for the dispersion of light caused by its refraction through glass. Possibly at this time too, and almost certainly in 1691−2, he proposed to conclude the work with the Fourth Book already described. But he also considered devoting Book IV (in the series as it was then) to the difficult topic of diffraction.

It was presumably at this point also that Newton performed his last optical experiments: on the colours of thick plates (1952: Book II, Part IV) and on diffraction (Book III, Part I). For a while accounts of these two sets of experiments were placed in a new Book IV, written out in Newton's holograph, while the then Book III, Part III was completed to Proposition 10. Various drafts indicate Newton's wish to incorporate in this Book his hypothesis of colour-related vibrations which, in the "Hypothesis" of 1675, he had attributed to the aether. Since that time he had rejected the aether as an *explicans* in physics, and, though sometimes tempted to transfer the vibrations positively to the transparent matter itself, finally in ten propositions extending the then Book III, Part III, he developed the theory of "fits" with no affirmation about their vehicle. It might be that the particles of the light-transmitting substance vibrated, he wrote, but he would leave the question open. The date of the composition of these ten propositions and of the drafts of a possible "Fourth Book" on optical mechanics as a conclusion to the whole can be established, from Newton's correspondence with Flamsteed and Gregory about the possible dependence of the velocity of light upon its colour, as being between the autumn of 1691 and the winter of 1692.

At this stage, presumably, the inclusion of this "Fourth Book" would have entailed the exclusion of a "Book IV" on thick plates and diffraction. With the latter Newton was dissatisfied, and therefore he set aside the drafted matter for this book, leaving a now virtually completed work in three Books; the highly speculative "Fourth Book" was never fully drafted.

David Gregory examines Opticks

In contrast to the position in the 1670s, little of Newton's preparation of a new book immediately after the *Principia* was known to the world. In June 1689 Newton told Christiaan Huygens that he had in hand a book on optics—he was certainly not engaged upon it at that moment; perhaps Halley and Fatio de Duillier knew of it, but certainly the first person to examine *Opticks* was Newton's young Scots protégé, David Gregory, who spent a few days in Cambridge with Newton in May 1694. In a Latin memorandum Gregory wrote:

I saw three books of *Opticks*. If they were printed they would equal the *Principia mathematica*. He has pursued catoptrics and dioptrics with concision and elegance. He puts forward marvellous and unheard-of things about colours. This work is to be published within five years of his retirement from the University, or (if he is still there) in a Latin translation which he will make. He has sent the Royal Society a paper about the colours of natural bodies [the "Discourse of Observations"]. He has finished with the treatise at this point, [although] he is not yet quite satisfied about a certain kind of colours and the manner of producing them. But the earlier part he is pleased with. The ray [sic] of light have 'fits' [*paroxysmos*] of reflecting or refracting, even indeterminate ones. Every kind of colour in natural bodies is from the size of the component atoms or particles. There is no coloured thing whose atoms are not pellucid, the atoms of black things are the smallest. The sizes of these atoms of air, water and glass are defined [in] a table. He has made experiments on children's soap-bubbles, on air in the space between a convex and a plane lens, and on water by analogy (Letter 446).

Now that Alan Shapiro has revealed the true arrangement of the Books of *Opticks* in 1694, it is clear that Gregory saw less than the complete printed text. Confirmation is found in another note of his, recently printed by Shapiro (1992, p. 220) in which Gregory recorded the incompleteness of the fourth Book on diffraction.

From Gregory the word about *Opticks* soon spread. Newton was pressed by the Royal Society and by the elderly Oxford mathematician John Wallis to print his book at once; Wallis was scornful of Newton's plea that its publication would bring him trouble. Abroad, he wrote, Leibniz was admired for his differential calculus, whereas the praise would have gone to Newton's fluxional calculus, if only Newton had not been so negligent in publication of his mathematical discoveries. (On this point at least, surely Wallis was right.) Did Newton wish the same fate to meet his optical discoveries too? 'I own that modesty is a Vertue; but too much Diffidence (especially as the world now goes) is a Fault' (Letter 503). Wallis returned to the charge two years later (Letter 567), again in the context of Leibniz, unbraiding Newton for continuing to suppress his book 'after more than 30 years'; it would be a noble accession to natural philosophy and the public deserved to read it.

The printing of Opticks

Newton was not to be hurried. His prefatory note to *Opticks* states the reason for his reluctance to publish the book: "To avoid being engaged in Disputes about these Matters, I have hitherto delayed the printing, and should still have delayed it, had not the Importunity of Friends, prevailed upon me." The harassment he had suffered (as he saw it) through six years after printing the "New Theory" in 1672 was not forgotten, while Hooke's assertion of priority in the concept of universal gravitation (1686) had left an unhealed wound. Some months before Hooke's death (March 1703), when he was wretchedly ill and incapable, Newton at last promised his friends that *Opticks* should be published.

In the last months of 1702 or early in the next year Newton made the final changes to its text, bringing the book to its initial printed form. Now the original Book II became Book I, Part II; the new Book II now included as its final Part (IV) Newton's splendid investigation of the colours of thick plates—which further buttressed his theory of vibrations or "fits"; while the unfinished "Book IV, Part II", on diffraction, was revised to appear as Book III, Part I. (It does not appear that Newton at this time took steps to prepare a 'Part II' from any of the other draft material he had to hand.) After his "Observations" on diffraction Newton explained how he had designed to repeat his experiments "with more care and exactness, and to make some new ones for determining the manner how the Rays of Light are bent in their passage by Bodies, for making the Fringes of Colours with the dark lines between them. But I was then interrupted, and cannot now think of taking those things to further Consideration." Therefore leaving his design unfinished, Newton concluded by "proposing only some Queries, in order to a further search to be made by others".

Opticks was presented to the Royal Society by its author on 16 February 1704. Newton had been President of the Society, in succession to Lord Somers, since 30 November of the previous year.

The success of Opticks

Opticks aroused enormous interest among English readers. It was reprinted, with additional Queries, in 1717 (re-issued 1718) and again in 1721. The fourth English edition (1730) claims to have been printed from a copy of the third revised by the author. For the benefit of foreign readers a Latin translation appeared in 1706 (see Appendix I). David Gregory had hoped, years before, to translate the book into Latin, just as he had hoped (vainly) to edit a second edition of the *Principia*. Instead, Newton preferred the friend, scholar, and divine Samuel Clarke, whom Newton is said to have rewarded with a gift of £100 to each of his five children. The task of supervising the printers of this translation was undertaken by another young disciple, the able refugee mathematician Abraham de Moivre. The reason for Newton's adding long, important passages as afterthoughts to this text is unknown.

On the Continent also *Opticks*, and especially the Latin *Optice*, aroused an interest not limited to mathematicians only, as had been the case (at first) with the *Principia*. The English text was read in French translation to the Paris Académie Royale des Sciences and later two editions in that language were published. A number of copies of *Optice* were sent by Newton to Italy, while in Germany Gottfried Wilhelm Leibniz reviewed the first edition in the *Acta Eruditorum* of Leipzig; though his chief interest was in the two mathematical treatises that Newton had annexed to *Opticks* and their bearing on the disputed question of the origins of the calculus, he was by no means critical of Newton's new ideas in optics, and admired his experimental genius. As Gregory had predicted a generation before, the influence of Newton's second book was hardly less than that of his first.

§2. The text of *Opticks*

The publishing history of Opticks

Like Newton's *Principia mathematica*, his *Opticks* evolved as a book in a rather complex way. The first edition was prepared for the Press by Newton himself, who presumably oversaw the printing. To it were added a pair of mathematical tracts written long before: "An enumeration of lines of the third order" and "A treatise on the quadrature of curves"; these never re-appeared with *Opticks* after the Latin version, *Optice* (1706). In *Optice* Newton declared: "having read the book over, changed some things, especially for the sake of clarity, and added not a little matter, chiefly to be found in the Addenda and Corrigenda, I besides enlarged the number of the Queries at the end of the book". Presumably all these changes passed into the next English edition, 1717; to this second English text yet more Queries were added (see Appendix II). The third edition (1721) again claims on the title-pages to be corrected by the author, as does the fourth (posthumous) edition of 1730. While the extension of the Queries in successive editions is certainly important, it has not yet been shown that Newton's substantial changes to the 1704 text were numerous. In this respect the case of the *Principia* was quite different.

Although it may be argued that the original *Principia* of 1687 was imperfect in a number of ways, so that Newton fell short of obtaining all his objectives, these imperfections were to a large extent removed in subsequent editions. *Opticks*, on the other hand, free of major errors to be corrected later, appeared as a book reporting an unfinished investigation when Newton let it go to press, and was so to remain for ever. He used the growing number of Queries both to enlarge the scope of the first edition—conspicuously so by his discussion of double refraction introduced in *Optice* (1706), a topic which would otherwise have remained a notable omission —and to enrich it conceptually, often with material having no direct bearing upon optics at all. But the incomplete investigation of diffraction remained so for ever.

The arrangement of the book

Like the *Principia, Opticks* is divided into three books, the first of them preceded by Definitions and Axioms. But there are no Laws of Light to match the Laws of Motion. Historically, Newton's first sketch of a formal, axiomatic treatment of physical optics is to be found in a letter to Henry Oldenburg (destined for Christiaan Huygens) of 23 June 1673 (Letter 116, pp. 292–4). Definitions 1 to 4 in this letter re-appear as Definitions VII and VIII in *Opticks*. The letter continues with an array of ten propositions, all to be demonstrated in the book. This is one scrap of evidence revealing the effect of the long debate during the 1670s upon the writing of the first Book of *Opticks*; the criticisms of such a man as Huygens were perhaps felt particularly keenly by Newton.

Newton's opening sentence in the book is a statement of method:

My Design in this Book is not to explain the Properties of Light by Hypotheses, but to propose and prove them by Reason and Experiments; in order to which I shall premise the following Definitions and Axioms.

Here Newton implies (both by his positive assertion and by his omission of any reference to geometry) that his treatise will be concerned with physical, not geometrical optics. The implication is made stronger by Newton's first Definition, of a *Ray of Light,* for it carefully distinguishes the ray from a geometrical line:

By the Rays of Light I understand its least Parts, and those as well Successive in the same Lines, as Contemporary in several Lines.

Evidently Newton prefers the similitude with matter-theory: the ray is a least part, just as an atom is the least part of matter. It is not a line because that is continuous, whereas light, Newton says, is discontinuous, that is, it is a physical entity not a mathematical abstraction. Newton would of course have denied strenuously that, by thus asserting light to be physical, he is necessarily also asserting it to be material rather than a form of motion. It is possible, for example, that the least part might be conceived as the minimum pulse of motion. In practice, he often uses the word 'ray' conventionally as signifying the least *line* of light.

The method of investigation, being neither hypothetical nor geometrical, is experimental. Clarke in *Optice* made this clearer from the first by adding the clause:

sed ut abditas nec antea observatas eius Proprietates simpliciter proponerem, & propositas Ratione duntaxat Experimentisque comprobarem [*but that I might simply propound hidden and hitherto unobserved Properties* [of light] *and demonstrate by reason and experiments only that which has been propounded—my italics*]

Hypotheses (Newton says in the Latin version) are built upon the known properties of things; he will put forward discoveries of new properties and prove them by reason and experiment alone. A further limitation of the mathematicians' treatment of light as geometrical lines is noted in Definition II: Newton asserts it to be compatible only with the instantaneous propagation of light, whereas experientially it appears that light travels in time.

Definitions II and III are concerned with the physical properties possessed by light of being refracted and reflected; Newton at this point does not consider another mode of interaction between light and matter: absorption. Neither refraction nor reflection were treated by Newton simply as mathematical properties, however, to be subjected to fixed rules: rather Refrangibility and Reflexibility are "Dispositions" of the rays to be bent or turned back, hinting at a certain physical subtlety of behaviour. Definitions IV to VI define angles of incidence and refraction/reflection and their sines. Definitions VII and VIII associate uniformity of refrangibility and colour with the descriptive terms "Simple, Homogeneous and Similar" while diversity of refrangibility and colour between the rays is associated with the words "Compound, Heterogeneal and Dissimilar".

Hence from the first Newton was making provision for, not the abandonment of geometry in favour of the qualitative language in which colour had traditionally been discussed, but the greater complexity of geometrizing light-rays when they were no longer to be treated as physically uniform and homogeneous.

The eight Axioms that follow give (in Newton's words) "the sum of what hath hitherto been treated of in Opticks", meaning geometrical optics. After postulating the equality of the angles of incidence and reflection, and the refraction of the ray towards the perpendicular when the second medium is denser—Newton accepted that density and reflectivity are roughly correlated—in Axiom V he explains the sine-law of refraction without attempting to derive it from any simpler principle. It is curious that at this point Newton was content to state that though the proportion of refraction alters with the colour of the ray, "the difference is so little that it need seldom be considered". It is a difference, however, upon which much of Newton's subsequent account of colour-phenomena will depend, being what we call dispersion (a term unknown to Newton). Axiom VI postulates that given the focus of rays falling almost normally upon an interface, after reflection or refraction the new focus may be found, or conversely the two foci being given the position and curvature of the interface may be found. Axiom VII states the convergence of rays coming from an object after reflection or refraction, yielding the "Picture of the Object" seen, as in the *camera obscura*, and also explaining image-formation in the eye. Finally, Axiom VIII postulates the position of an image-point, "which Consideration unfolds the Theory of Microscopes and Telescopes". Everything expressed in these Axioms had been handled more thoroughly in the Optical Lectures, as is signified by a footnote first inserted in the fourth edition of *Opticks*, after the posthumous printing of the Lectures. It is clear that Newton was eager to embark as directly as might be on the main business of his book, experimental physical optics, without too much delay over geometrical details inessential to the study of the interactions of light and matter in their chief manifestations, colours.

Whereas in both versions of the Optical Lectures and in the "New Theory" paper Newton had presented his work in a synthetic form, not at all respecting the historical path of his discoveries (indeed, misrepresenting that path), in *Opticks* he elected to begin with those experiments upon reflected coloured light seen through a prism which were, I believe, the first that he made in optics (above, pp. 36,38). Possibly Newton chose yet another way of introducing his optical researches at this, his third, attempt because it seemed to offer the most accessible approach, and not at all because it was autobiographical. The experiments with which Newton opens *Opticks* are indeed the simplest possible, both for the reader and the would-be experimenter. The beginner requires a prism, to be sure, but it is impossible to initiate the study of refraction without employing both the prism and the lens. Otherwise, for these first experiments no darkened room is required, nor a narrow beam, nor even direct sunlight, and that may be why Newton put them first. The "crucial experiment" (Fig. 9, p. 55) upon which the credibility of the "New Theory of Light and Colours" of 1672 so largely turned is, in comparison, a difficult one to contrive, as Mariotte discovered.

Differential refrangibility of colours

The point of the first few experiments is to show that when light reflected from variously coloured patches reaches the eye through either a prism or a lens, blue light is more markedly refracted than is red. In one experiment with a lens Newton finds it impossible to focus the image of black silk-thread lines upon a blue background at the same distance as when the same lines are placed against a red background; the distance between the two positions of sharp focus was as much as one and a half inches. Later, in Experiment 16, Newton devised an arrangement with a prism and a lens to form a very elongated spectrum; using a white screen and carefully selected spectral colours forming patches upon it he once more satisfied himself (by performing essentially the same experiment as before) that

it's certain that the Rays which differ in Refrangibility do not converge to the same Focus; but if they flow from a lucid Point, as far from the Lens on one side as the Foci are on the other, the Focus of the most refrangible [blue] Rays shall be nearer to the Lens than that of the least refrangible [red] by above the fourteenth part of the whole distance . . . (1952, p. 94)

—that is, as much as $5\frac{1}{2}$ inches. This demonstration acts as a prelude to the explanation of the superior merits of the reflecting telescope, and its construction.

However, Newton was now careful to note that appearances can be deceptive in these experiments: some rays emanating from a blue patch of colour may be less refracted than those from a red patch:

For both Lights are mixed of Rays differently refrangible, so that in the red there are some Rays not less refrangible than those of the blue, and in the blue there are some Rays not more refrangible than those of the red . . . (1952, pp. 25–6).

But such untypical rays in each colour are few, and "serve to diminish the Event of the Experiment, but are not able to destroy it".

In Propositions II to VI of Part I Newton developed his thesis concerning the relation between refrangibility and colour by means of experiments involving a spectrum cast by a prism, now turning the argument round to adduce new ideas about the nature of white light. The "doctrine" of the heterogeneity of white light, the chief topic of the "New Theory", is now expressed at greater length, with more prudence, and with wider experimental evidence. When Newton turns to a deeper consideration of the origin of the dispersion of the coloured rays after refraction, taking for demonstrated the association between apparent colour and degree of refrangibility, he asks

whence this inequality arises, whether it be that some of the incident Rays are refracted more, and others less, constantly, or by chance, or that one and the same Ray is by Refraction disturbed, shatter'd, dilated, and as it were slit and spread into many diverging Rays . . . .

Remembering Newton's idea of the ray as a kind of atomic unit of light, we may understand that he is enquiring whether each unit is marked by its own constant degree of refrangibility, or whether its degree of refraction depends upon some fortuitous circumstance in its passage through the glass, or whether its passage in some way dilates and modifies each ray, some more, some less, in order to create dispersion where there was parallelism and colour where there was whiteness. There is of course imperfection in Newton's statement of the hypothesis of the shattering and dilation of light: if the ray is a "least Part" of light, it cannot be imagined to be split into still smaller parts. Rather it would seem such writers as Robert Hooke imagined a homogeneous *beam* (a visible entity) to be modified or divided so as to make diverse rays.

Newton took trouble to demonstrate that experiment speaks for the first of these choices. They are of course experiments taken from the Optical Lectures, of which the most important is the fifth, where a beam shone through crossed prisms forms, not a rectangular spectrum, but a normal elongated spectrum whose axis is at a half-right-angle to the axes of both the prisms (Fig. 10, p. 67). On this experiment Newton bases the important point that if sunlight were of a single, pure, homogeneous colour, it would when shining through a prism form upon a screen a single circular image of the hole through which it has passed; because sunlight is heterogeneous its spectrum consists of an infinity of such circular images, dispersed and coloured according to the variety of refractions undergone by the infinite number of rays leaving the prism. Each ray forming such an image is always refracted as a unit, not blending with or splitting from other rays. This again conforms to Newton's notion of the "atomicity" of light. The formation of the oblique spectrum by the second prism is easily accounted for by tracing the individual paths of every coloured ray; but if these rays had been formed from homogeneous white light by splitting and blending one would expect the result of two such processes occurring successively at right angles to be a square spectrum.

The 'crucial experiment'

The 'crucial experiment' of the "New Theory" reappears with much less importance as Expt. 6. The lesson now drawn from it is that though the rays passing through the two diaphragms to the second prism are sensibly parallel, still dispersion is seen after the second refraction, blue more, red less, as before. Expt. 7 like Expt. 16 is a version of an earlier experiment of viewing coloured patches through a prism, the colours now being those of the spectrum rather than paints. Another version of the same, demanding great skill in manipulation, requires a paper disk to be illuminated with the red of one prism and the deep violet of a second, at the same time; when viewed from a suitable distance through a prism the doubly illuminated disk appears as two separated images.

Expt. 9 (p. 54) introduces an important concept of Newton's: that reflexibility, like refrangibility, is related to colour and is a connate property of each distinct ray (though of course there is no dispersion among the reflected rays). This is the first experiment in *Opticks* upon the critical angle, where reflection and transmission (refraction) both occur. In Lecture 6 of the Optical Lectures Newton had devoted some effort to explaining and justifying by such experiments as these his contention that easily refrangible rays are also easily reflexible rays, and vice versa, even showing (in a version of the crucial experiment) that when the rays issuing from a first prism are so collimated as to become almost parallel, some still disperse by refraction while others are reflected at the critical angle in a second prism, the blue being more easily reflected than the red. I have already noted the difficulty in the sixth Optical Lecture that refraction is made to occur *before* the light is reflected and transmitted (with dispersion) at the critical angle; therefore, though these experiments may be held to justify the basic notion that blue light is more reflexible than red, they do not serve—beyond logical cavil—to demonstrate that the coloured rays are together in a pre-existent combination in white light before refraction.

In *Opticks*, in a much briefer treatment of this class of experiments, Newton seeks to block the cavil; as Fig. 12 shows, the beam of light is now passed through a first, right-angled 45° prism, so arranged that the beam penetrates at right angles its two faces *AB, AC* (if it is internally reflected from the face *BC*), that is, without refraction. Further, the prism *ABC* can be so turned that the beam through *F* is either internally reflected at *M* to *N*, or refracted through *M* to form the spectrum *HG*, *H* being the violet end of the spectrum, *G* the red end. When the light is internally reflected at *M* to *N* it falls upon a second, similar prism *VXY*, placed in the same way as *ABC*, so that light in passing through it from *M* is refracted only at the second face *VX*, forming a partial or full spectrum *t* (red), *p* (blue). Newton reported that by careful axial rotation of *ABC* he could initially cause a spectrum to appear at *HG*; and then, as rotation continued and the angle of refraction at *M* increased, reflection of the blue rays in the beam *FM* from *M* to *N* and so to *p* began to occur, leaving the other colours to appear at *HG*; more rotation still abstracted further light from *HG* and at last enabled a full spectrum to be seen at *tp*.

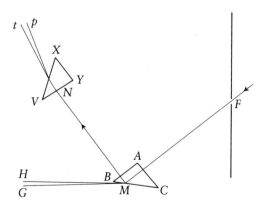

Fig. 12. Another experiment upon the critical angle: the light reflected from *M* to *N* by the base of the 45° prism *ABC* is not refracted. Its composition is analysed by the second prism. After *Opticks*, p. 56.

Newton understood that the variously coloured rays reaching *tp* had followed a path involving only reflection at *M*; they were therefore undifferentiated in nature from the white light reaching *M*. He wrote: "And therefore the Light *MN* admits into its composition, first the more refrangible Rays, and then the less refrangible Rays, and yet after this Composition is of the same Nature with the Sun's immediate Light *FM*, the reflexion of the specular Base *BC* causing no alteration therein" (1952, p. 57). That is to say, light "of the same Nature" can be both white and coloured, contrary to those who assert that a coloured ray is a modified ray. We may all agree with Newton's earlier affirmation that "no Man ever doubted" the identity of direct sunlight and the same reflected from a perfect mirror; but the point surely is that "the specular Base *BC*" is a very peculiar mirror indeed, reflecting some rays, and transmitting others, in a way that Newton will have to explain later.

The critical angle

The significance of the critical angle in this experiment was that it allowed Newton to divide a beam of white light so that its coloured rays (in the beam *MN*) appeared without their having to suffer refraction. Though the beam *MN* might be bluish, Hooke had to agree with Newton that it was unmodified.

Thus Newton is forcing Hooke's admission that colour is not indicative of the "Nature" of light. Newton's argument is puzzling, because it is strange to declare "bluish" to be of the same nature with white, and the same conclusion could have been based on the common observation that grass appears green—no one ever supposed that the colour had been created by a modification due to refraction. Further, the coloured ray *MN* cannot be manifest without transmission, that is refraction, of reddish light to *HG*; might not Newton's opponents have maintained that the beam *FM* was surely modified by the separation from it of this refracted ray? Indeed, if Robert Hooke had been still alive, might he not have argued that Newton's experiment clearly showed that when white light is divided or split into different rays, colour is created?

It is perhaps unnecessary to remark further that Newton's experiment depends on the singular fact of the critical angle for the light in the beam's being 45°. Or that in the enunciation of it he plainly writes of there being refraction at the base when a ray is transmitted towards *HG*.

The existence of coloured rays in white light

The truth is that the theoretical debate towards which Newton's experimental discussion was directed turned upon words such as 'modified', 'dilated', and 'split', used ambiguously and without clear meaning. Some of them, such as 'modified' and 'split', seem just as applicable to Newton's idea of dispersion of the coloured rays by refraction as to his opponents' ideas of the creation of colour. For clearly refraction both modifies and splits the incident white beam. This modification—call it analysis to suit Newton's interpretation—is clearly subtle, as is its converse, the synthesis of white light from the spectral rays, since Newton proved that white light can be constituted which has different properties from sunlight. It is possible for Newton to demonstrate all the properties of the infinitely numerous separate rays between deep purple and red as revealed by refractive analysis, and all his experiments are consistent with the existence, *after refraction*, of the heterogeneous rays as he characterizes them. Yet there is no single experiment known to Newton or his opponents demonstrating positively that white light *before refraction* consists of homogeneous rays. Therefore it is open to question (and has indeed been strongly questioned by Sabra 1967) whether Newton could claim with all his efforts to have proved positively that white light *before refraction* consists of just those same heterogeneous rays that are manifest after. The assertion that this is so depends upon a 'principle of continuity' whose applicability in this case has not been proved, though common sense indicates that it must apply.

Inevitably the experiments concluding Proposition II are cited in confirmation of the following Proposition III:

The Sun's Light consists of Rays differing in Reflexibility, and those [same] Rays are more reflexible than others which are [also] more refrangible.

The ambiguity of the enunciation without my addition is corrected in the Latin:

Lumen Solis constat ex Radiis, qui Reflexibilitate inter se differunt: Et qui Radii magis Refrangibiles sunt, iidem quoque sunt magis Reflexibiles.

Despite the generality of this proposition, Newton offered no evidence of its holding in the normal reflection of light: the only cases demonstrated are when refraction is associated with reflection. It is notable too that the parallel words 'reflexible' and 'refrangible' do not have parallel significations for Newton. 'More refrangible' means 'bent through a greater angle by refraction', while 'more reflexible' means 'yielding sooner to reflection'. When, in an appropriate experimental arrangement, a prism is rotated about its axis while a beam of light shines through it, in such a way that (as Newton reports in Experiment 9) bluish light is reflected from the base internally while reddish light is transmitted, in this event it might well be said that the latter is more easily transmitted (refracted) while the former is more easily reflected. But such a description would clash with Newton's normal language, in which the bluish light is described as more easily refracted because it is bent through a greater angle. In short, 'more easily' may mean both 'responding more readily' and 'responding to a greater extent': it is ambiguous.

Experiment 11, in Proposition IV, describes a technique for elongating the spectrum in proportion to its breadth which might, perhaps, have been described earlier with advantage. Newton employed a long-focus lens to create a cone of light in which he placed the prism. Receiving the spectrum upon a screen placed at the focal length of the lens away from it, the spot of light cast by each component ray in the sunlight becomes of small diameter (and also intensely bright); but, the dispersion remaining unaffected, Newton now formed a spectrum whose length exceeded its breadth by forty or even seventy times, he writes. At this point he discusses the manufacturing defects introduced into lenses and prisms, which may perhaps be overcome by making 'prismatick Vessels' of plate glass, filled with a saturated solution of lead acetate.

The same device appears in Proposition VI (Experiment 15) whose object is to demonstrate that the sine-law of refraction holds true for each and every separate coloured ray; that is to say, given any transparent, refracting substance (for example, pure water) we can establish for it, within precise limits, an infinity of indexes of refraction each appropriate to a particular hue in the refracted beam. This proposition is also interesting because Newton brings into it a dynamical argument based on the same assumption that Descartes had adopted: "That Bodies refract Light by acting upon its Rays in Lines perpendicular to their Surfaces" (p. 79). The sine-law follows when it is postulated that a force in the transparent medium either accelerates or decelerates the rays of light passing into or out of it. This demonstration, Newton insists, is "general, without determining what Light is, or by what kind of Force it is refracted, or assuming any thing further than that the Refracting Body acts upon the Rays in Lines Perpendicular to its Surface" (pp. 81–2), that is, the demonstration postulates a dynamic action of matter upon light. It also assumes that the velocity of light is finite and variable.

The errors of telescopes

The reflecting telescope is also a prime concern of Propositions V to VIII. The fundamental reason for its superiority over the refractor—the greater confusion in vision when looking through optical instruments that is caused by chromatic aberration as compared with spherical aberration— is the subject of Proposition VII. Newton had first covered this ground long before in the "New Theory" of 1672 and subsequent discussion with Christiaan Huygens. He had insisted that "the greatest laterall error of the [dispersed] rays from one another [was] about 1/50 of the glasses [lens's] diameter", which he supposed to be an error

some hundreds of times greater, than a circularly figured *Lens* of so small a section as the Object glasses of long Telescopes are, would cause by the unfitness of its figure, were Light *uniform* (Letters 40 and 103, pp. 95, 266).

Proposition VII is a lengthy and elaborate proof of his assertion (evidently Newton never forgot Huygens's doubts) showing—in the later editions of *Opticks*—that the ratio of the two kinds of error is very precisely 5449 to 1, so small is the relative effect of spherical aberration in telescopes; in the early editions this ratio was computed to be even higher: 8151 to 1. At about the same time in the early seventies, responding to Hooke's criticisms of the "New Theory", Newton had likewise calculated that reflection to a focus is sixteen times more accurate than refraction to a focus; but this argument is not repeated in the book. Newton did there, however, explain more elaborately than he had before how it is that our vision accepts the images formed by ordinary simple lenses, though so imperfect, because the widely dispersed rays are so few in number.

Turning now to the practicalities of telescope design, Newton noted that experience teaches the desirability of proportioning both the aperture and magnification of a refracting telescope to the square root of its length (or of the focal length of its objective): so, if a telescope one foot long, aperture one-third of an inch, gives a good image at magnification ×15, the same quality might be expected of another 64 feet long, aperture 8/3 inches, magnification ×120. This accords with the theory that chromatic aberrational effects increase directly with the aperture.

If spherical aberration were the chief problem with telescopes, it might be much reduced by employing a compound meniscus lens, the two outer components being separated by a fluid of different refractive index from glass, such as water.

Correction of the errors

The idea of such a compound lens had been introduced into optics by Robert Hooke; Newton, reading Hooke in the *Philosophical Transactions*, studied it geometrically in the late 1660s (Whiteside 1967, pp. 575–6). The likely chronology, and the fact that Newton speaks of "difforme rays" of light, indicate that he was examining a possible way of correcting chromatic aberration, of whose existence Hooke had been unconscious. But Newton did not achieve his result. The compound meniscus of *Opticks*, to reduce *spherical* aberration, is composed of convex, rather than the concave elements of the earlier trial:

And by this means might Telescopes be brought to a sufficient perfection, were it not for the different Refrangibility of [the] several sorts of Rays (p. 102).

For chromatic aberration Newton now thought no correction possible, though its effects could be alleviated by giving the objective-glass of the telescope a long focal length. This negative view seems to have been held by Newton for some years. In the *Principia* (1687) he had written:

If the objective glasses of telescopes be made of two spherically figured lenses and water fill the space between them, it can be arranged that the errors occurring in the refractions of the outside sufaces of the glasses can be pretty well corrected by the refractions of the water.

Obviously Newton refers to the spherical errors of the lenses. He continues:

Such [compound] objective lenses are to be preferred to elliptical and hyperbolic ones, not only because they may be figured more accurately and more easily but also because they refract more accurately the rays that fall far away from the axis of the lens. But in truth the diverse refrangibility of the separate rays is an impediment against the perfection of optics by lenses that are either spherical or of another figure. Unless the errors arising from this source can be corrected, all labour to correct the others is quite vain (*Principia* (1687), pp. 234–5).

Consistently, Newton affirmed in print that the gross source of error in lenses was chromatic aberration and that compound lenses could not correct more than spherical aberration. The latter was to him no more than a red herring so far as the improvement of telescopes is concerned. True, as Whiteside has remarked, it is not impossible that impediments may be removed; but Newton offered no hope that this was possible.

In fact, the chief criticism made by Newton of the 'writers on dioptrics' in the Optical Lectures long before was precisely that they were ignorant of "a certain irregularity" in refractions "that upsets everything, [and] not only causes the figures of conics to be little superior to spherical ones but also makes spherical lenses perform far less well than they would if this refraction were uniform" (Shapiro 1984, pp. 49, 283). Accordingly, the efforts of opticians to figure improved lenses have been all in vain, since colours would appear "no differently in glasses however perfect" (ibid., pp. 81, 433).

Why was Newton when writing *Opticks* still as convinced that "the Improvement of Telescopes of given lengths by Refractions is desperate"— he does not say *impossible*—as he had been in 1666 when he gave up "glassworks" (according to the "New Theory")? Over roughly forty years (1666–1704) Newton formalized both theoretical and experimental reasons for thinking that dispersion and refraction were inseparable properties of light. Here Newton was in error: the dispersive powers of transparent substances are highly variable, and not proportional to their refractive powers. An accidental point helped to put him astray. The dispersive powers of water and of glass (as handled by Newton) are nearly identical; indeed, no compound lens constructed of water and this glass could be achromatic. If Newton had happened to experiment with a prism made of flint glass or of natural materials, he might have found a dispersive power different from that of water. In this instance Newton generalized from a too-limited experience; he experimented with prisms of several different shapes, but made no serious attempt to explore a variety of refractive materials. That being said, it must be added that having taken his position against the possibility of achromatism, Newton went unreasonably out of his way to nail down its coffin (compare Mills 1981).

Achromatism impossible

The hammer was Book I, Part II, Proposition 3, Experiment 8 of *Opticks*. The critical point is contained in a theorem here enunciated (though with the curiously hesitant expression 'I seem to gather . . .'):

The Excesses of the Sines of Refraction of several sorts of Rays above their common Sine of Incidence when the Refractions are made out of divers denser Mediums immediately into one and the same Rarer Medium, suppose Air, are to one another in a given Proportion (*Opticks* 1952, p. 130).

Newton offers a gloss upon this forbidding sentence; by this Theorem

the Refractions of the Rays of every sort made out of any Medium into Air are known by having the Refraction[s] of the Rays of any one sort.

He means (as is shown by the example following in his text) that given the refractive index (n, n') for the red rays in any two different transparent mediums, and beams of white light incident upon each at angles I, I', the sines of the angles of refraction into air of this pair of least refracted rays will be related as

$$\frac{\sin R}{\sin R'} = \frac{n\ (n' - 1)}{n'\ (n\ - 1)}$$

This is a statement of the proportionality of the refractions between the two media in which Newton has, however, abandoned (without explanation) the ordinary Law of Sines. Newton goes on—after this calculation of the red ray in the second medium—to suppose the dispersion of the more-refracted rays equal in the two mediums; in either case the addition of a certain quantity to the refraction for red yields the refraction for the other colour. In Newton's numbers, with $n = \dfrac{5}{4} = \dfrac{135}{108}$ and $n' = \dfrac{4}{3} = \dfrac{108}{81}$ for red rays, the sines of these least refracted rays in the two media are 135 and 108, and those of the corresponding violet rays 136 and 109, the dispersion in each case being 1. (Newton correctly appreciated that, as a consequence of his theory, the refractive index of each ray varies slightly according to the colour of the light.)

Dispersion in the Lectures

The Optical Lectures contain an elegant geometrical representation of the relationship between refraction and dispersion in which, however, the angular dispersion of the extreme rays of the spectra does vary with the refractive index of the media. Newton's diagram (Fig. 13) illustrates the production of several refracted beams from a single incident beam IX, narrowly inclined to the interface, which is imagined to be entering three different media having the mean refractive indices n_1, n_2, n_3. The three mean refracted rays so formed are XR', XR, Xr. These points R', R, r lie on the straight line Dr, parallel to the axis XG, so that

$$n_1 = \frac{XD}{XR'} , n_2 = \frac{XD}{XR} , n_3 = \frac{XD}{Xr}$$

Cp and Et, lines parallel to Dr, indicate the limits of the red rays (T', T, t) and the violet rays (P', P, p) respectively, lying on normals to Dr. Hence the *linear* dispersion of the coloured rays between the limits indicated is postulated as being equal in all media, but it is obvious from the figure that the angular dispersion of the three beams is unequal (see Shapiro 1984, p. 200 note).

And in Opticks

To return to *Opticks*, the formal foundation of its treatment of dispersion is based upon the unique Experiment 8, baldly enunciated with no details. Newton claims that however many refractions a beam of light undergoes, provided that at the end of them the beam emerges

in Lines parallel to those in which it was incident, [it] continues ever after to be white. But if the emergent Rays be inclined to the incident, the Whiteness of the emerging Light will by degrees in passing on from the Place of Emergence, become tinged in its Edges with Colours. This I try'd by refracting Light with Prisms of Glass placed within a Prismatick Vessel of Water (1952, p. 129).

Bechler (1975) gives the figure from a manuscript: note that the bases of the prisms are parallel, and the path of the light-beam nearly symmetrical either side (Fig. 14). Curiously, the figure ignores the simpler version of the experiment with the glass V point-downwards, so that the top could be open. In this manuscript of 1672 Newton declared that if the passage of light through the compound prism is arranged so that "the contrary refractions [air to water and water to glass] are as neare as may be equall to one another"—colours appear in the emergent beam.

But if the Refractions of [the] interior Prism be something lesse then those of the exterior the transmitted light may be without any colours at all (Bechler 1975, pp. 113–14).

Since in the latter case the incident and refracted beams are no longer parallel, *Opticks* stands in diametric contradiction of Newton's MS of 1672. The MS seems to be concerned to refute Hooke's contention that

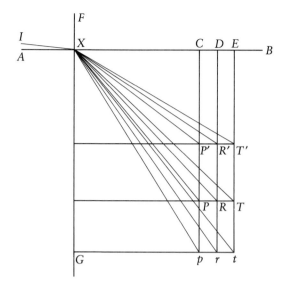

Fig. 13. The dispersion model in the Optical Lectures. After Shapiro (1984), pp. 198, 336.

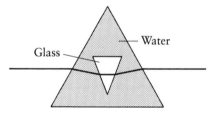

Fig. 14. Refraction in opposed prisms of glass and water. After Bechler (1975), p. 114 from Cambridge University Library MS Add. 3970, fo. 443r.

colour (in beams passing from one medium to another) can occur only when refraction occurs; in refutation of Hooke, Newton is *ipso facto* claiming that parallel beams may show colour, and a refracted beam may be white—if this were true, an achromatic lens could be constructed. In *Opticks* Newton went back on himself in the theorem just quoted to adopt Hooke's contention—without of course mentioning Hooke's name!

A doubtful experiment?

Whether Newton ever performed this delicate experiment—which requires the glass prism to be rotated *inside* the water-filled prism—or obtained his results by supposition and calculation, is uncertain; Bechler denies its reality. Nor is it certain why Newton moved from one dogmatic experimental result to another, opposite to the first but equally dogmatic. Alan Shapiro has failed to find the single sentence that in *Opticks* refers to the experiment of a prism within a prism in the Latin precursor of *Opticks*, the *Fundamentum opticae*; evidently this sentence was an afterthought. However, as he also points out, it is in conformity with an earlier passage in *Opticks* where Newton asserts that the length of a spectrum is independent of the material used for the prism:

Now the different Magnitudes of the hole in the Window-shut, and different thickness of the Prism where the Rays passed through it, and different inclinations of the Prism to the Horizon, made no sensible changes in the length of the Image. Neither did the different matter of the Prisms make any: for in a Vessel made of polished Plates of Glass cemented together in the shape of a Prism and filled with Water, there is the like Success of the Experiment according to the quantity of the Refraction (1952, pp. 30–1).

No such assertion is made in the "New Theory", nor in the Optical Lectures, where the use of such a water-filled prism was first described (Shapiro 1979, p. 97, 1984, pp. 104–5).

As I have already noted, this last result is justifiable, though Newton's readiness to base a generalization of such range and importance as the invariability of the length of the spectrum in proportion to the refraction in all transparent materials whatever upon a single experiment implies excessive credulity in his own Platonic idea of Nature. He was also, in fact, aware that, as between two glass prisms, the lengths of the spectra are not always proportionately the same; or, to be more precise, he found reason to cite measurements in *Opticks* which yield a value for the dispersion of $27\frac{1}{2}$ where in the Optical Lectures similar measures gave a value of 25. (Newton of course never recognized the dispersion of a refracted ray as a separate parameter to be calculated from the ratio of the least and the greatest refractions; but the parameters can be calculated from the spectrum lengths and other figures that he quoted.) One might imagine that in checking earlier results Newton had found them to differ systematically from his new measurements, and simply decided to adopt the latter as the more accurate without looking into the cause of the discrepancy. But this 'verification' seems to have entailed the falsification of earlier experimental results, that is their recalculation to accord with shorter spectra. Alan Shapiro has found (compare Chapter 3, §1 above):

from the manuscript of *Opticks* that Prop. VII (and Prop. VIII which also concerns telescopes) was added to the end of Part I, Bk. I after the rest of that book was composed, and it was this measurement of chromatic aberration that caused him to adopt a new value for the dispersive power, . . . (1979, p. 121 note);

having done so, Newton had to revise the manuscript already written, amending the numbers stated to make them accord with this new dimension now taken as standard: the changes can still be seen (ibid.).

Dispersion not an independent parameter

In writing *Opticks*, Newton was just as much concerned as he had been when writing the *Principia* to attain the highest degree of mathematical consistency (a trivial example is his choice of the conjoint ratios 3/4, 4/5 in the example a few pages back). Everything had to fit precisely: discrepancies were ironed out by unacknowledged 'adjustments' to experimentally-derived figures (Westfall 1973). At an early stage Newton excluded from the range of possibilities the notion of dispersion as an independent parameter. Shapiro endorses Brewster's phrase of long ago (1855, I, p. 110) that this rejection was axiomatic:

For Newton colors and degree of refrangibility were innate, immutable properties of light. These were properties of light and not matter. To admit otherwise would undermine the very foundation of his theory of color: the one-to-one correspondence between color and degree of refrangibility and their immutability. The index of refraction alone, according to Newton, depended on the properties of matter and indicated how strongly a particular substance acted on light to bend it. Newton accepted these principles as axioms . . . (Shapiro 1979, p. 124).

I do not mean that Newton ever entertained the concept of dispersion as a parameter, which he was later to reject (contrary to the evidence as we see it). I think that he never considered the possibility of such a parameter at all. When, at a late stage, he made certain measurements in connection with the writing of Proposition VII, and found that the prism he had taken up for his experiments with a refracting angle of $62\frac{1}{2}$ degrees gave a spectrum shorter by one-eighth than he had found before, he discovered that this new spectrum length fitted so well with his dimensions of the rainbow and other things that he resolved to take this new, shorter length as his standard. To standardize in this way, setting aside experimental aberrations, was the best way to make the essential mathematical structure of Nature appear in sharp clarity (Shapiro 1979, pp. 119–21).

A dynamical model of refraction

There is another point. As the last quotation from Alan Shapiro's paper of 1979 hinted, Newton's physical ideas of light obstructed recognition of dispersion as a distinct parameter. I have already drawn attention to Newton's conjectural use of a dynamical model, and this matter will be taken further elsewhere (§4 below). One form of such a model supposes that different materials exert different degrees of short-range optical force; these various degrees of force are made manifest in experiments by the different refractive indices of various transparent media. The model assumes that among such media this is the sole variable parameter relevant to the passage of light through them. The light itself is supposed to consist of extremely minute particles differentiated one from another by their inertial mass, their velocity, or some other mechanical characteristic, causing them to respond variously to the force exerted upon them by transparent media. The third postulate contained in this model is that light-particles sorted by their mechanical characteristics are also systematically sorted by 'colours' (as we apprehend the difference). Accepting these postulates, we may argue that a medium exerting a refractive force upon a light-ray sorts its particles into coloured bands in the manner discovered by Newton, that is, all the particles possessing a certain range of values of the defining mechanical characteristics fall into a specific band of the spectrum, endowing it with their own 'colour'. (There is here a possible analogy with the mass-spectrometry of later physics.) The angle of inclination of the refracted beam to the incident beam will depend upon the strength of the attractive force of the medium only; the dispersion of the refracted beam—the length of its spectrum—will depend upon the physical characteristics of the light-particles only. The latter cannot possibly be varied by any property of the medium. Two parameters are concerned—force in the medium, mass (say) in the particles—and there is no room for a third.

Some elements of such a model are suggested by Newton in Section XIV of Book I of the *Principia*, and in the text of *Opticks*; other thoughts of his on the mechanical interaction of light and matter are found in the manuscripts, carefully analysed by Zev Bechler (1973, 1974). Although simple, the model is nevertheless appealing, even if there is an obvious difficulty in explaining why a *reflected* beam does not also display colours, when reflection is treated (as in the *Principia*) as an extreme case of refraction. I am far from suggesting that Newton was committed to any such mechanical model of light. However, since he certainly was convinced of the truth of the particle theory of light, and also of the existence of (at least one) optical force, it is hard to deny that his speculative thoughts ran to such a model, excluding dispersion as a separate parameter.

A discovery missed

It seems that Newton was in the kind of situation that has occurred more than once in the history of science, where a strong physical imagination combined with good circumstantial evidence has led an investigator of genius into making fundamentally unsound statements, even to the extent of making experimental claims that run to the edge of truth; as in Newton's case, countervailing evidence could have been, perhaps was, available for consideration, but seemed too trivial or too uncertain. Newton's biographer, Sir David Brewster, an expert in optics, remarked that 'trifling circumstances often arrest the philosopher when on the very verge of a discovery'. Newton had mixed lead acetate with water in the prism-within-a-prism experiment,

so that if Newton had completed the experiment, the use of the sugar of lead would have prevented him from making an important discovery, which was almost in his possession (Brewster 1855, I, p. 110).

In reality, Newton made no such claim that his experiment was 'incomplete' and was reluctant to make the 'discovery' which would have upset his fundamental understanding of light.

The discovery of achromatism

Newton's error was made public knowledge less than thirty years after his death. The Swedish mathematician Samuel Klingenstierna (1698–1765) demonstrated in 1754 that either the prism-within-a-prism experiment was incorrect, or Newton's dispersion theorem was false. His effort to support one by the other was a mistake. Other mathematicians, of whom Leonhard Euler was the most distinguished, rejected Newton's corpuscular theory, and with it Newton's belief in the invariability of dispersion. In order to refute such criticisms of Newton's optics, John Dollond, a practical optician, repeated Experiment 8 in 1758 using a flint-glass prism with a dispersive power markedly different from that of water or 'common' glass; to his amazement he found it possible to produce a white, refracted ray (as, unknown to him, Newton had already claimed in 1672!). Within a short time Dollond had made a two-element achromatic lens of crown and flint glass, described (1759) in the *Philosophical Transactions* of the Royal Society, which elected Dollond a Fellow and awarded him two of its medals. For his part, Klingenstierna went on to lay the foundations of the mathematical theory of the correction of aberrations in lenses. Opticians have since worked with great success on their elimination from both telescopes and microscopes.

The Boundary of a beam does not affect colour

After devoting the last pages of Book I, Part I to the construction of reflecting telescopes, Newton opens Part II—into which we have already trespassed in dealing with his treatment of dispersion—with a fresh attack upon an old enemy, the idea that differences of colour "arise from the different Confines of Shadow, whereby Light is variously modified, as hath hitherto been the Opinion of Philosophers" (1952, p. 114). Some of his experiments require the large fluid-filled prism already mentioned, or a very large lens. In one of the former Newton again shows how variations in apparent colour may be effected by reflection alone: a broad beam was refracted through the large prism, illuminating a screen close by and normal to the screen with white light. However, when the screen was held very obliquely to the refracted beam it appeared reddish or bluish according to the orientation, the colour being caused by the selective incidence of the rays resulting from their differences in refraction. Newton's object throughout these experiments is to bring forward colour-formation independent of the bounds of the colour. One experiment (rather curiously) cites the changing colour of soap-bubbles (p. 119). Newton's position that no "Colours [can] arise from any new Modifications of the Light by Refractions" of course implies the unchangeability of homogeneous light, which is established by his next proposition: Homogeneous light cannot be changed by refraction or reflection and colours all objects with its own hue.

From all of which it is manifest, that if the Sun's Light consisted of but one sort of Rays, there would be but one Colour in the whole World, nor would it be possible to produce any new Colour by Reflexions and Refractions, and by Consequence that the variety of Colours depends upon the Composition of Light (1952, p. 124).

Colour itself is "nothing else than a certain Power and Disposition to stir up a Sensation of this or that Colour" in the mind, or in other words "to propagate this or that Motion into the Sensorium, and in the Sensorium they are Sensations of those Motions under the Forms of Colours" (ibid., pp. 124–5).

The musical analogy once more

Proposition III, "To define the Refrangibility of the several sorts of homogeneal Light answering to the several Colours" leads to the statement about dispersion already considered. The enunciation here already takes it for granted that there is a constant relation between colour and refrangibility which clearly cannot hold if dispersion is variable, for in this event (supposing the red rays always to be kept constant in position when using prisms of different dispersion) the refraction of the blue rays cannot be uniform. It is here, in delineating the boundaries of the seven spectral colours through the extent of the spectrum (Fig. 15), that Newton declares "this Operation being divers times repeated, both in the same and in different Papers, I found that the Observations agreed well enough with one another, and that the [spectrum was] by the said cross Lines divided after the manner of a Musical Chord" (1952, p. 126). This notorious assertion, not otherwise justified in *Opticks*, but present in the revised Optical Lectures (Chapter 2, §2, p. 56), is mysterious to physicists, though less so to those who would number Newton among the Platonists, alchemists, and magicians. The analogy between colours and musical harmony—as old as

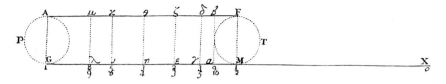

Fig. 15. The spectrum divided according to the musical scale, the 'just diatonic', with the successive intervals GX, λX, ιX, etc. as 1, 8/9, 5/6, 3/4, 2/3, 3/5, 9/16, 1/2; that is, the violet, indigo, blue, green, yellow, orange, and red spaces have the successive lengths of 80, 40, 60, 60, 48, 27, and 45 units, each unit being 1/360th of the whole length of the spectrum. From *Opticks*, p. 127.

Aristotle—provided Newton with a convenient rationale enabling him to choose precise fractions for the limits of the colours, where unambiguous determinations are difficult and perhaps impossible for the eye. It was from this analogy with the division of the octave into notes that he derived the fractional 'excesses' in the dispersion of the refracted rays, already discussed (p. 105); specifically, Newton makes (for the rays passing from glass into air)

$$\sin r = n.\sin i + d$$

where d successively equals 0/0, 1/8, 1/5, 1/3, 1/2, 2/3, 7/9, 1/1. The seven colours red, orange, yellow, green, blue, indigo, and violet occupy the spaces between each successive pair of fractions. The analogy certainly accorded with his conviction that Nature is ever consonant to herself (Shapiro 1984, pp. 546–7 note).

Newton also used the analogy in describing the colour-mixing circle (*below*), in defining the thicknesses of the thin films producing the various colours in 'Newton's rings' (1952, pp. 211–12) and in soap-bubbles (p. 225), and in explaining the colours of thick plates (p. 295—this is couched in a different form). The Proposition ends with an extended comment by Newton upon the usefulness of its theorems about the complex refraction of rays:

these Theorems being admitted into Opticks, there would be scope enough of handling that Science voluminously after a new manner, not only by teaching those things which tend to the perfection of Vision, but also by determining mathematically all kinds of Phaenomena of Colours which could be produced by Refractions. For to do this, there is nothing else requisite than to find out the Separations of heterogeneous Rays, and their various Mixtures and Proportions in every Mixture. By this way of arguing I invented almost all the Phaenomena described in these Books, beside some others less necessary to the Argument . . . (1952, pp. 131–2).

Note Newton's claim that a proper "way of arguing" leads to the discovery of new phenomena, not experimental serendipity!

In the Optical Lectures Newton had also considered the whole question of the classification of the colours in the spectrum more thoroughly than he was willing to do in *Opticks*. In the book it appears that the seven bands of colour with the names he has attached to them are obviously visible to every normal eye, whereas in the lectures Newton had distinguished the "five more prominent colours" (red, yellow, green, blue, and violet) from the other two, and explained why it was necessary to add orange and indigo as valid colours; these are "eminent", they occupy spaces "sufficiently wide according to the perfection of their species" (whatever that may mean), and they balance the whole spectrum in a symmetrical way.

Combinations of colours

After the analysis of colour, Newton next takes up its synthesis. For example, prismatic yellow and red may be combined to form an orange indistinguishable by the eye from the homogeneous orange of the spectrum, but resolvable by the prism into its elements in a way that the prismatic orange is not. The addition of white light to a simple or compound colour merely dilutes it: this is one of the points where Newton comes close to stating that the intensity or saturation of a colour is a variable distinct from its brightness. All the coloured rays of the spectrum are necessary for the formation of natural white light, but persistence of vision can make white appear where in reality it is not. Newton describes the experiment with a large 'comb' whereby colours are momentarily removed from the spectrum.

Newton recognized that because pigments absorb a part even of the light they reflect best, it is impossible to form a pure white by mixing them. At best the result is

a grey or pale white, [verging] to no one of the Colours more than to another. For thus it becomes of a Colour equal in Whiteness to that of Ashes, or of Wood newly cut, or of a Man's Skin (1952, p. 151).

Such a mixture of powders, under illumination by the full sun, might appear whiter than paper in shadow.

For when I was trying this, a Friend coming to visit me, I stopp'd him at the Door, and before I told him what the Colours were, or what I was doing; I asked him, Which of the two Whites were [*sic*] the best, and wherein they differed? And after he had at that distance viewed them well, he answer'd, that they were both good Whites, and that he could not say which was the best, nor wherein their Colours differed (1952, p. 153).

These tests again reveal the importance of the brightness of the reflected light in our sense of colour. The nameless friend must have been one of the few individuals to encounter Newton engaged in his experimental work.

The colour-circle

In Proposition VI, on the use of the colour-circle for defining hues and shades, Newton returned to two of the dominant interests in his study of colour from the earliest days in 1664. One is the possibility of balancing two colours so as to make a third or white; the other the definition of heterogeneous pigments in terms of homogeneous primary colours. In an early notebook Newton had written (1664–5): "Try if two Prismes the one casting blew on the others red doe not produce a white" (Hall 1948, p. 247; Hendry 1980, p. 235). Possibly because he lacked a second prism at that time, Newton devised a reverse experiment—looking at two patches painted red and blue through his single prism—which taught him much about the differences between prismatic colours and pigments. In the Optical Lectures Newton did not develop a theory of colour-mixing, though he did there affirm (rather too boldly) that primitive (that is, spectral) colours may always be reproduced by the compounding of the neighbouring colours on either side, repeating the same with more caution in Proposition 4, Book I, Part II of *Opticks*. The point of the colour-circle was that it enabled Newton to fix intensity as well as hue. The circumference of the circle is coloured exactly like a spectrum bent round upon itself; the centre of gravity of each band or arc of colour is noted, then circles drawn about each of these points denote by their size the strength of that colour in the mixed hue under consideration (Fig. 16):

the Circle *p* proportional to the Number of the red-making Rays in the Mixture, the Circle *q* proportional to the Number of the orange-making Rays in the Mixture, and so of the rest.

Fig. 16. Newton's colour-circle, not found in the Optical Lectures. The partitioning of the colours is "proportional to the seven Musical Tones or intervals of the eight Sounds", but not identical with that of Figure 15. The successive circumferential spaces now have the proportional lengths (violet) 80, 45, 45, 80, 72, 45, 80 (red). Newton did not explain this discrepancy.

Next, the common centre of gravity Z of all these little circles is found, and a radius drawn from the centre of the colour-circle passing through it. Where this meets the arc, at Y, the hue of that particular mixture will be found. Newton rather curiously remarks: "This Rule I conceive accurate enough for practice, though not mathematically accurate . . .". I find it hard to understand how Newton proposed to determine empirically the number of rays in any particular colour, or as he later puts it, the "parts". The rule, of course, applies only to homogeneous, that is spectral, colours, all pigments being of uncertain heterogeneity.

So far as I know, Newton never proposed to compound painted colours by rotating a disk swiftly, as in the 'colour-top' of James Clerk Maxwell (and indeed the toys of my childhood). In this way he could have examined experimentally the matching of mixtures with any given hue, including white. It seems that for him the colour-circle was a purely conceptual device.

Newton concludes the first Book of *Opticks* with the declaration that all colours in Nature are either those of homogeneous light, or compounded of these in the manner he has explained. To illustrate this declaration he reviews again the formation of colours by the prism (Proposition 8) and especially the blue 'bow' of light seen when illumination coming from the clouds is partially reflected from the base of a prism, and then the formation of the rainbow colours by atmospheric moisture, a matter that occupies several pages. A final curious effect accounted for is the different colour of some solutions (Newton instances *lignum nephriticum*, following Boyle) when seen by transmitted or reflected light.

Book II of Opticks

Turning to Book II, its first three Parts (so far as the middle of Proposition 8, Part III) are derived, almost word for word, from the so-called "Discourse of Observations" sent to the Royal Society at the end of 1675, as I have already said, with some use also made of the "Hypothesis explaining the Properties of Light" which had preceded it. Most of the differences between the two printed versions—the earlier in Birch's *History of the Royal Society* (III, pp. 272–305), the later in *Opticks*—are of a few lines only, but some are longer: for example, Newton rewrote Observation 14, introducing the statement that

it agrees something better with the Observation to say, that the thicknesses of the Air between the Glasses, where the Rings are successively made by the limits of the seven Colours, red, orange, yellow, green, blue, indigo, violet in order, are to one another as the Cube Roots of the Squares of the eight lengths of a Chord, which sound the Notes in an eighth [octave] *sol, la, fa, sol, la, mi, fa, sol*; that is, as the Cube Roots of the Squares of the Numbers 1, 8/9, 5/6, 3/4, 2/3, 3/5, 9/16, 1/2 (1952, p. 212).

Similarly, at the opening of Part II Newton again brought in the musical chord as a means of dividing his scale of colours, where in the "Discourse" he had been satisfied with proportional parts. Systematically, many of the dimensions were revised throughout the Book. Certain of these differences are, it seems, reflected in the manuscripts, but these have not yet been carefully collated (Turnbull 1959–77, I, p. 387, note 1). I quote here one example, which shows Newton delicately emphasizing his superiority as an exact quantitative scientist over Robert Hooke. In 1676 the passage read to the Royal Society was:

Mr Hooke, in his Micrographia, observes, that a faint yellow plate of Muscovy glass, laid upon a blue one, constituted a very deep purple. The yellow of the first order is a faint one, and the thickness of the plate exhibiting it, according to the table, is $5\frac{1}{4}$, to which add $9\frac{1}{2}$, the thickness exhibiting blue of the second order, and the sum will be $14\frac{3}{4}$, which most nearly approaches $14\frac{4}{5}$, the thickness exhibiting the purple of the third order (Birch 1757, III, p. 290).

In *Opticks* the phraseology is virtually identical but the numbers run . . . $4\frac{3}{5}$, 9, $13\frac{3}{5}$ . . . and the concluding words are: which is the thickness exhibiting the purple of the Third Order (1952, p. 234).

The numbers are different in the two versions because Newton had revised his measurements for the table (mentioned in the quotation) of the sizes of the thin plates (or the particles) producing the seven orders of coloured rings; to me, at least, it seems that the changes reveal no obvious pattern (apart from the fact that the numbers are always less in the book than in the "Discourse") and therefore were not produced by the use of a constant multiplier.

Aether waves become "fits"

A major feature of Book II is the transformation of the aether-model of the 1675 "Hypothesis" into the theory of "fits". It seems fairly obvious that the seat of these mysterious alternations must be in either (1) the rays of light themselves; or (2) the air, water, glass, or other transparent medium between two interfaces; or (3) an aether supposed to be latent in all such media. Statements compatible with each of these discrepant hypotheses can be found in *Opticks*. Much else is far from clear in the theory of "fits", not least the fact that the easy reflection or easy transmission of light at either surface of a thin plate is conditioned by the other surface: for the "fit"

depends on both the Surfaces of every thin Plate, because it depends upon their distance . . . It is therefore perform'd at the second Surface; for if it were performed at the first, before the Rays arrive at the second, it would not depend upon the second. It is also influenced by some action or disposition, propagated from the first to the second, because otherwise at the second it would not depend upon the first (*Opticks* (1952), p. 279).

"Fits" connate with light

Obviously the simplest treatment of the "fits" would have been to separate them altogether from the 'body' of light, as Newton had done in the "Hypothesis". But *Opticks* was written and published during the interval of roughly thirty years (1680–1710) in which Newton eschewed aetherial hypotheses in favour of force-mechanics; therefore, though strong traces of the older view remain in the book, logic compelled him now to make the "fits" elements of light itself. Accordingly it is both a wave and a particle! (Westfall 1980, pp. 522–3; Shapiro 1989, pp. 238–9). In Newton's own words:

what is said of [the rays'] Refrangibility may also be understood of their Reflexibility, that is, of their Dispositions to be reflected, some at a greater, and others at a less thickness of thin Plates or Bubbles; namely, that *those Dispositions are also connate with the Rays, and immutable* (*Opticks* (1952), pp. 242–3; my emphasis).

It had happened by chance that Newton's abandonment of the aether in favour of dynamics had coincided with the sighting of a new comet in 1680–1, which was to be the accidental occasion of Newton's investigating the coloured rings formed by scattered light in *thick* plates (see below). Extending his early ideas about 'Newton's rings' to the new phenomena, Newton at this time rejected the aether hypothesis and took up "fits". From this change he derived important conceptual gains (Shapiro 1989, p. 39).

Reflection as the equivalent of refraction

To return to more solid ground, we may again pick up a point in the last quotation that has been touched upon before, that is, the importance of the refraction – reflection equivalence in Newton's theory of light. It is equally central to his study of the light-force exerted by matter in his *Principia*, Book I, Section XIV, and to his theory of the colours of natural bodies in *Opticks*, Book II, Part III. Proposition 1 of this Part asserts that the reflecting power of transparent bodies is proportional to their refracting power; Proposition 9 that these powers are in fact one and the same "variously exercised in various Circumstances" (p. 269). The identity is established by reference to Proposition 1, by the continuous transition from total transmission to total reflection at the critical angle of incidence, and (interestingly) by 'Newton's rings', for in them

the thickness of the Glass determines whether that Power by which Glass acts upon Light shall cause it to be reflected, or suffer it to be transmitted (pp. 269–70).

This is a rather rare Newtonian conjunction of the theory of "fits" with the dynamic theory of light. Further (Proposition 10) this optical power is roughly proportional, in different substances, to their density; only unctuous materials are a little more powerful in proportion than others.

The colours of bodies

Whereas in elucidating the true nature of light and the true character of the interaction between light and matter the refracting manifestation of this power had been of prime importance, now (since refraction plays little part in our perception of the colours of opaque bodies) the reflecting manifestation comes to the fore for a few propositions, and in particular the reflectivity of the surface structure of bodies. The suggestion that colour (like other properties) is determined by the mechanical form of the surfaces, the constituent parts of these surfaces being in themselves colourless, was made by Robert Boyle. Newton showed how this could come about by the selective reflection of light from surface corpuscles, intrinsically transparent, which become coloured in just the same way that transparent thin plates become coloured; from this fact their magnitudes may be deduced (Propositions 5, 7). Thus the green of a natural body may be a third-order green (referring to Newton's table), in which case its surface corpuscles have a diameter of $1625/10^8$ inches (p. 255). Newton added, too optimistically:

In these descriptions I have been the more particular, because it is not impossible but that Microscopes may at length be improved to the discovery of the Particles of Bodies on which their Colours depend, if they are not already in some measure arrived to that degree of perfection. For if those Instruments are or can be so far improved as with sufficient distinctness to represent Objects five or six hundred times bigger than at a Foot distance they appear to our naked Eyes, I should hope that we might be able to discover some of the greatest of those Corpuscles. And by one that would magnify three or four thousand times perhaps they might all be discover'd, but those which produce blackness (p. 261).

The best microscopes of Newton's age, the lenses of Antoni van Leeuwenhoek, could resolve about one micron, at a magnification of about 250 times; if Newton hoped to see corpuscles of about half this length— half a millionth of a metre—at a magnification about twice as great, his hope was not absurd. Light-microscopes exceeded this hope by the mid-nineteenth century without, however, yet penetrating to the corpuscles of matter or surface molecules.

Absorption

If only a small proportion of the beam of sunlight is reflected to the eye by even the most reflective surface, should it be coloured by a fraction of the whole spectrum, what happens to the rest of the incident sunlight?

Newton's answer is that the light is "stifled or lost", that is, it is absorbed (pp. 266–7). The best reflectors are white metalline substances

which by reason of their excessive density seem to reflect almost all the Light incident on their first Superficies, unless by solution in Menstruums [solvents] they be reduced to very small Particles, and then they become transparent (pp. 248–9).

Other bodies are in general transparent to light in very thin sections; they become opaque by "the multitude of Reflexions caused in their internal Parts" and so ultimately by absorption. Absorbed light produces heat, Newton indicates elsewhere, knowing that differently coloured bodies absorb heat from sunlight to different extents. Proposition 8 of this Part contains important information about Newton's idea of the physical constitution of matter, notably (as already mentioned) his assurance that corpuscles and particles are widely separated in the densest substances. Although polished metals reflect efficiently, reflection (unlike refraction) is not in general proportional to density; Newton maintains that air reflects more strongly than water or glass, and a vacuum perhaps more than air (pp. 262–3). Reflection is not caused by light's impinging directly on the solid particles of bodies: if it were so

it would be impossible for thin Plates or Bubbles, at one and the same place, to reflect the Rays of one Colour, and transmit those of another . . . For it is not to be imagined that at one place the Rays which, for instance, exhibit a blue Colour, should have the fortune to dash upon the part[icle]s, and those which exhibit a red to hit upon the Pores of the Body; and then at another place, where the Body is either a little thicker or thinner, that on the contrary the blue should hit upon the Pores, and the red upon its part[icle]s.

Moreover, reflection from smooth surfaces is so perfect that some effect must smooth over the confusion that must necessarily arise by reflection from the microscopic scratching and irregularity of polishing processes;

this Problem is scarce otherwise to be solved, than by saying, that the Reflexion of a Ray is effected, not by a single point of the reflecting Body, but by some Power of the Body which is evenly diffused all over its Surface, and by which it acts upon the Ray, without immediate Contact.

This is, of course, the optical force of matter.

The optical force of matter

Forces act through solid matter, as though it were transparent to their action:

The Magnet acts upon Iron through all dense Bodies not magnetick nor red hot, without any diminution of its Virtue; as for instance, through Gold, Silver, Lead, Glass, Water. The gravitating Power of the Sun is transmitted through the vast Bodies of the Planets without any diminution, so as to act upon all their part[icle]s to their very centres with the same Force and according to the same Laws, as if the part[icle] upon which it acts were not surrounded with the Body of the Planet. The Rays of Light, whether they be very small Bodies projected, or only Motion or Force propagated, are moved in very right Lines; and whenever a Ray of Light is by any Obstacle turned out of its rectilinear way, it will never return into the same rectilinear way, unless perhaps by a very great accident. And yet Light is transmitted through pellucid solid Bodies in right Lines to very great distances. How Bodies can have a sufficient quantity of Pores for producing these Effects is very difficult to conceive, but perhaps not altogether impossible (pp. 267–8).

Supposing the ultimate, solid particles of matter to be arranged in a primary open cluster or corpuscle of the first order, let these in turn constitute others of the second order and so on; if the matter of experience is composed of corpuscles of a high order the proportion of the ultimate solid matter within them will be very small, and there will be wide gaps through which the light-rays can travel.

Thick plates and their rings

One might expect Newton to make more effort at this point to characterize the optical force at which he has hinted, and its manner of acting, but he does not. Instead, the fourth and last part of Book II takes up the specialized and intricate study of the coloured circles that can be formed by *thick* plates. These "very strange and surprizing" effects were a late discovery, probably of 1681, when (in pursuit of a new comet) Newton attempted to construct a large reflecting telescope using a glass mirror silvered on the convex side (Westfall 1980, p. 392). This mirror had been prepared by "one of our *London* artists", not by Newton himself (*Opticks* (1952), p. 106); it was of about six feet focal length. Perhaps he originally set up the following arrangement to examine the quality of this mirror, which was not high: Newton darkened his room as usual, admitted a narrow beam of light, and sent this to the concave side of the mirror through a small hole in a white screen. This he placed at the mirror's focus, so that the beam of sunlight was reflected straight back on itself and only scattered light reached the screen, where it formed coloured circles, analogous to the familiar 'Newton's rings' of thin plates. As always, the blue light was the most refrangible, the red the least; and as before these new rings could be fitted to the musical octave (Fig. 17; p. 295). The mirror without the silver backing made the same rings more faintly, but a metal speculum made none —clearly both surfaces of the glass were necessary, the silver intensifying the reflection from the rear surface.

It seemed to me therefore that these Rings were of one and the same original with those of thin Plates, but yet with this difference, that those of thin Plates are made by the alternate Reflexions and Transmissions of the Rays at the second Surface of the Plate, after one passage through it; but here the Rays go twice through the Plate

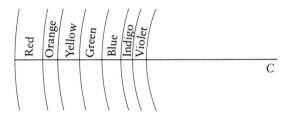

Fig. 17. The coloured circles produced by *thick* plates reduced to the octave. Newton here makes the spaces occupied by the seven colours (red to violet) follow "the Tones in an Eight . . . [that is,] as the Numbers 1/9, 1/18, 1/12, 1/12, 2/27, 1/27, 1/18"; that is, if the scale be of 360 parts, the divisions are placed after 80, 40, 60, 60, 53, 27, and 40 parts (approximately). This is close to the series of Figure 15 *reversed*. Newton's music was highly versatile and elastic!

before they are alternately reflected and transmitted. First, they go through it from the first Surface to the Quick-silver, and then return through it from the Quick-silver to the first Surface, and there are either transmitted to the [screen] or reflected back to the Quick-silver, accordingly as they are in their Fits of easy Reflexion or Transmission when they arrive at that Surface (p. 299).

The test of the correctness of this identification was to calculate the diameter of the successive rings from the thickness of Newton's mirror. He measured this thickness "and found it every where $\frac{1}{4}$ of an Inch precisely", a barely credible result if "precisely" be understood in terms of the magnitudes of 10^{-5} inches with which Newton was concerned. Rounding off Newton's over-extended figures, he had formerly found the "fits" associated with the primary yellow ring in thin plates to be 1/140 000 inches long, therefore 35 000 "fits" succeed each other in the thickness of the mirror at the centre. The rings are formed because the depth of glass penetrated by the light—before and after reflection from the rear surface—increases away from the centre, as the parallel rays fall more and more obliquely upon the first surface of the glass, and refraction occurs there. The diameters of the rings measured on the screen must also increase as the radius of the mirror increases and the screen is further away. A rather tedious geometrical computation taking all this into account permits Newton to discover that the first yellow ring (35 000 "fits") should have a diameter of 1.688 inches, the second (34 999 "fits") 2.389 inches, the third (34 998 "fits") 2.925 inches, and so on:

Now these Diameters of the bright yellow Rings, thus found by Computation are the very same with those found in the third of these Observations by measuring them, *viz.* with 1 11/16, 2 3/8, 2 11/12, and 3 3/8 Inches, and therefore the Theory of deriving these Rings from the thickness of the Plate of Glass of which the

Speculum was made, and from the Obliquity of the emerging Rays agrees with the Observation.

The agreements are indeed very close: I put the decimal equivalent of Newton's first three fractions as 1.687, 2.375, and 2.917 inches. That Newton should have measured the coloured circles to one-sixteenth of an inch is believable; a comparison with theory to a third place of decimals, a thousandth of an inch, does not make sense. The calculation is an example of Newton's tremendous energy and ingenuity in bringing experimental results to an exact numerical concord with his theoretical model. In this case he repeated all the above steps with a different mirror, to the same satisfactory effect. We need not follow Newton through more complex ring-formations of the same generic kind.

The halo

Only one example in Nature of the formation of colours by this mechanism is proposed, the atmospheric halo. Consider a water-droplet of 1/500th inch diameter: a red-making ray passing through its diameter has "250 Fits of easy Transmission within the globule"; other red rays, with successively integral numbers of "fits", would depict circles about this. If the sun or moon under clear conditions shines through a cloud of such uniform droplets, it should appear to be surrounded by a circular halo of colours, the diameters of successive red rings (as computed by Newton; I pass over the details) being $7\frac{1}{4}°$, $10\frac{1}{4}°$, and $12\frac{1}{2}°$. He himself had twice witnessed such a halo; the first occasion indicates the early beginning of his scientific observation:

in the beginning of the Year 1664, *Febr.* 19th at Night, I saw two such Crowns [haloes] about her [the Moon]. The Diameter of the first or innermost was about three Degrees, and that of the second about five Degrees and an half . . .

The second must be near to the time of writing *Opticks*:

in *June* 1692, I saw by reflexion in a Vessel of stagnating Water three Halos, Crowns, or Rings of Colours about the Sun, like three little Rainbows concentrick to his Body. The Colours of the first or innermost Crown were blue next the Sun, red without, and white in the middle between the blue and red. Those of the second Crown were purple and blue within, and pale red without, and green in the middle . . . The Diameter of the second Crown measured from the middle of the yellow and red on one side of the Sun, to the middle of the same Colour on the other side was 9 1/3 Degrees, or thereabouts. The Diameters of the first and third I had not time to measure, but that of the first seemed to me about five or six Degrees, and that of the third about twelve . . . (*Opticks* (1952), pp. 313–4).

Newton's was indeed a very long life of scientific experiment and observation.

Diffraction

The last optical phenomenon discussed by Newton in the main text of *Opticks* is diffraction, discovered not by Newton but by Grimaldi. As we have already seen, Newton's early knowledge of diffraction effects seems to have derived from books alone, unless we suppose him to have made some untypically careless trials. My own opinion is that only after completing the *Principia* (where diffraction is explained in rather cavalier fashion in Book I, Section XIV) did Newton at last undertake the exact but frustrating series of experiments described in *Opticks*, Book III (pp. 317–36), from which (typically) he was able to present to his readers a clearer, more exact, and more detailed account of diffraction than any of his predecessors.

Newton began by preparing a very narrow beam of light, admitting it into his room through "a small hole made with a Pin" in a piece of lead. He verified at once the paradoxical broadening of the shadow of a hair "and such like slender Substances placed in this beam of Light" reported previously. He concluded that rays passing close by the hair were bent away from it (Fig. 18), this action being

strongest on the Rays which pass by at least distances, and grows weaker and weaker accordingly as the Rays pass by at distances greater and greater . . . For thence it comes to pass, that the Shadow of the Hair is much broader in proportion to the distance of the Paper [screen] from the Hair, when the Paper is nearer the Hair, than when it is at a great distance from it (*Opticks* (1952), pp. 319–20).

In this beam, the shadows of all bodies when cast on the screen were edged with "three Parallel Fringes or Bands of colour'd Light, whereof that which

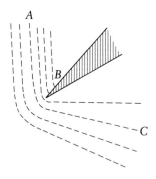

Fig. 18. The *Principia*'s dynamic model of diffraction: parallel rays of light at *A* are segregated at *C* because those passing very close to the sharp edge are more tightly curved round it than those more remote, by the action of the attractive optical force of the edge. Rays striking the edge at an angle are bent inwards at *B* by the same force. After *Principia* (1687), p. 230.

was contiguous to the Shadow was broadest and most luminous". Newton examined the order of the colours in these fringes as carefully as possible. Typically, he also measured the breadth of the shadows and fringes scrupulously; by arranging his screen very obliquely to the beam, he was able to magnify the effects twelvefold, and so measured fringes down to 1/340th of an inch. It seemed to him that the fringes and the intervals between them formed a "continued progression of the Numbers 1, $\sqrt{\frac{1}{2}}$, $\sqrt{\frac{1}{3}}$, $\sqrt{\frac{1}{4}}$, $\sqrt{\frac{1}{5}}$", etc.

More novel phenomena followed; to obtain these, Newton used a larger aperture ($\frac{1}{4}$ inch), the beam passing through a blackened diaphragm with a square hole of $\frac{3}{4}$ inch side. Fixing a knife edge centrally in the beam, he "saw two streams of faint Light shoot out both ways from the beam of Light into the Shadow, like the Tails of Comets" (p. 326). He improved the effect and described it in detail. Next he formed a narrow slit, as little as 1/400th of an inch broad, between the edges of two knives placed parallel. Now,

the stream parted in the middle, and left a Shadow between the two parts. This Shadow was so black and dark that all the Light which passed betwen the Knives seem'd to be bent, and turn'd aside to the one hand or to the other . . . And hence I gather that the Light which is least bent, and goes to the inward end of the streams, passes by the Knives at the greatest distance, and this distance when the Shadow begins to appear between the streams, is about the 800th part of an Inch. And the Light which passes by the edges of the Knives at distances still less and less, is more and more bent, and goes to those parts of the streams which are farther and farther from the direct Light (pp. 327–8).

In other experiments Newton attempted to define the course of the diffracted rays more precisely; in some he formed the slit into a narrow angle. He learnt that each edge of the slit seemed to have a separate effect on the fringe-pattern, and "that the Light which makes the Fringes upon the Paper is not the same Light at all distances of the Paper from the Knives . . .". Finally, he experimented upon diffraction with monochromatic light from a prism. Red made the largest fringes, violet the least. From this Newton concluded that

the Hair in causing these Fringes acted alike upon the red Light or least refrangible Rays at a greater distance, and upon the violet or most refrangible Rays at a less distance

and so made larger or smaller fringes without in any way changing the colour of the light. Hence some of his earliest notions about light were once more validated; when fringes of various colours were created by sunlight

those Colours arose not from any new modifications impress'd upon the Rays of Light by the Hair, but only from the various inflexions whereby the several sorts of Rays were separated from one another, which before separation . . . composed the white beam of the Sun's Light . . .

Very soon after this follows the end of the unfinished text:

When I made the foregoing Observations, I design'd to repeat most of them with
more care and exactness, and to make some new ones for determining the manner
how the Rays of Light are bent in their passage by Bodies, for making the Fringes
of Colours with the dark lines between them. But I was then interrupted, and cannot
now think of taking these things into farther Consideration (p. 338).

The gain of England's Mint was a loss to British science.

Over-extension of the idea of optical force

But perhaps there was an element of self-deception involved when Newton,
seeking to put the best face on the destruction of his hope of writing a
complete and final treatise about the physical nature of light and colours,
suggested that if only he had had more time for experiments and reflection
he might have solved the problem of diffraction as well as he had solved the
problems of coloured rings. For in fact the phenomena of diffraction put a
new strain upon a conceptual structure that was already breaking down. As
we shall see later, Newton's earliest experiments on refraction were
conducted in the context of dynamical speculations about light—concealed
as thoroughly as might be from readers—which both stimulated and
explained his observations. The final expressions in print of such
speculations are to be found in the Queries and in the *Principia*. Particularly
Newton seemed to see his way through the confusing thickets of facts with
the aid of a theory of a short-range optical force of attraction. Upon this
simple and satisfactory conceptual basis, which had the merit of uniting
reflection and refraction, Newton had been compelled to graft the
undynamic, indeed inexplicable, "fits", in order to rationalize 'Newton's
rings'. Now, it seemed, diffraction forced him to reconsider his dynamical
conceptions. The quotations from *Opticks* Book III just presented make it
clear that for Newton (fairly enough) the bending of light implied the action
of a force. But it could not be (and again he was right) the force responsible
for refraction. Its characteristics were quite different. A section added to the
optical section of the *Principia* in 1726 makes Newton's late understanding
of what was involved even plainer:

And those [rays] which pass at greater distances are less bent, and those at still
greater distances are a little bent the contrary way and form three fringes of colours
(*Principia*, 1726, p. 226).

Newton is clearly imagining a force which at very close range is attractive, at a slightly greater distance sinks to zero, then becomes a repulsive
force as the distance increases still more. This is of course in accord with
a general principle stated elsewhere by Newton, but clearly the complexities
are increasing and attainment of a unified explanation has become a

vanishing hope. True, the precious first discovery of the unique, durable specificity of each pure colour has survived intact through all vicissitudes, indeed was confirmed by all the new phenomena revealed to Newton after 1664; but the original promising model of particles acted upon by a force seems to have been overwhelmed. If Newton in the 1690s really had any ideas for solving the remaining problems of optics in a consistent manner—and to those already mentioned that of birefringence, of which Newton was certainly aware by now, must be added—he was no longer eager to pursue them.

§3. The Queries

Modernizing early work

Nothing is more certain about *Opticks* than that Newton had no original intention of concluding his book with a series of questions and conjectures, a dubious method of suggesting to the reader possible resolutions of the problems that the text had left unsolved, or even untouched. There is a poignant contrast between *Opticks* and the *Principia mathematica*. The latter was a work begun in a mood of white-hot enthusiasm and written with a feverish intensity of concentration, while Newton was carried forward by the power of new ideas and constantly stimulated by the renewed successes rewarding his mathematical method; *Opticks* was a book formalizing ideas whose inception was thirty years before and whose experiments were for the most part twenty years old. To a large extent, indeed, its writing was a literary labour, the revision of papers composed long before. It is amazing that *Opticks* reads as freshly as it still does. The book as we have it—though not as Newton first envisaged it—is in the main an exposition of Newton's two great studies of refraction and interference colours; Grimaldi's diffraction, of which Newton was barely or not at all aware when writing his 1672 manuscripts, probably seemed of little importance to him until after the completion of the *Principia*, while of birefringence at that time (when *Opticks* was begun) he knew nothing, though it had been described in a book by Erasmus Bartholin in 1669, noticed in the *Philosophical Transactions* (no. 67, January 1671, pp. 2041–8).

The Queries represent, in part, Newton's attempt to compensate for the effects of his twenty years' delay in writing and publishing his book on optics—which was yet to remain in cold storage for a further twelve. The science of optics had by no means stood still in the interval between Hooke's *Micrographia* (1665) and Huygens's *Traité de la Lumière* (1690), and more work appeared in the 1690s. Perhaps in all this there was not a great deal, other than Huygens's investigations, that touched Newton closely; but it can hardly be denied that the lacunae left by the two first Books of *Opticks* were more significant in 1704 than they would have been thirty years earlier. As for the *Traité de la Lumière,* it left no trace upon the main text of *Opticks.*

Opticks *broken off: its dynamical theory incomplete*

The Queries, then, represent afterthoughts, modernizations, the filling of gaps; but even more they surely reflect Newton's need, before the book left his hands, to say something deeper and therefore more speculative about the natural philosophy of which it was one aspect. Just as he had been unable to print the *Principia* without some hints in the Preface and elsewhere of a metaphysics and a philosophy of Nature that far outran the axiomatic, mathematical method, hints much expanded in the General Scholium added to the second edition (1713), so with *Opticks* he failed to suppress thoughts ranging far beyond the experimental scope of his design, again much enlarged in successive editions of the book (see Appendix II). Scholia and Queries gave their author a freedom to express himself forbidden in the main text, whether its preferred method was mathematical or experimental. I have alluded to the evidence that Newton at one stage intended the final Book of *Opticks,* then numbered IV, to treat of the optical force and the mutual interaction of light and matter at a distance, topics barely hinted at in the main text. No doubt this Book would have set this particular force in a broad contextual discussion of the universal role of physical force in Nature. Because this final, dynamical Book of *Opticks* remained unfinished and unpublished, the chief public evidences of Newton's grand philosophy of forces were released through the growing body of the Queries. For all his commitment to the Boylean philosophy of nature since his earliest studies, and his personal faith in his own new, mathematical and dynamic version of that philosophy, Newton remained ever reluctant to assert the truth of ideas of this kind, to affirm it as a "doctrine". He left his ideas to be confirmed or refuted by his successors (Boas and Hall 1959; Westfall 1980, pp. 640–1).

The overt reason for the abrupt abandonment of *Opticks* after the remarkable series of eleven experimental "Observations" on diffraction was an unexplained shortage of leisure; having been once interrupted, Newton could not resume his work: "To communicate what I have tried, and leave the rest to others for farther Enquiry, is all my Design in publishing these Papers" (*Advertisement*). Newton accordingly ended his book with the Queries which, Alan Shapiro has found, were drafted only shortly before its publication.

It is obvious that in 1703 days of experimentation were long past for Newton. It is less obvious why his time was so suddenly taken up by other things eleven or twelve years before. If it were possible to suppose that the diffraction experiments had been made in 1687–8, then again it would be obvious why they suddenly ceased, never to be resumed.

Extending them hypothetically, the Queries, originally sixteen in number, open with speculation about the interaction of light and matter: Do not bodies attract light inversely in proportion to the distance, the more refrangible (blue) rays being the more strongly attracted? Are not oscillations "with a motion like that of an Eel" thereby produced? Does not this action extend into the space surrounding matter? Then Newton's thoughts begin to stretch further, for he now asks: Is there not a common principle in matter that either reflects, refracts or inflects the rays of light according to circumstances, and conversely does not light act upon bodies to heat them? (Query 5). The particulate surface structure of bodies that we perceive as colour also comes into this, since the absorption of heat and light varies with the hue of the absorbing and reflecting surface (Query 6).

Heat, light, and electricity

By means of this transition Newton passes rapidly from optics to heat and photochemistry: Is not the peculiar susceptibility of sulphureous bodies to the heating action of light the reason why they take fire so readily? Is not fire merely "a Body heated so hot as to emit Light copiously?" (Query 9). For just as the impact of light sets the particles of a body vibrating, creating the effects of heat, so when vibrating rapidly enough the particles emit light. In the *Addenda* to *Optice* (1706) Newton inserted a long passage into Query 8 about this light-emitting motion, sometimes associated with heat, but also occurring in cold bodies:

As for instance; Sea-Water in a raging Storm; Quicksilver agitated *in vacuo*; the Back of a Cat, or Neck of a Horse, obliquely struck or rubbed in a dark place; Wood, Flesh and Fish while they putrefy; Vapours arising from putrefy'd Waters, usually call'd *Ignes Fatui*; Stacks of moist Hay or Corn growing hot by fermentation; Glow-worms and the Eyes of some Animals by vital Motions; the vulgar *Phosphorus* agitated by the attrition of any Body, or by the acid Particles of the Air; Amber and some Diamonds by striking, pressing or rubbing them; . . . (p. 340).

Then, to the second English edition (1717) Newton added still more about this light associated with frictional electricity, which had by then been explored by the Royal Society's experimenter, Francis Hauksbee:

So also a Globe of Glass about 8 or 10 Inches in diameter, being put into a Frame where it may be swiftly turn'd round its Axis, will in turning shine where it rubs against the palm of ones Hand apply'd to it; And if at the same time a piece of white Paper or white Cloth, or the end of ones Finger be held at the distance of about a quarter of an Inch or half an Inch from that part of the Glass where it is most in motion, the electrick Vapour which is excited by the friction of the Glass against the Hand, will by dashing against the white Paper, Cloth or Finger, be put into such an agitation as to emit Light . . . (p. 341; cf. Guerlac 1977, pp. 113–14).

Once launched into chemical notes upon heat and fire, Newton seemed unable to stop. Query 10 is a little essay on fumes and flames, which are only red-hot fumes, including the observation (relating to colour) that flames are specifically tinged by certain burning substances, "as that of Sulphur blue, that of Copper . . . green". Query 11 suggests that intensity of heat is a function of mass and of an interaction between hot matter and the light emitted by it occurring within the mass:

the Reflexions and Refractions of its Rays within the Pores [causing the massive body] to grow still hotter, till it comes to a certain period of heat, such as that of the Sun?

This passage too was enlarged in *Optice* by the suggestion that such an intense heat in massive bodies may be conserved by the gravitating power of the body's preventing vapours and exhalation from escaping into space.

Vision effected by vibrations

Query 12 turns from the macrocosm to the microcosm, man, and his mechanism of vision: "do not the Rays of Light in falling upon the bottom of the Eye excite Vibrations in the *Tunica Retina?*" Vibrations which, when transmitted by the optic nerves to the brain, cause sight. There is a connection with heat, however, because the persistence of these vibrations "along solid Fibres of uniform dense Matter to a great distance" is possible because dense bodies maintain their heat for a long time. (I confess incomprehension of this notion, even if we allow a sort of equivalence between heat and light.) In Query 13, recalling his "Hypothesis" of 1675, Newton proposes that colour-sensation is determined by the wavelength of the vibrations, the shortest waves being excited by the most refrangible or deep violet rays. He makes the expected comparison with sound, where high pitch accords with short waves, and suggests also (Query 14) that, as sounds have their harmonies and discords, so too do colours—an idea of recurrent if elusive fascination. The next two Queries are wholly physiological, dealing with the combination of images from two eyes into a single visual picture, and the production of sensations of light by pressure upon the eye, phenomena which Newton thought confirmed his mechanical theory of light.

At this point, after sixteen Queries, the first edition of *Opticks* ended abruptly. Two years later, in *Optice*, Newton increased the number of Queries to 23, adding 48 pages to this translation (see Appendix II). I shall consider this important group of new Queries next, after noting that because of the insertion of yet another group of eight more Queries into the second English edition of *Opticks* in 1717 the new Queries of *Optice* appear (revised) in the subsequent English editions as Queries 25 to 31. I shall therefore refer to them here by these numbers of the English editions.

Double refraction

Queries 25 and 26 contain Newton's attempt to resolve the problem of birefringence, or double refraction, that is, the appearance of an extra, "unusual", refracted ray, in addition to the ray expected from Snel's Law, when a beam of light is shone through the crystalline substance then called Iceland (or Island) crystal, or Icelandic spar, calcite (or indeed less conspicuously with rock-crystal). The "unusual" ray had been discovered by Erasmus Bartholin. I do not know why Newton's attention in print to this strange effect was deferred to 1706; it is on record that both he and Christiaan Huygens addressed the Royal Society upon this topic on 12 June 1689 (Shapiro 1989, p. 223). What Newton then said is unrecorded. Query 25 opens rather feebly: "Are there not other original Properties of the Rays of Light, besides those already described?" Typically, Newton begins with a scrupulous examination of the angles of the crystal and advice on how to polish its faces. Then he defines the emergent angle of the "unusual" ray, and finds that on a second refraction through a second crystal, each of the two refracted rays leaving the first crystal either preserves or exchanges its character according to the orientation of the pair of crystals; therefore "The unusual Refraction is . . . performed by an original Property of the Rays" (p. 358). Query 26 goes on to propose what this property may be:

Have not the Rays of Light several sides, endued with several original Properties? For . . . there are not two sorts of Rays differing in their nature from one another, one of which is constantly and in all Positions refracted after the usual manner, and the other constantly and in all Positions after the unusual manner (pp. 358–9).

Because the relative orientation of the crystals determines the character of each of the pair of refracted rays Newton argues that

every Ray may be consider'd as having four Sides or Quarters, two of which opposite to one another incline the Ray to be refracted after the unusual manner, as often as either of them are [*sic*] turn'd towards the Coast of unusual Refraction; and the other two, whenever either of them are turn'd towards the Coast of unusual Refraction . . . incline it to be refracted . . . after the usual manner.

By "Coast" (Latin *plaga*) Newton means 'area, region' (cf. French *côté*) as determined by the orientation of the crystals: the rays are, as it were, keyed into passages within the crystal.

Every Ray of Light has therefore two Opposite Sides, originally endued with a Property on which the unusual Refraction depends, and the other two opposite sides not endowed with that Property (pp. 360–1).

Thus the ray can present itself to the crystal in two orientations, but the crystal can offer more than two to the ray, one of which actually results in the production of *four* refracted rays (two usual, two unusual), as Newton noted at the end of Query 26. Any physical beam of light is of course composed of rays presenting both orientations to the crystal.

In Query 29, on forces, Newton added further detail to this hypothesis of relative orientations:

. . . the unusual Refraction of Island-Crystal looks very much as if it were perform'd by some kind of attractive virtue lodged in certain Sides both of the Rays, and of the Particles of the Crystal. For were it not for some kind of Disposition or Virtue lodged in some Sides of the Particles of the Crystal, and not in their other Sides, and which inclines and Bends the Rays towards the Coast of unusual Refraction, the Rays which fall perpendicularly on the Crystal, would not be refracted towards that Coast rather than towards any other Coast, both at their Incidence and at their Emergence, so as to emerge perpendicularly by a contrary Situation of the Coast of unusual Refraction at the second Surface; the Crystal acting upon the Rays after they have pass'd through it, and are emerging into the Air; or, if you please, into a *Vacuum*. And since the Crystal by this Disposition or Virtue does not act upon the Rays, unless when one of their Sides of unusual Refraction looks towards that Coast, this argues a Virtue or Disposition in those Sides of the Rays, which answers to, and sympathizes with that Virtue or Disposition of the Crystal, as the Poles of two Magnets answer to one another. And as Magnetism may be intended and remitted, and is found only in the Magnet and in Iron: So this Virtue of refracting the perpendicular Rays is greater in Island-Crystal, less in Crystal of the Rock, and is not yet found in other Bodies. I do not say that this Virtue is magnetical: it seems to be of another kind. I only say, that whatever it be, it's difficult to conceive how the Rays of Light, unless they be Bodies, can have a permanent Virtue in two of their Sides which is not in their other Sides, and this without any regard to their Position to the Space or Medium through which they pass (pp. 373–4).

This makes plain Newton's idea—in which he had been anticipated by Huygens, and indeed it is obvious enough—that it is the peculiar structure of the calcite crystal that effects these extraordinary refractions, as Newton supposed by variously pulling the rays this way and that. Many writers (including Mach 1926, p. 189) have attributed the concept of polarization to Newton on the basis of this passage, on account of its analogy with magnetic *poles*. Clearly Newton did, as Mach said, attach 'lateral asymmetry' to the rays, but the nineteenth-century concept of optical polarization is applicable only to the waves of light that Newton still so firmly rejected (as we shall see). It is obvious that one can imagine wave-motion occurring in a plane which possesses a definite orientation in space, but it less easy to imagine force confined to a plane (though Kepler did this). Newton's hypothesis of "Sides" seems, in truth, to be a rather crude mechanical analogy compared with Huygens's sophisticated (if lengthy) geometrical analysis. It reminds one of Descartes's theory of magnetism, with left-hand and right-hand screwed particles and matching passages in magnetic bodies; replace the screw asymmetries by the asymmetry of forces and the likeness is close. It is perhaps not surprising that most commentators upon Newton's writings (including Smith 1738) either omitted double refraction altogether or passed over it lightly.

The modification of light again rejected

So that the reader should not misunderstand his position by supposing him to mean that the rays of light are modified by their passage through the complexities of the crystal, Newton reiterated his fundamental axiom of optics in Query 27: phenomena are not to be explained by imaginary processes in which the character of the rays is altered:

For those Phaenomena depend not upon new Modifications, as has been supposed, but upon the original and unchangeable Properties of the Rays (p. 361).

Query 28 contains Newton's main critique of the undulatory theory of light. Years before, his chief targets of criticism, as proponents of this type of erroneous theory, had been Hooke and Grimaldi; now it is Christiaan Huygens, whose *Traité de la Lumière* appeared as *Opticks* was being written. (When this Query was printed the *Traité* had been issued for sixteen years and Huygens dead for eleven!) The double refraction of Icelandic spar had been a challenge to the explanatory capabilities of his wave-theory because 'the refractions of this crystal *seemed* to overturn our preceding explanation of regular refraction; which explanation, on the contrary, they strongly confirm . . .' As far as it went, Huygens's treatment was indeed superior to Newton's in being geometrical: 'For the wave theory of light it was indeed an *experimentum crucis*' which Huygens was able to resolve, though he could not resolve *all* the phenomena of the spar, which he was compelled to leave to others (Shapiro 1980, pp. 215, 217). His geometrical triumph was also at the cost of physical economy. Huygens had to account for two rays: therefore he had to propose two different advancing wave-fronts (one for each ray) of different forms, and consequently two different media (one for each wave-train), though only a single aether.*

And Huygens refuted

While Newton justly noted that Huygens was unique in offering an explanation of double refraction "by Pression or Motion" he naturally rejected Huygens's twin media, which in any case failed to cope with the phenomena of the superposed crystals. One of the few quotations in French in Newton's writings is of Huygens's ultimate admission of incomplete success: 'Mais pour dire comment cela se fait, je n'ay rien trouvé jusqu'ici

---

* One medium included the solid particles of the spar, the other excluded them.

qui me satisfasse' (p. 364; *Optice*, p. 309). Rather strangely to modern minds Newton wrote that

Pressions or Motions, propagated from a shining Body through an uniform Medium, must be on all sides alike; whereas by those Experiments it appears, that the Rays of Light have different Properties in their different Sides (p. 363).

Moreover, Huygens (Newton thought) had flirted with the axiomatically inadmissible idea of the physical modification of light in its passage through a medium.

Rejection of waves and aether

Query 28, the exposure of the fallacy of theories alternative to Newton's, is based on the axiom of the unchanging ray:

Are not all Hypotheses erroneous, in which Light is supposed to consist in Pression or Motion, propagated through a fluid Medium? For in all these Hypotheses the Phaenomena of Light have been hitherto explain'd by supposing that they arise from new Modifications of the Rays: which is an erroneous Supposition (p. 362).

Whether or not this sweeping generalization is fair, Newton hurries on to assert (again surprisingly in our eyes) that pressure could not by itself heat bodies, and that instantaneous motion would require the action of an infinite force. On the other hand, pressure or motion propagated in time would bend into the shadows of obstacles—Newton's perennial objection—as do the waves of water and sound. They could not carry the "dispositions" of polarization. The "fits" of easy transmission and easy reflection must present no less a difficulty to the wave theorist,

unless perhaps one might suppose that there are in all Space two Aetherial vibrating Mediums, and that the Vibrations of one of them constitute Light, and the Vibrations of the other are swifter, and as often as they overtake the Vibrations of the first, put them into those Fits. But how two *Aethers* can be diffused through all Space, one of which acts upon the other, and by consequence is re-acted upon, without retarding, shattering, dispersing and confounding one anothers Motions, is inconceivable (p. 364).

Another oblique blow against Huygens's wave analysis of double refraction!

Moreover, that there is no fluid medium of this kind at all, I gather from the fact that the planets and comets are borne in so regular and lasting a motion everywhere in the celestial spaces, following all paths in all directions. Hence it is manifest that the heavens are void of all sensible resistance, and by consequence of all sensible matter (*Optice*, p. 310).

So declared Newton in 1706. Later (as we shall see) he weakened this vacuist assurance considerably.

In order to justify this last point—that a material aether must fairly quickly destroy the motion of any body travelling through it—Newton now entered upon a little essay on the theory of resistance. After taking other factors into account, he finds that the resistance of fluid media is nearly proportional to their density. Accordingly, the resistance of air is some 800 or 900 times less than that of water, "as I have also found by Experiments made with Pendulums". These experiments also failed to detect the existence of any universal "dense and subtile Fluid" filling the pores within ordinary fluids, and all space. Supposing there is no such thing, we can rarefy air in pumps to 10^{-4} times its usual density and reduce the resistance that it offers to motion in the same proportion. In the heavens, the density of matter must be far less still, since barometric data and computation indicate that the density of the Earth's atmosphere is reduced by a factor of 10^{24} at an altitude of only 300 miles above its surface. Hence in space the resistance offered by such highly tenuous matter must approximate to zero. But if the celestial space were filled with matter, "let the Matter be never so subtil and fluid, they would have a greater resistance than Quick-silver".

And therefore to make way for the regular and lasting Motions of the Planets and Comets, it's necessary to empty the Heavens of all Matter, except perhaps some very thin Vapours, Steams, or Effluvia, arising from the Atmospheres of the Earth, Planets, and Comets . . . (p. 368).

Here again, for the English edition of 1717 Newton was constrained to weaken this clear and positive statement. And so (he goes on) such a dense, space-filling medium is useless to natural philosophy; it can only arrest all those motions which it is the object of philosophy to account for. But if such a medium is rejected, then "the Hypotheses that Light consists in Pression or Motion, propagated through such a Medium, are rejected with it." Such a medium was spurned by the earliest philosophers,

who made a *Vacuum*, and *Atoms*, and the Gravity of Atoms, the first Principles of their Philosophy; tacitly attributing Gravity to some other Cause than dense Matter (p. 369).

Natural theology furnishes ultimate explanations

Rather than invent mechanical or metaphysical fictions—Newton strikes at Descartes and Leibniz—we should argue "from Phaenomena without feigning Hypotheses" and in the final steps as we approach the search for the First Cause of all things "which is certainly not mechanical" we must address ourselves to questions about the purpose and design of the Universe:

What is there in places empty of Matter? Whence is it that the Sun and Planets gravitate towards one another, without Matter between them? Whence is it that

Nature does nothing in vain? Whence arises all that Order and Beauty which we see in the World? To what end are Comets? Whence is it that Comets move everywhere and in all manner of ways through the Heavens in Orbs very excentrick while Planets move all one and the same way in Orbs concentrick? And what is it that hinders the Sun and fixed Stars from falling upon one another? Who caused the Bodies of Animals to be contrived with such exquisite Art and Wisdom? And for what ends were their several Parts formed? Was the Eye contrived without Skill in Opticks? Or the Ear without Knowledge of Sounds? Who caused the Motions of the Body to obey the Rule of the Will? And whence comes what we call the Instinct in Animals? Is not the Sensory of Animals that place to which the sensitive Substance is present, and into which the sensible Species of Things are carried through the Nerves and Brain, that being presented there they may be perceived by what is present? And these things being rightly dispatch'd, does it not appear from the Phaenomena that there is a Being incorporeal, living, intelligent, omnipresent, who in infinite Space, as it were in his Sensory, sees the things themselves intimately, and thoroughly perceives them, and comprehends all things by their immediate presence to himself: Of which things the Images only, as carried through the Organs of the Senses into our little Sensoriums, and there seen and beheld by that [*Id*] which in us perceives and thinks.

(I have translated this famous passage from *Optice* using so far as possible the language of the later English texts. I am sure that Newton originally wrote it himself in Latin, and that it was later rendered into English. There are one or two differences in the two versions.)

A reader and his criticism

One reader who followed these sentences of Newton's with great interest was Gottfried Wilhelm Leibniz. He had already been caused by the *Principia* both to admire and to deplore Newton's genius for mathematics and physics; the experimental part of *Opticks* he admired unreservedly, but his main interest in 1704 was in the two mathematical treatises annexed to the book. However, when he read *Optice* (1706) he found in the new Queries an opportunity to score a philosophical point in his long-continued dispute with Newton and his expositor, the same Samuel Clarke. For to this translation Newton added further Queries, and in that there numbered 20 (but 28 in the final text) Newton originally printed on page 315 the question:

Annon Spatium Universum, Sensorium est Entis Incorporei, Viventis, & Intelligentis; quod res Ipsas cernat & complectatur intimas, totasque penitus & in se praesentes perspiciet; quarum id quidem, quod in Nobis sentit & cogitat, Imagines tantum in Cerebro contuetur?
[Is not universal space the *sensorium* of a Being Incorporeal, Living and Intelligent, because 'he sees and discerns, in the inmost and most Thorough Manner, the Very Things themselves, and comprehends them as being entirely and immediately

Present within Himself; Of which Things, the Perceptive and Thinking Substance
that is in Us views nothing but the Images' in the brain.]

The Latin word *sensorium* signifies either 'the organ of sensation'
(Leibniz) or 'the place of sensation' (Newton and Clarke). The distinction
within the highly speculative nervous anatomy of the age is somewhat
nebulous: for if that which actually senses things is the soul or spirit, it may
be supposed to occupy (within an animal body) an organ, seat, or place.
We know that the comparison contained in the sentence was one dear to
Newton: God, pure universal Spirit, in immediate contact with all the
matter in the Universe, is immediately aware of every event within it,
whereas the human spirit, localized in an organic brain, knows only what
a material nervous system reports to it. God is everywhere and fills all space
and all matter (since this is preponderantly space); the human soul is
individual and (we might say) localized in a point.

However, after page 315 had been printed and all the rest of *Optice*, and
the sheets assembled into a number of complete volumes, Newton or Clarke
decided that the statement about space being the place of God's knowledge
of things was theologically dubious, and took steps to remove it. Yet they
left untouched the parallel sentence only 30 pages later (p. 346) that space
is God's boundless, uniform sensorium:

quod [Deus] sit ubique, scilicet praesens, possitque Voluntate sua corpora omnia
infinito suo *Sensorio* movere,. . .
['because God is everywhere, that is to say present, and can by his will move all
things in his infinite sensorium,. . .!]

In order to remove the offending passage on page 315 a 'cancel sheet' was
printed (obviously with p. 316 on its verso) which was inserted into
fascicule *Ss* in place of the original; in at least one copy of *Optice* both the
original and the cancel are present! The new text read, in the significant
place (giving the later English version of it):

It is not the Sensory of Animals that place to which the sensitive Substance is present,
and into which the sensible Species of Things are carried through the Nerves and
Brain, that there they may be perceived by their immediate presence to that
Substance? And these things being rightly dispatch'd, does it not appear from
Phaenomena that there is a Being incorporeal, living, intelligent, omnipresent, who
in infinite Space, as it were in his Sensory, sees the things themselves intimately, and
thoroughly perceives them, and comprehends them wholly by their immediate
presence to himself: Of which things the Images only carried through the Organs
of Sense into our little Sensoriums, are there seen and beheld by that which in us
perceives and thinks (*Opticks*, p. 370).

Unfortunately, we do not know whether Newton wrote this English, or the
Latin text first printed, which is clearer in meaning.

It seems likely that the publisher of *Optice*, finding some copies on his hands that the author and editors regarded as imperfect, quietly shipped them overseas; one such almost certainly reached Leibniz (Koyré and Cohen 1961). He read the original and stronger statement in his book, and he protested to Clarke against it: how could Newton attribute *organs* to God? Clarke in reply, unconscious of the imperfect copy in Leibniz's hands, simply denied that Newton had made any such attribution. Newton had only written that space was God's place—unexceptionable enough. After these exchanges, Newton took care to add in the next (English) edition of *Opticks* a further disclaimer to Query 31, after the passage just quoted in Latin; God

is more able by his Will to move the Bodies within his boundless uniform Sensorium, and thereby to form and reform the Parts of the Universe, than we are by our Will to move the Parts of our own Bodies. And yet we are not to consider the World as the Body of God, or the several Parts thereof, as the Parts of God. He is an uniform Being, void of Organs, Members or Parts, and they are his Creatures subordinate to him, and subservient to his Will; and he is no more the Soul of them, than the Soul of Man is the Soul of the Species of Things carried through the Organs of Sense into the place of its Sensation . . .

The whole of this passage, besides being a riposte to Leibniz, is an attempt by Newton to detach his philosophy from pantheism.

Light-atoms and force again

From this very lofty ground, one of the most sublime and eloquent series of rhetorical questions that Newton (or anyone else) ever proposed, in Query 29 Newton came back to the physical nature of light:

Are not the Rays of Light very small Bodies emitted from shining Substances? For such Bodies will pass through uniform Mediums in right Lines without bending into the Shadow, which is the Nature of the Rays of Light.

Particles can possess a variety of properties, such as light reveals. Chief of these is an attractive force-interaction with matter. If, writes Newton, refraction is effected by an attractive force, the Snel proportionality of the sines of incidence and refraction follows, as was proved in the *Principia mathematica*, Book I, Section 14. Suppose a ray to fall so obliquely upon a glass–vacuum interface that it is totally internally reflected within the glass; this happens because the attractive force of the glass bends the ray backwards. But if a clear fluid such as oil is applied to the glass surface, the ray passes through the glass boundary and enters it: "because the Attraction of the Glass is almost balanced and rendered ineffectual by the contrary Attraction of the Liquor" (p. 371).

Similar results are obtained by applying a second glass closely to the first, instead of the fluid. Further (Newton continues) it is easy to explain colour-phenomena by the attractive force, if the size (and consequential inertia) of the light-particles be attended to:

Nothing more is requisite for producing all the variety of Colours, and degrees of Refrangibility, than that the Rays of Light be Bodies of different Sizes, the least of which may make Violet the weakest and darkest of the Colours, and be more easily diverted by refracting Surfaces from the right Course; and the rest as they are bigger and bigger, may make the stronger and more lucid Colours, blue, green, yellow, and red, and be more and more difficulty diverted (p. 372).

'Newton's Rings' and other phenomena of thin plates can equally well be accounted for in this dynamic hypothesis:

Nothing more is requisite for putting the Rays of Light into Fits of easy Reflexion and easy Transmission, than that they be small Bodies which, by their attractive Powers, or some other Force, stir up Vibrations in what they act upon, which Vibrations being swifter than the Ray, overtake them successively, and agitate them so as by turns to increase and decrease their Velocities, and thereby put them into those Fits (pp. 372–3).

That the vibrations might be stimulated in transparent fluid or solid bodies is clear enough, perhaps also in air; but Newton did not declare whether the vibrations might be carried across the extreme tenuity of empty space.

Ordinary matter and the matter of light

Query 30 makes even more of the relationship between matter and light, preparing the way for the essentially chemical content of the final Query:

Are not gross Bodies and Light convertible into one another, and may not Bodies receive much of their Activity from the Particles of Light which enter into their Composition?

For hot bodies shed light while cold bodies absorb it:

The changing of Bodies into Light, and Light into Bodies, is very conformable to the Course of Nature, which seems delighted with Transmutations (p. 374).

So Water, "a very fluid tasteless Salt" by heat becomes vapour (that is, air) or by cold becomes ice "a hard, pellucid, brittle, fusible Stone", changes that are all reversible. Fermenting bodies yield airs, which may again be solidified. Mercury (not now called Quick-silver by Newton!) is protean in its forms. All living things are composed of transmuted water and salts, to which substances they revert by putrefaction. "And among such various and strange Transmutations, why may not Nature change Bodies into Light, and Light into Bodies?" (p. 375).

There ends Query 30 in the English texts, but not so its Latin base, Query 22 in *Optice*. There Newton continued with a long paragraph detailing the relatively enormous force exerted at close range by the minuscule particles of light:

Now the attractive force of bodies of the same kind and virtue is the stronger, in proportion to their size, as the bodies are smaller. It is found to be stronger in small magnets, in proportion to their weights, than in greater ones: For the particles of small magnets, as they are closer to one another, more easily combine their forces together. For this reason, the rays of light, as they are the most minute of all bodies with which we are acquainted, may be expected to possess the strongest of all attractive forces. It is possible to gather from the following rule how strong these forces are. The attraction of the rays of light, in proportion to their mass, is to the gravity which some projectile has (likewise in proportion to its mass), in the compound ratio of the velocity of the ray of light to the velocity of that projectile and the bending or curvature of the line that the ray describes at the place of refraction to the bending or curvature of the trajectory that the projectile describes: bearing in mind that the angle of inclination of the rays to the refracting surface must be the same as that of the projectile's trajectory to the horizontal. And from this [compound] ratio I gather that the attraction of the rays of light is more than 10^{15} times greater than the gravity of bodies at the surface of the Earth, in proportion to their masses, supposing that light travels from the sun to the Earth in about seven or eight minutes. And in the actual contact of the rays, their forces [of attraction] might be much greater still. Now such a great force in the rays cannot but have immense effects upon those particles of matter with which they are combined in compound bodies, in causing those [material] particles to attract each other, and causing them to move with respect to one another. That this matter might be better understood I propose the following Query [31] (*Optice*, pp. 321–2).

In this passage deleted from the English editions Newton developed the projectile theory of light with a vengeance; but, more important, he had found a way of explaining why the short-range forces between material particles, such as the chemical force whose operations he now goes on to illustrate at length, are so much stronger than the gravitational force. The increase comes from the great virtue of the light-particles imprisoned in matter.

The dynamical philosophy of Nature affirmed

So Newton approaches his last great question, the final statement of his dynamical philosophy of Nature:

Have not the small Particles of Bodies certain Powers, Virtues or Forces, by which they act at a distance, not only upon the rays of Light for reflecting, refracting, and inflecting them, but also upon one another for producing a great Part of the Phaenomena of Nature? (pp. 375–6).

Newton had so often wished to embark on the extension of his dynamic philosophy to the microscopic realm, substantiating the hints that had been allowed to remain in the *Principia mathematica*. A well-known document explains why he had not pursued his object further in that book, as he had planned to do (Hall and Hall 1962); it may well belong to the drafts rejected from *Opticks* about 1692. The "principle of nature" with which it begins is that of the analogy in particulate dynamics between the microscopic and the macroscopic:

This principle of nature being very remote from the conceptions of Philosophers I forebore to describe it in that Book least I should be accounted an extravagant freak & so prejudice my Readers against all those things which were the main designe of the Book: But & yet I hinted at it both in the Preface & in the book itself where I speak of the inflection of light [Book I, Section 14] & of the elastick power of the Air [Book II, Prop. 23] but the design of that book being secured by the approbation of Mathematicians, I had not scrupled to propose this Principle in plane words. The truth of this Hypothesis I assert not, because I cannot prove it, but I think it very probable because a great part of the phaenomena of nature do easily flow from it which seems otherwise inexplicable (Cambridge University Library, MS. Add. 3970, fo. 338; McGuire 1968, pp. 165–6).

It seems strange that Newton should suddenly term his "principle" an "Hypothesis". The document continues with a list of the inexplicable phenomena of chemistry and physics which the principle resolves, most of them (and others) figuring in the Queries, especially in Query 31.

Attraction a phenomenon, force its cause

As always, and first in the *Principia mathematica*, Newton is reluctant in Query 31 to speculate on the causality or mechanism of forces; the word *Attraction* "I use . . . to signify only in general any Force by which Bodies tend towards one another, whatsoever be the Cause". But effectively Newton's position is that while attraction is a phenomenon demonstrable to the senses, force is its invisible cause. The attractions of gravity, magnetism, and electricity are manifest, and indicate

the Tenor and Course of Nature, and make it not improbable but that there may be more attractive Powers than these. For Nature is very consonant and conformable to her self.

By investigation we can discover the "Laws and Properties" of such attractions, indeed we necessarily must do so before seeking for their causes; but we cannot expect readily to discover other attractions moving macroscopic bodies at considerable distances, as gravity, magnetism, and electricity do. We must search more narrowly and among other types of phenomena for other attractions and the forces causing them.

We may confidently identify a chemical force, Newton declares:

For when Salt of Tartar runs *per Deliquium*, is not this done by an Attraction
between the Particles of the Salt of Tartar, and the Particles of the Water which float
in the Air in the form of Vapours? And why does not common Salt, or Saltpetre,
or Vitriol, run *per Deliquium*, but for want of such an Attraction? (pp. 376–7).

Many more examples follow. Exothermic chemical reactions argue
violent motion of the invisible particles, as when acids dissolve metals, and
in turn the violence of the motion argues a powerful attraction between the
particles of acid and those of the metal:

the acid Parts of the Liquor rush towards the Parts of the Metal with violence, and
run forcibly into its Pores till they get between its outmost Particles and the main
Mass of the Metal, and surrounding those Particles loosen them from the main
Mass, and set them at liberty to float off into the Water . . .

That an easy heat will not dissociate the corpuscles of metallic salt so
formed confirms the existence of a strong attractive bond between their compounded particles. Some experiments can be explained by invoking relative
strengths of attraction, the less yielding in exchange to the greater, but we
need not follow Newton into the chemical development of this notion of
variable 'affinity'. An almost poetic ink flows from Newton's pen as he
sketches the violence of attractive force in gunpowder, or in the natural
sulphureous compounds of Earth whose explosions cause it to shake

and makes Tempests and Hurricanes, and sometimes causes the Land to slide, or
the Sea to boil, and carries up the Water thereof in Drops, which by their Weight
fall down again in Spouts.

In the lofty regions above the Earth sulphureous rising steams ferment
with acid vapours abounding there "as appears by the rusting of Iron and
Copper in it, the kindling of Fire by blowing, and the beating of the Heart
by means of Respiration". When the fermenting mixture of vapours takes
fire it causes lightning, meteors, and thunder.

. . . the above-mention'd Motions are so violent as to shew that in Fermentations
the Particles of Bodies which almost rest, are put into new Motions by a very potent
Principle, which acts upon them only when they approach one another, and causes
them to meet and clash with great violence, and grow hot with the motion, and dash
one another into pieces, and vanish into Air, and Vapour, and Flame.

*The force in chemical reactions**

The purchases of chemicals recorded in his early notebooks, the long hours
which he had spent in the little garden by the Great Gate of Trinity College,
Cambridge, watching over the furnaces, retorts, and crucibles assembled

---

* Newton's role in the development of chemical theory has been studied in great detail—see,
for example, Thackray (1970).

there by his own hands (did no curious passer-by ever stay to observe the Lucasian Professor at his pyrotechnical labours?) found their due expression in print at last, not in the language of the alchemists, by no means soaring with Diana's Doves and hunting with the Green Lyon, but in yielding prosaic evidence for the true existence of chemical force:

When *Aqua fortis* dissolves Silver and not Gold, and *Aqua regia* dissolves Gold and not Silver, may it not be said that *Aqua fortis* is subtil enough to penetrate Gold as well as Silver, but wants the attractive Force to give it Entrance; and that *Aqua regia* is subtil enough to penetrate Silver as well as Gold, but wants the attractive Force to give it Entrance? . . . And is it not for want of an attractive virtue between the Part[icle]s of Water and Oil, of Quick-silver and Antimony, of Lead and Iron, that these Substances do not mix; and by a weak Attraction, that Quick-silver and Copper mix difficultly; and from a strong one, that Quick-silver and Tin, Antimony and Iron, Water and Salts, mix readily? And in general, is it not from the same Principle that Heat congregates homogeneal Bodies, and separates heterogeneal ones? (pp. 382–3).

Gradually drifting away from the principle of attraction, Newton delivers himself of many notions about chemical structure and the formation of chemical compounds. So he would have it that "Sulphur is composed of an inflammable thick Oil or fat Bitumen, an acid Salt, a very fix'd Earth, and a little Metal." And similarly all kinds of earthy minerals are compounded of sulphur and other things, held together by mutual attraction:

all the Parts of Animals and Vegetables are composed of Substances volatile and fix'd, fluid and solid, as appears by their Analysis; and so are Salts and Minerals, so far as Chymists have been hitherto able to examine their Composition (pp. 384–5).

Old ideas refurbished still do good service:

Do not the sharp and pungent Tastes of Acids arise from the strong Attraction whereby the acid Particles rush upon and agitate the Particles of the Tongue (pp. 385–6)?

Such small invisible bodies may have an internal structure whose nature may be inferred, just as the greatest do:

So that a Particle of Salt may be compared to a Chaos; being dense, hard, dry, and earthy in the Center; and rare, moist, and watry in the Circumference. And hence it seems to be that Salts are of a lasting Nature . . . (pp. 386–7).

As Newton had declared in other places before, force is not attractive merely: we find repulsions also. Thus the particles of salt diffuse uniformly through a large volume of water:

does not this Endeavour imply that they have a repulsive Force by which they fly from one another, or at least, that they attract the Water more strongly than they do one another?

Why, when this water is evaporated off, do the salt particles appear in solid shape, cohering in regular figures? The salt crystal must be the product of the forces acting in the particles diffused in the water before they contracted together into a solid. In the solution, they

acted upon one another by some Power which at equal distances is equal, at unequal distances unequal. For by such a Power they will arrange themselves uniformly, and without it they will float irregularly, and come together as irregularly.

Again Newton's thoughts return to the puzzling optical phenomenon of Icelandic spar:

may it not be supposed that in the Formation of this Crystal, the Particles not only ranged themselves in rank and file for concreting in regular Figures, but also by some kind of polar Virtue turned their homogeneal Sides the same way (p. 388).

The force of cohesion

Pursuing this lead into physics away from chemistry, Newton next examines the problems of cohesion and rigidity. Why do the adhering particles of matter form a firm mass? Rejecting all the various notions of the Epicurean, Cartesian, and Leibnizian philosophers as erroneous, Newton would

rather infer from their Cohesion, that their Particles attract one another by some Force, which in immediate Contact is exceeding strong, at small distances performs the chymical Operations above-mention'd, and reaches not far from the Particles with any sensible Effect (p. 389).

For my part, I do not find what Newton here writes about cohesion being due to a force which is immensely strong at the point of contact between two particles (or corpuscles) easy to reconcile with the views he states elsewhere about the great rarity of even the most solid matter. Moreover, if the particles of solids were in close contact, how would one account for the fact that certain bodies are compressible, yet possess considerable tensile strength? It seems to me that, at least momentarily, Newton, in hypothesizing about different problems of structure, proposed contradictory ideas.

The ultimate particles and perhaps some compound corpuscles seem to be hard, for all fluids solidify: "Even the Rays of Light seem to be hard Bodies; for otherwise they would not retain different Properties in their different Sides" (p. 389). All uncompounded particles at least may be reckoned hard, indeed must be far harder than the hardest bodies of our experience, whose particles can only touch and cohere at a few points. How could such hard particles stick together into compounds without a force of cohesion? The same force seems to be evident in the tight adhesion of flat polished surfaces even *in vacuo* and the anomalous suspension of mercury in a tube, far above one metre. By the same force [which we call surface tension] water rises into narrow spaces, the attraction being reciprocal to the distance:

if slender Pipes of Glass be dipped at one end into stagnating Water, the Water will rise up within the Pipe, and the height to which it rises will be reciprocally proportional to the Diameter of the Cavity of the Pipe,

because the centre of the water column is further removed from the attraction of the glass, as the diameter increases. By the same principle,

a Sponge sucks in Water, and the Glands in the Bodies of Animals, according to their several Natures and Dispositions, suck in various Juices from the Blood (p. 392).

Second thoughts in 1717

In several passages of the Queries the English text of 1717 departs considerably from its Latin precursor. Newton deleted the following sentences critical of the aetherial hypothesis:

Some think that the pieces of marble are compressed by a certain circumambient aether, and that the quicksilver is driven upwards in the tube by the same aether. But in truth if this aether be supposed to pass through either the quicksilver or the glass [of the tube] it cannot be that which drives the quicksilver upwards in the tube; and if it is supposed to pass through neither, then it cannot allow the quicksilver to subside, as it does subside if the glass tube be lightly tapped so that the quicksilver is detached from it, or if the quicksilver contains some bubbles of air, which prevent its particles from touching one another and cohering. And further the same experiment has succeeded with water which had first been thoroughly purged of all air. When quicksilver is solidified by the fumes of lead, or water by cold, the particles of the congealed fluid so cohere as to constitute a solid body. And in the experiments just mentioned of the fluids anomalously suspended in the barometer, it seems that the particles even of fluids can cohere one to another. Whence it may readily be deduced that whatever agent causes the particles of ice and of two metals to cohere one to another, also causes the same bodies to cohere when they are in the fluid state, though perhaps less firmly; normally the particles of fluid bodies perpetually glide hither and thither among themselves (*Optice*, pp. 337, my translation).

However, he also expanded some topics in the English, for example the capillary ascent of water in pipes. All this new material had been prepared for another purpose. In 1713 Newton had put the last touches to the second *Principia*, then in the press at Cambridge. To this he proposed to add a concluding General Scholium. Much material on the short-range forces and on the electric force in particular, first drafted for this Scholium, was ultimately transferred to Query 31.

Exactly as with drafts of the Preface and the abortive long "Conclusion" to the *Principia*, Newton played with an exposition of short-range attractive force, illustrated by experiments and stressing the importance of the electric force (to which we shall return later). Thus, in one of the tentative versions of the General Scholium, we read:

Proposition 1. That very small particles of bodies, whether contiguous or at very small distances, attract one another.

Experiment 1. Of parallel pieces of glass. 2. Of inclined [planes of glass]. 3. Of tubes. 4. Of sponges. 5. Of oil of oranges.

Proposition 2. Or Scholium. That attraction is of the electric kind.

Proposition 3. That attraction of particles at very small distances is exceedingly strong . . . and suffices for the cohesion of bodies (Hall and Hall 1962, p. 361).

The similarity to the Queries is clear.

Hauksbee's influence

It was when engaged upon these *Principia* drafts that Newton asked the Royal Society's Curator of Experiments, Francis Hauksbee, to repeat carefully his investigation of capillarity (Hauksbee 1719; Guerlac 1977, p. 110). The pages added to the 1717 version of Query 31 were based (as Newton acknowledged on page 393) upon Hauksbee's experiments. The most important of these was that with 'oil of oranges': a drop of the oil was placed near one end of a long narrow strip of glass; a second similar strip was then gently lowered so that one of its ends touched the end of the former strip remote from the drop of oil, then gradually lowered further till the other end just made contact with the drop. The drop then flowed towards the junction of the two strips at their other ends. Tilting the pair of glass strips to the horizontal, the drop flowed up more slowly or not at all. The inclination of the strips could thus be used to give a measure of the force impelling the drop upwards towards the junction of the strips. Newton wrote:

By some Experiments of this kind, . . . it has been found that the Attraction is almost reciprocally in a duplicate Proportion of the distance of the middle of the Drop from the Concourse of the Glasses . . . The Attraction therefore within the same quantity of attracting Surface, is reciprocally as the distance between the Glasses. And therefore where the distance is exceeding small, the Attraction must be exceeding great . . . There are therefore Agents in Nature able to make the Particles of Bodies stick together by very strong Attractions. And it is the business of experimental Philosophy to find them out (pp. 393–4).

When, after this major interpolation of new material, Newton returned the text of the 1717 *Opticks* to that of the Latin Queries, he took up two ideas about the nature of matter that he had often expressed before. The first is its hierarchic structure—a concept established by modern physics since the end of the last century. The fundamental particles combine into corpuscles, these into molecules, then again into larger aggregates, and "so on for divers Successions, until the Progression end in the biggest Particles on which the Operations in Chymistry, and the Colours of Natural Bodies, depend . . ." (p. 394). The higher the order of the aggregate, the less strong its binding force. Newton also offers hints about the differences between the corpuscles of hard and soft solids, and of fluids: drops of fluid are spherical because of the "mutual Attraction of their Part[icle]s."

The second idea about matter is its repulsive force, already noted:

as in Algebra, where affirmative Quantities vanish and cease, there negative ones begin; so in Mechanicks, where Attraction ceases, there a repulsive Virtue ought to succeed (p. 395).

Optical phenomena argue the existence of such a force; "It seems also to follow from the Production of Air and Vapour." If airs [gases] are elastic it cannot be because their particles are inherently springy, but must be because they repel each other (compare *Principia*, Book II, Prop. 23). Heat assists the natural tendency of some fluids and solids to fly apart. The bodies which the chemists call fixed, rarefied by fermentation, become true permanent air

those Particles receding from one another with the greatest Force, and being most difficultly brought together, which upon Contact cohere most strongly (p. 396).

Vapours contain larger corpuscles than airs, are more readily condensed, and weigh specifically less than airs. Then Newton recites again the litany of repulsive effects which we attribute to surface tension:

From the same repelling Power it seems to be that Flies walk upon Water without wetting their Feet; and that the Object-glasses of long Telescopes lie upon one another without touching; and that dry Powders are difficultly made to touch one another so as to stick together, unless by melting them, or wetting them with Water, which by exhaling may bring them together; and that two polish'd Marbles, which by immediate Contact stick together, are difficultly brought so close together as to stick (pp. 396–7).

But the play of particles, corpuscles, attractive force, and repulsive force, rich and complex as it is, is not enough to maintain the Universe in perpetuity. Nature performs the great

Motions of the heavenly Bodies by the Attraction of Gravity which intercedes those Bodies, and almost all the small ones of their Particles by some other attractive and repelling Powers which intercede the Particles.

The Active Principles

As he has previously explained the motions could be neither aroused nor continued by the mere inertia of matter, and so "certain Powers, Virtues or Forces" are required. These, now called "active Principles", must continually supply fresh motion to the parts of the Universe to compensate for that motion which, despite the assertions of Descartes, is actually destroyed or rendered unavailable (this is the Newtonian equivalent of the modern thermodynamic law of the irreversible increase of entropy). Among such "active Principles" are

the Cause of Gravity, by which Planets and Comets keep their Motions in their Orbs, and Bodies require great Motion in falling; and the Cause of Fermentation, by which the Heart and Blood of Animals are kept in perpetual Motion and Heat; the inward Parts of the Earth are constantly warm'd, and in some Places grow very hot; Bodies burn and shine, Mountains take Fire, the Caverns of the Earth are blown up, and the Sun continues violently hot and lucid, and warms all things by his Light. For we meet with very little Motion in the World, besides what is owing to these active Principles. And if it were not for these Principles, the Bodies of the Earth, Planets, Comets, Sun, and all things in them, would grow cold and freeze, and become inactive Masses; and all Putrefaction, Generation, Vegetation and Life would cease, and the Planets and Comets would not remain in their Orbs (pp. 399–400).

Given the continued recruitment of motion from these sources, we may (Newton suggests) expect the invisible, hard, primitive particles created by God to last for ever, and so the Universe may endure without ruin.

Such active principles, he insists, are not lightly to be dismissed as occult qualities, inexplicable characteristics of things, rather they possess the epistemological status of

general Laws of Nature, by which the Things themselves are form'd; their Truth appearing to us by Phenomena, though their Causes be not yet discover'd (p. 401).

The occult quality, Molière's *virtus dormitiva*, is (Newton agrees) a mere empty label, and the concept has rightly been rejected by modern philosophers,

But to derive two or three general Principles of Motion from Phenomena, and afterwards to tell us how the Properties and Actions of all corporeal Things follow from those manifest Principles, would be a very great step in Philosophy, though the Causes of those Principles were not yet discover'd . . . (p. 401).

The 'mechanical philosophy' re-established

In those words Newton made his final attempt to set his revolutionized mechanical philosophy of Nature against the mechanical philosophy developed in the seventeenth century by Gassendi and Descartes, Boyle and

Hooke, Huygens and Leibniz, and many more. That philosophy had been kinematic, its essence being a restless motion of particles and great bodies wherein each movement was generated by a preceding movement, and in turn generated another. Motion, all activity in things, could spring only from immediate contact, the impact of particle upon particle. It admitted force only as the momentum of some body in motion with respect to a second. It denied the possibility of absolute motion. Seeming force without causal motion preceding it (as in the force of a compressed spring) was to be accounted for by postulating minute, invisible 'intestinal' motions, and magnetic force was translated into a stream of minute, invisible, 'effluvial' particles. Since it had been impossible to realize the ambitious explanatory programmes of pre-Newtonian mechanical philosophers without a great reliance upon imagination, it had been correspondingly impossible to geometrize their hypotheses. Newton wrought a new pattern. The imagined invisible mechanisms of his predecessors were subsumed under the simple label of 'forces', and force (in general principle and particular example) could be geometrized. The kinematic view of Nature submitted to the dynamic. The force exerted by body B at point P was something that the mathematical philosopher could compute upon Newtonian principles, and confirm by experiment.

Nevertheless . . . epistemological doubts remained, the doubts that prevented Newton's older contemporaries from becoming converts to his new dynamical science. What *is* a power, virtue, force, or active principle? The profusion of names itself suggests an uncertainty in Newton's own mind. Is not the sentence 'The force of gravity causes the apple to fall' painfully like that ridiculed by Molière: 'The dormitive virtue causes the patient to sleep'? True, Newton had a quantitative theory of gravitation and brought far more than apples within its grasp, but dormitive virtue too can be measured in milligrams. Is there not always some risk that the philosopher may be tempted to discover a new force or virtue whenever he encounters a fresh difficulty: the 'life-force', for example? Especially, how does a force which is immaterial exist and act where no matter is (but in association with matter which is somewhere else), where nothing but force is? If the philosopher admits that force is immaterial (or as the seventeenth century said, incorporeal) yet an effective agent, has not natural philosophy left the world of material entities which it is supposed to investigate and explain for the world of spirits?

Newton could surely have written a large volume about these and other questions both metaphysical and epistemological that (whether they are directly faced or not) constitute the foundations of physical theories. He did not do so, though some answers were given by his friend Samuel Clarke in his letters to Leibniz (Clarke 1717). An indirect approach to the resolution of such questions was, however, provided by Newton in the last pages of *Optice*, the conclusion of Query 31.

God the Creator

In the concluding paragraphs of *Optice*, as also in those of the second *Principia mathematica* which he was to pen a few years later, Newton turned from Nature to Nature's God. Here, like his fellow-countryman Henry More half a century before, he argued from the manifest evidence of Design to the existence of a Designer, an "intelligent Agent" who has not only created the particles of this world, set them in order and prescribed their laws, but could create different particles obeying other laws and so "make Worlds of several sorts in several Parts of the Universe" (p. 404). The world we know is the product of the divine choice and purpose. The evidence of Design recited by Newton is familiar enough from the almost identical English text (1717):

blind Fate could never make all the Planets move one and the same way in Orbs concentrick . . . Such a wonderful Uniformity in the Planetary System must be allowed the Effect of Choice. And so must the Uniformity in the Bodies of Animals, they having generally a right and a left side shaped alike . . . Also the first Contrivance of those very artificial Parts of Animals, the Eyes, Ears, Brain, Muscles, Heart, Lungs, Midriff, Glands, Larynx, Hands, Wings, swimming Bladders, natural Spectacles, and other Organs of Sense and Motion; and the Instinct of Brutes and Insects, can be the effect of nothing else than the Wisdom and Skill of a powerful ever-living Agent . . . (pp.402–3).

(The bizarre allusion here to natural spectacles may be clarified by reading *Optice*, where Newton wrote of "the very clear membranes in animals by which their eyes are covered as though with spectacles".)

Now if Design necessitates a Designer, the idea of a planned, intelligent creation follows also:

it's unphilosophical to seek for any other Origin of the World, or to pretend that it might arise out of a Chaos by the mere Laws of Nature (p. 402).

Moreover, God the Creator has not withdrawn from his Creation but is everywhere present within it, for the Universe is within space and there is no space without God, who

is more able by his Will to move the Bodies within his boundless uniform Sensorium [that is, space], and thereby to form and reform the Parts of the Universe, than we are by our Will to move the Parts of our own Bodies (p. 403).

(In the English edition of 1717 Newton in reply to Leibniz extended this passage in sentences explaining that God is not the soul of the world, nor the world his body because he is "everywhere present in the Things themselves".)

And upholder of the Universe

The hint is surely plain, that the ultimate source of the active principles must be God himself. God did not wind up the Universe like a clockwork toy and set it going, but is himself involved in the workings of the Universe as a man's soul is engaged in the workings of his body. (But this is an analogy not a simile.) Forces are God's immediate agents to fulfil his ends in Nature, though they do not constitute what More called the Spirit of Nature. To confirm the hint we have David Gregory's memorandum. On 21 December 1705 Newton told his friend Gregory about his new extension of Query 31 for *Optice*. Gregory recorded:

His Doubt was whether he should put the last Quaere thus. *What the space that is empty of body is filled with.* The plain truth is, that he believes God to be omnipresent in the literal sense; And that as we are sensible of Objects when their Images are brought home within the brain, so God must be sensible of every thing, being intimately present with every thing: for he supposes that as God is present in space where there is no body, he is present in space where a body is also present.

Matter and spirit: Charleton

The co-presence of matter and spirit is a perfectly orthodox idea. Walter Charleton, whose *Physiologia* was carefully read by Newton as a very young man, affirms that the incorporeal, spiritual form of an angel is able

to penetrate the Dimensions of any the most solid Bodes, so that the whole substance of an Angel may be *simul & semel*, altogether and at once in the same place with that of a stone, a wall, the hand of a man, or any other body whatever, without any necessity of mutual *Repugnancy* (Charleton 1654, p. 71).

If an angel can be accidentally present in a wall, God must be so of necessity. Gregory continues with two more sentences, which also illuminate Newton's thoughts about his precursors in antiquity:

But if this way of proposing this his notion be too bold, he thinks of doing it thus. *What Cause did the Ancients assign of Gravity.* He believes that they reckoned God the Cause of it, nothing els, that is no body being the cause; since every body is heavy (Hiscock 1937, pp. 29–30).

Again, we have to read a little between the lines—and we are entitled to believe that Newton's speech was somewhat more subtle than Gregory's rather bald record of it. Newton imagined that in broad terms his ideas about universal gravitation had been anticipated by the Pythagoreans; he was following their tradition also in asserting that God is the cause of gravity and other forces.

Warily, Newton was less specific about this conjecture to the reading public than he was to David Gregory in private. Even so, Queries 28 and

31, with their talk of space as God's sensorium, were to provide trouble for him. Leibniz thought the attribution to the Deity of a neural mechanism appropriate to man and animals was intolerably jejune, if not impious; Clarke defended Newton's ideas in his letters of apologia to Leibniz. Accordingly, when the 1717 English *Opticks* was in preparation, Newton was tempted to adopt a less vulnerable position than he had adopted in 1706, though he let the relevant passages stand—Leibniz being dead by now—even to the obtrusive duplication of material about the divine design at the ends of Queries 28 and 31.

Hauksbee again: the electric fire

Newton cared less about Leibniz's metaphysical criticisms, it seems, than he did about Francis Hauksbee's experimental demonstrations. His work on capillarity—not long before his death in 1713—has already been mentioned. Now we are concerned with electrostatic experiments that he began at the end of 1706, after the publication of *Optice* (Guerlac 1977, pp. 107–17). Hauksbee showed that electric attraction could occur in the vacuum, and then, by means of a simple electrostatic machine of his own devising, he produced more dramatic effects. A hollow sphere of glass was rotated rapidly by a handle and a pulley; with a dry hand placed against it as a rubber the electric fire appeared profusely: in Newton's words (Query 8):

the electric Vapour which is excited by the friction of the Glass against the Hand, will by dashing against [a] white Paper, Cloth or Finger, be put into such an agitation as to emit Light, and make the white Paper, Cloth or Finger appear lucid like a Glow-worm; and in rushing out of the Glass will sometimes push against the Finger so as to be felt (p. 341).

When the glass sphere was evacuated of air before spinning it against the hand, the electric fire would illuminate it brilliantly from within.

There can be no question but that Newton (and others) were enormously impressed by these electrostatic fireworks. The statement that "attraction is of the electric kind" appeared in the abortive drafts for the Scholium Generale of 1713, and much about electricity was added to the revision of the Queries about 1716. Quite why Newton was so deeply impressed by Hauksbee's new phenomena it is hard to say. He had himself experimented upon electrostatic attraction and repulsion forty years before, and he must have been familiar with the sparks produced by frictional electricity. Perhaps Newton was particularly struck by the fact that the electric force was the unique one known to result from a mechanical manipulation: friction. He guessed that the electric vapour, fluid, or spirit was present everywhere and that it only became manifest by effects when, as it were, raised to a height of intensity by friction. It could not, of course, be condensed into a liquid or solid as chemical vapours and spirits could be. All this suggested to Newton an idea towards which he may have been highly receptive—for it promised a solution to many difficulties about the action-at-a-distance of forces—the idea of a state of matter almost infinitely less dense than chemical vapours and spirits or than the aether of the Cartesians which he had refuted. Such a form of matter, the "electric and elastic spirit", must occur everywhere, in all bodies and in space, because the electric spirit seems to be found in all bodies just as forces are certainly found everywhere.

Newton's return to an aether

Such ideas, while by no means marking a return to the Cartesian plenum or to such fluid media as Newton had previously entertained, involved a counter-revolution in Newton's speculations. In the early 1680s he had enthusiastically adopted a mathematical, dynamic view of Nature which was also positivistic, thereby renouncing his (unpublished) aetherial hypotheses of 1675 and 1679. Though he had consented formally to acknowledge that forces *might* have a mechanical explanation, that what seemed to be performed by attraction might really be performed by impact, for example, this had not been a notion that he regarded as plausible. Time and again he declared that he could offer no physical account of gravity and other forces, while privately believing that none could be found. We have examined the hints in Query 31 of his true opinion—up to 1706.

Now the concept of an active "electric and elastic spirit" offered a way of avoiding this negative position, of going beyond the idea of force without subverting it. Newton's reversion to the language of aether or spirit—an agent of a rather different kind from that which he had proposed in 1675–9—need not be read as indicating a rejection of the ideal of a dynamics of optical motions towards which he had striven for so long. Nor did the aether or spirit contravene the notion of "active Principles" invoked elsewhere in the Queries by Newton as the causes of forces. 'Newton's commitment to active principles did not conflict with this theory of the aether, for indeed the aether itself can be viewed as a kind of active principle' (Heimann 1973, p. 5). In his imagination, Newton could reduce the mass of this new aether to any level of minuteness; all that he required was that this aether fill space with centres of repulsive force.

In brief, what the new aether did was to substitute a universal repulsive force attached to aether-particles of virtually zero mass for a variety of attractive forces attached to material particles of finite (though very small) mass. There was some economy in this ontological modification, but also some increase of complexity and a multiplication of hypotheses. In the end, repulsive force is as much a final term of explanation as attractive force had formerly been.

The first signs of Newton's change of mind came in the last paragraph of the second edition of the *Principia* (1713), containing Newton's cautious substitution for the longer versions of the *Scholium Generale* that he had drafted, but now rejected:

It would be possible now to add something about a certain very subtle spirit that permeates dense bodies and lies within them, by whose force and actions the particles of bodies when separated by the smallest distances attract each other mutually and after making contact, cohere; and at greater distances electric bodies become active in attracting and repelling light objects near by; and by which also light is emitted, reflected, refracted, inflected and heats bodies; and all sensation is stimulated and the limbs of animals are moved in accordance with their Will, in this case by the vibrations of this spirit spreading within the solid fibrils of the nerves from the external organs of sensation to the brain, and from the brain to the muscles. But these matters cannot be explained in a few words, nor do we have available an adequate body of experiments by which the laws of motion of this spirit might be adequately determined and demonstrated (*Principia* (1713), p. 484, my translation).

While the word *spirit* is ambiguous, there can be little doubt that Newton's "electric and elastic spirit"—the phrase first appeared in the English translation of the *Principia* of 1729—is as material a spirit as the spirit of wine (alcohol), though far more subtle; in fact, it foreshadows the aether about which Newton writes in Queries 17 to 24 in the late English editions. It is not known why Newton chose to use the word *spirit* in one book and *aether* in a later one. Perhaps, under Leibniz's pressure, he was now anxious to avoid the metaphysical overtones of the term *spirit*, while *aether* was in some sense a concession to the neo-Cartesians. That the two terms were equivalent in Newton's mind is certain from a sentence in a draft for a proposed Part II of Book III of *Opticks* which Newton had in hand in 1716 while preparing the second English edition. There he wrote that "gross bodies contain within them[selves] a *subtile Aether or Aetherial Spirit* which by friction they can emit to a considerable distance . . ." as had been shown by the experiments of Mr Hauksbee. The elastic spirit is therefore also electric, and we have clear proof that this whole revival of Newton's interest in the attribution of all forces to a single universal "active Principle" was occasioned by Hauksbee's experiments (Guerlac 1977, pp. 120–30 [1967], p. 122).

As this document found by Henry Guerlac also shows, Newton's original intention for the material that eventually found its way into the revised Queries of 1717 was to continue the main text in a Book III "Part II. Observations concerning the Medium through which light passes, & the Agent emits it". (The rubric "Part I" survives in the text of *Opticks* Book III to this day as a reminder that it was once to have had a sequel.) Like Part I, this Part would have contained a series of numbered Observations. At first these were limited to an account of and comments upon Hauksbee's discoveries in electroluminescence. Later Newton placed before these Observations two more upon the thermometer in *vacuo* (Query 18).

In the final English text of *Opticks* Newton inserted before his account of these important experiments an initial new Query, no. 17. This contains no fresh material but serves to introduce the idea of there being a single universal medium or aether which is the vehicle of light. It marks a return to the 1675 explanation of 'Newton's rings' by a physical mechanism, now a far finer aether. A disturbance in water or air, Newton writes, creates waves spreading in concentric circles or spheres to great distances:

And in a like manner, when a Ray of Light falls upon the Surface of any pellucid Body, and is there refracted or reflected, may not Waves of Vibrations, or Tremors, be thereby excited in the refracting or reflecting Medium at the point of Incidence, and continue to arise there, and to be propagated from thence as long as they continue to arise and be propagated . . .

since such vibrations are excited in the "bottom of the Eye by the Pressure or Motion of the Finger . . ." (p. 348). Newton seems to me to propose a *non sequitur*. If the neural process of transmission of the sense of vision from the eye to the brain involves vibrations, why should that be grounds for supposing that the transmission of light through transparent bodies involves vibrations? Newton continues:

and are not these Vibrations propagated from the point of Incidence to great distances? And do they not overtake the Rays of Light, and by overtaking them successively, do they not put them into the Fits of easy Reflexion and easy Transmission described above?

This idea is taken straight from the "Hypothesis" of 1675 (Cohen 1958*a*, p. 193, from Birch 1757, III, p. 263). As transferred to Query 17, however, Newton has simply postulated a "pellucid Body . . . or Medium" without any explanation of what this might be. However, since he goes on to say that the vibrations extend to great distances, a transparent substance like glass or water can hardly be meant, or even air, and so we are left to presume that this "Medium" is an aether filling both space and bodies, and accordingly everywhere continuous, though not necessarily uniform.

The supposed passage of heat through a vacuum

To confirm that there is such a medium Newton in Query 18 quotes disastrously misleading experiments. Let two small thermometers be suspended in tall cylindrical jars without touching the walls. Let one jar be sealed and the air extracted from it. It was found that this thermometer isolated in the vacuum responds to changes in the external temperature almost as readily as that surrounded by air within the jar. The vacuum did not stop the heat reaching the thermometer. Accordingly Newton wrote:

Is not the Heat of the warm Room convey'd through the *Vacuum* by the Vibrations of a much subtiler Medium than Air, which after the Air was drawn out remained in the *Vacuum*? And is not this Medium the same with that Medium by which Light is refracted and reflected, and by whose Vibrations Light communicates Heat to Bodies, and is put into Fits of easy Reflexion and easy Transmission? And do not the Vibrations of this Medium in hot Bodies contribute to the intenseness and duration of their Heat? And do not hot Bodies communicate their Heat to contiguous cold ones, by the Vibrations of this Medium propagated from them into the cold ones? And is not this Medium exceedingly more rare and subtile than the Air, and exceedingly more elastick and active? And doth it not readily pervade all Bodies? And is it not (by its elastick force) expanded through all the Heavens? (p. 349).

Newton has in these words indeed given definition and function to the aether, still not yet so termed, introduced into Query 17 and now given universal range and great importance. The experiments which appeared so decisive to Newton in establishing its existence were made (at Newton's suggestion) by J. T. Desaguliers in November 1716 (Guerlac 1977, p. 124). In one he was careful to warm the pair of jars containing the thermometers by a heat source shedding no visible light. They may at first surprise us, because we accept the idea that a high vacuum is a near-perfect heat insulator; a point that has become very familiar (and practical) since Sir James Dewar introduced the vacuum flask in 1872.

Nevertheless, Desaguliers's experiments were accurate and Newton's hypothesis of heat-radiation by vibrations (or waves) in order to explain them is an acute one. We now know that to use the vacuum as an insulator the radiation must be prevented from entering it by a bright reflective coating upon its exterior wall. This Desaguliers could not possibly divine. Newton's error was in imagining that the radiation of heat through the vacuum thus discovered is different in kind from that of light through the vacuum, which he took for granted. Had Newton accepted one hypothesis of light put forward in the seventeenth century, by Galileo among others, Newton might have thought of 'fire-particles' radiating from the heat-source through the vacuum to the thermometer just as he supposed the light-particles to do, in this way maintaining the similitude of the radiations. But Newton was as convinced that heat is a 'mode of motion', an intense vibration of the particles of the hot body, as that light is particulate. Therefore he could not see that the transmission of light through the vacuum was of the same kind as the transmission of heat. Because the thermometer grew warm *in vacuo*, it must be that the vibrations of the heat-source reached it, and therefore a medium to convey them must permeate the wall of the jar and fill the void inside. Such a medium was not in Newton's view required for the passage of light into the jar because light was a stream of minute particles. Thus a discrepancy of theoretical notions, of great damage to the development of physics, was widened and perpetuated by Desaguliers's correct experiments.

The new aether and light

As we shall see later, scholars dispute over the exact meaning of Newton's various terms in draft and print: aether or plain spirit, electric spirit, and electric force. Sometimes, even after 1713, Newton seems to have written as though aether is simply an *explicans* for force, at other times (and especially in relation to light) as though aether could possess the properties of matter. Partly for this reason, I find it useful to preserve a distinction between Epicurean empty space, which Newton had in 1687 filled with immaterial forces, and his post-1713 aether-filled space, which certainly contained some active matter, however small its relative mass.

Having once decided to renounce the Epicurean vacuist philosophy, Newton went on with enthusiasm to reformulate in terms of his new, extremely tenuous aether his long-neglected hypotheses of 1675, introducing them into the remainder of the 1717 group of Queries. If we postulate a repulsion between matter and aether, it follows that the aether—whose particles must of course strongly repel one another—will be thinner within the pores of material bodies than in empty spaces, and if also light avoids the denser parts of the aether it will bend towards and enter matter, thus explaining both refraction and reflection (always, as we have seen, identified by Newton as regards their ultimate physical causation). Total internal reflection (Query 19 alleges) is evidence of the flight of light from the aether; it

ought to proceed rather from the density and vigour of the Medium without and beyond the Glass, than from the rarity and weakness thereof (p. 350).

Query 20 brings Grimaldi's inflection of light into the scope of the same hypothesis:

doth not the gradual condensation of this Medium extend to some distance from the Bodies, and thereby cause the Inflexions of the Rays of Light, which pass by the edges of dense Bodies, at some distance from the Bodies?

This again is a revival of 1675: compare Cohen (1958*a*), p. 199, after Birch (1757), III, p. 269, where Newton's careless treatment of his figure requires obvious corrections. Rashly still reverting to the notions of a younger self Newton in Query 21 makes the aether the cause of gravity also: because the aether becomes very dense in the remote regions of space far from the celestial bodies, matter flees from these spaces and so tends to coalesce into great bodies.

And though this Increase of density may at great distances be exceeding slow, yet if the elastick force of this Medium be exceeding great, it may suffice to impel Bodies from the denser parts of the Medium towards the rarer, with all that power which we call Gravity (p. 351).

How exceedingly great the elastic force of the aether is Newton calculates by comparing the velocity of sound in air with that of the vibrations that cause the "fits" associated with light. We know (says Newton) that the lowest possible velocity of these vibrations is greater than that of light, since they outrun the light particles. Therefore the minimum ratio between the two speeds is (by conservative data) 7.10^5. Newton's mathematical investigations of wave-motion in the *Principia mathematica* long before had taught him that in proportion to the density of the medium its elastic force must be as the square of the velocity of waves in it, and so the elastic force of the aether in space must be 49.10^{10} times greater than the elasticity of air (in proportion to its density).

Its resistance is negligible

In the final paragraph of Query 22 of *Optice* that was not transferred to Query 30 of 1717 (see above pp. 140–1) Newton had argued the huge attractive force of the particles of light from their minute size; now in Query 21 in its final form he briefly repeats the same argument on behalf of the even smaller particles of aether. But now the force of the particles is taken to be *repulsive*, and thereby

that Medium [becomes] exceedingly more rare and elastick than Air, and by consequence less able to resist the motions of Projectiles, and exceedingly more able to press upon gross Bodies, by endeavouring to expand it self (p. 352).

The objection to a space-filling aether just suggested is faced squarely in Query 22. If space were completely filled even by the most freely fluid matter little movement would be possible, but if the aether Newton postulates be supposed as rare as it is elastic (in proportion to the air), that is, 7.10^5 less dense than air,

its resistance would be above 6.10^8 times less than that of Water. And so small a resistance would scarce make any sensible alteration in the Motions of the Planets in ten thousand Years.

If so open a scattering and so minute a size in the particles of aether seems outrageous, Newton goes on, consider how rare a magnetic effluvium must be to pass through a plate of glass without the least impairment of its force (p. 353).

The new aether and gravity

In detail, the aetherial explanation of gravity and the computations in it are new to Queries 21 and 22. That the aether as conceived by Newton in the 1670s might be the cause of gravity he had argued in his letter to Robert Boyle of 28 February 1679, the earlier part of which summarizes the "Hypothesis" of 1675. But that earlier aether—though many of its functions were to be transferred to the revived aether of 1717—had been of a very different physical constitution. Newton had defined it by saying only that it was "much of the same constitution with air, but far rarer, subtler, and more strongly elastic." He had thought *this* medium to resist the motion of a pendulum "in a glass exhausted of air" almost as much as the atomosphere does (Cohen 1958*a*, p. 179). Such a medium could not permit the almost uninhibited revolutions through it of planets and comets moving inertially, especially as it became more dense in empty space (like its successor of 1717). This first Newtonian aether belongs, in fact, to a period when he not yet embraced dynamical concepts or abandoned the notion of a solar vortex. In any event, Newton suggested to Boyle a quite different mechanism from that proposed in *Opticks*, by which this aether might create the effect of gravity (ibid., p. 253).

However, the immensely rare and elastic aether of 1717 clearly owed much to the cruder hypothesis of the 1670s, and indeed the connection of this aether with electric phenomena had been anticipated also, for Newton had remarked in 1675 that "the [electric] effluvia seem to instruct us, that there is something of an aetherial nature condensed in bodies" (ibid., p. 180). (The word printed in the text is *elastic*, clearly a literal error committed by Newton or the printer.) Newton continues with an account of some phenomena of attraction and repulsion by the electric effluvia that he had recently studied.

Its physiological functions

Newton has by no means yet finished with the wonderous powers attributable to what we might well call Newton's 'spirit of Nature', (distinguishing it sharply, nevertheless, from that of Henry More): he has still to restate its physiological functions, already tersely adumbrated in the Scholium Generale to the second *Principia* of 1713. And long before that they had been anticipated in the functions attributed to the aether of 1675. In the "Hypothesis", read to the Royal Society on 9 December 1675, Newton had averred that his newly introduced elastic aether might cast light upon

that puzzling problem: *By what means the muscles are contracted and dilated to cause animal motion* . . . For, if there be any power in man to condense and dilate at will the aether, that pervades the muscle, that condensation or dilat[at]ion must vary the compression of the muscle . . . and cause it to swell or shrink accordingly (Cohen 1958*a*, p. 182).

Newton went on to describe in some imaginary detail how this physiological aether might be controlled and operated upon by the soul (does this imply the existence of a soul in animals as well as men?), involving an "unsociableness" between the "aetherial vital spirit" and the "coats of the brain, nerves, and muscles" with a counterpart "sociableness" between the spirit and the "marrow and juices".

But we need stay no longer with these jejune speculations. The Queries do not range so far. In Query 23 Newton simply asks whether this new aether does not transport the vibrations of sight and sound as received by the eye and ear to the brain, "through the solid, pellucid and uniform Capillamenta of the optick" and auditory nerves. "And so of the other Senses". Query 24 transfers this reasoning from the afferent to the deferent nerves:

Is not Animal Motion perform'd by the Vibrations of this Medium, excited in the Brain by the power of the Will, and propagated from thence through the solid, pellucid and uniform Capillamenta of the Nerves into the Muscles for contracting and dilating them?

Newton thinks of each capillament as an 'optical fibre', perfectly transparent, through which the aether travels without disturbance. Many such fibres make the opaque, white body of the nerve.

At this point the 1717 *Opticks* returns to the already printed text. (On the above see M. Mamiani and E. Trucco (1991). 'Newton e i fenomeni de la vita'. *NUNCIUS: Annali di storia della scienza*, **VI**, pp. 69–96.)

It has long been, and is likely long to remain, a puzzling problem for Newton scholars to interpret Newton's reversal of allegiances between 1706 and 1717, whereby he partly returned to an earlier position, stimulated (it seems) by the banefully deceptive experimental demonstrations of Hauksbee and Desaguliers. Was he not by this reversal virtually making himself a neo-Cartesian? Had he not surrendered the principles of the great dynamical revolution which most historians have seen as the foundation of modern physical science?

The consistency preserved in Newton's thought

In answer to such questions as these many points may be made. Firstly, it is clear that Newton never surrendered anything of the mathematical architecture of his dynamical revolution. Putting the point in post-Newtonian language, we may agree with Stephen Toulmin (1959) that rational mechanics needs nothing beyond definitions and axioms as its basis; these Newton never altered, nor was any conclusion drawn from his arguments in the *Principia mathematica* ever substantially modified. The same may be said with equal force of Newton's use of observational and experimental data to demonstrate that the definitions and axioms were well chosen, and that the whole system he constructs corresponds to the world of experience. In fact Newton was always fully justified in maintaining that he could construct such a verifiable system of rational and celestial mechanics without postulating the physical causes—or any causes—of attractive and repulsive forces, and without declaring what the nature of force action is. And on this point too he never shifted his ground. Whether there is a substance filling all space and matter which is the cause of physical force, but is otherwise indistinguishable from the Epicurean void, was a question with which the Newtonian science of mechanics did not need to concern itself, any more than this science needed to concern itself with issues of metaphysics and theology about which nevertheless Newton the philosopher thought fit to speak his mind. Newton might have told us that red is the most pleasing of colours, but such a preference is of no relevance to the science of optics.

Nor did Newton in 1717 yield anything of the experimentally-assured physical theory of *Opticks*. Nothing in the text is retracted by the aether-theory of the late Queries. The dynamical theory of light was—as we shall see in the next section—always expressed at a rudimentary mathematical level as compared with the *Principia*, though Newton regarded it as strongly confirmed by his experiments, Newton never departed from the idea of optical forces, his only idea for handling the interrelations between matter and light. As with the science of mechanics, it seems that to the science of optics the 1717 aetherial speculations were largely irrelevant. We have no evidence, even, that such speculations guided Newton's experimental explorations in any way, since these explorations long preceded the aetherial speculations. As Newton was well aware, the value of what he had to reveal about the phenomena of refraction, reflection, inflection, and colours in the text of *Opticks* was independent of the merits of his latest brain-child, relegated to the new Queries. Later Newtonians might write as though the text of *Opticks* demonstrated the existence of an aether, as does Desaguliers for example:

That there is a subtile Medium even finer than Light which serves in the Reflection, Refraction and Inflexion of Light, may be deduced from Phenomena, as is evident to those who read Sir Isaac Newton's Optics with such attention and skill as thoroughly to understand them . . . (Guerlac 1977, p. 125).

but Newton himself made no such claim, nor (*pace* Desaguliers) did he register far greater confidence in an optical than a gravitational aether. The *Opticks* of 1704 speaks discreetly of the optical force; of the optical aether not at all. No one (to my knowledge) has ever claimed that this book is seriously defective because it lacks aetherial explanations of phenomena; and they play only the slightest part in the later editions of the book. In fact, aetherial speculations are an *addition* to Newton's dynamical theory of light, not second thoughts offered in substitution for it. Newton yielded nothing to which he had set his hand before.

In Newton's mind the distinction between his 1717 aether and all its precursors (his own aether of the 1670s among them) was its fantastically high elasticity–density ratio. It is an aether whose particles are extremely minute, with vast intervals between them. The aether-particles cannot act by contact, as neo-Cartesian aethers do, nor even by impulse. A powerful repulsive force between the particles is thus the essential of the hypothesis, which provides a unification of force not a replacement of force. We cannot read the 1717 hypothesis as removing the need for active principles in Nature: at the best it reduces these active principles to one only. The 1717 aether could only disguise the fact that Newton believed the government of the Universe to require an intelligent, immaterial agent, and that agent could only be God. What can the aether be but God's instrument?

It is clear that there can be no genuine antithesis between the 1717 aetherical speculations and the science of light and colours developed by Newton over fifty years. It is almost as certain that any apparent conflict between these speculations and his firmly-established convictions about the physical nature of light (Newton's dynamical theory) must be illusory. One should not therefore exaggerate the significance of these latest Queries, which indicate only Newton's vacillations from one set of familiar conjectures to another. McGuire has remarked that it is difficult to suppose Newton wholly serious in these aether speculations; his aether

was subject to obvious conceptual inconsistencies; it was a flagrant example of the sort of intermediary entity which Newton had always tended to reject; and more significantly it repudiated his basic metaphysics of God in an empty universe. To whatever extent it may have exonerated him from the continental charge of employing gravity as an occult quality, the 1717–18 aether remains the most puzzling of Newton's attempts at the problem of the cause of force (McGuire 1968, p. 147).

Puzzling, however, not because it seems to negate features of Newton's earlier thinking (I repeat, this cannot be its intention) but because it is philosophically superfluous. It removes no difficulty in the ontology of force. It does not obviate action at a distance. It solves none of those problems about the perpetuity of the universe of which Newton was conscious: how the universe might be preserved from gravitational collapse, the mutual disturbance of planetary orbits, and the slow annihilation of motion. In no way does the aether improve our understanding of the interaction between matter and the necessarily continuing active principle of creation, and therefore (worst of all) the aether cannot illuminate God's purposes with respect to his creation. What is the aether, in the last resort, if not a sop to prejudice?

§4. The nature of light and matter

Early speculations, mostly critical

To the Middle Ages optics, or *perspectiva*, had been the science of vision. To the Greeks, it had been a form of applied geometry, and Newton was thoroughly familiar with the height of sophistication to which Barrow had recently raised this study. His own endeavours in optics took (for the most part) different paths: his method was rather experimental than mathematical, his object the elucidation of the properties of light in its relations with matter. In this investigation he found no necessity to define the physical nature of light, as Descartes had done in his *Dioptrique* and *Principia philosophiae* (not quite identically) or as Hooke had done in his own different way in *Micrographia*. Newton did not, as they had done, attempt to deduce Snel's law of refraction from the chosen definition; he stated it as an axiom. And all the rest is postulated as definition or axiom or is "evinced from experiments". But (as we have already seen) Newton was from the first intrigued by the problem of the physical nature of light and, keeping his thoughts on this subject largely to himself, he constantly compared them with his experience of phenomena and adjusted them accordingly.

In the early manuscript *Quaestiones quaedam philosophiae* (1664–5) the earliest notes concerning optics are rebuttals of concepts of light presumably endorsed by Descartes or Gassendi (through Charleton):

Light cannot be by pression for then weè should see in the night as well or better than in the day we should see a bright light above us becaus we are pressed downewards . . . ther could be no refraction since the same matter cannot presse 2 ways the sun could not be quite eclipsed the Moone & planetts would shine like sunns. A man goeing or running would see in the night . . . (Hall 1948, p. 246; Hendry 1980, p. 232).

Similarly, when he became acquainted with Hooke's vibration-theory of light by reading *Micrographia* (1665) Newton objected:

Why then may not light deflect from streight lines as well as sounds &c ? How doth the formost weake pulse keepe pace with the following stronger & can it bee then sufficiently weaker? (Hall and Hall 1962, p. 403).

Kinematic hypotheses of colour

In the *Quaestiones* notes, mechanical action, perhaps even particulate motion, is first suggested by the following passage:

That darke colours seeme further of than light ones may be from hence that the beames loose little of their force in reflecting from a white body because they are powerfully resisted thereby, but a darke body by reason of the looseness of its parts give some admission to the light & reflects it but weakly & so the reflection from whiteness will be sooner at the eye. or else because the whit sends beams with more force to the eye and gives it a feircer knock (loc. cit., pp. 246, 233).

A precise kinematic hypothesis appears a little later in the same notes: "Note that slowly moved rays are refracted more than swift ones." Newton followed this by several lines explaining to himself in more detail how such a segregation of the rays by their respective velocities might be capable of forming the extended spectrum of colours by refraction.

The colours of bodies as seen by reflected light might correspondingly be caused by selective absorption (or "stopping") of the component rays of white light (for Newton had by now mastered the idea of the compound nature of white):

Hence rednes yellownes &c are made in bodys by stoping the slowly moved rays without much hindring of the motion of the swifter rays. & blew green & purple by diminishing the motion of the swifter rays & not of the slower. Or in some bodys all these colours may arise by diminishing the motion of all the rays in greater or lesse geometricall proportion, for then there will be lesse differences in theire motions than otherwise (loc. cit., pp. 248, 238–9).

Again, the physical differentiation between the rays that causes colour is in terms of the relative velocities of the incident rays composing white light. Newton hypothesizes that effects may also arise from the structure of the reflected surface; if its form is less elastic than another it will bounce back the light-particles less vigorously than the other does, and so it will appear darker than the more elastic surface. The text then enters upon a rather complex discussion of the possible effects of the pore structure of the reflecting surface upon the passage of the light-particles.

Colour seen as a function of mass

At this point in the *Quaestiones* Newton seems to have realized that the velocity of the light-particles could not well determine both the colour and the luminosity of the reflecting surface. He then chose to let velocity determine luminosity, while a new quantity, the mass of the light-particles, determined colour:

Though 2 rays be equally swift yet if one ray be lesse than the other that ray shall have so much a lesse effect on the sensorium as it has lesse motion than the other &c. (loc. cit., pp. 248, 240).

Note that a "ray" here is a particle of light, also called in the text a "globulus" (a word presumably borrowed from Descartes). Newton next embarked upon a calculation of relative momenta for large and small globuli, reconstructed by Hendry (1980, p. 241). The upshot seems to be that a preponderance of smaller globuli causes the light reflected from the surface to appear bluish; when the larger globuli preponderate the surface looks reddish.

To the extent that the violet end of the spectrum was taken to be the weaker, darker end, while red was the stronger, brighter, and more cheerful hue, Newton's new ideas matched conventional ideas of colour, conveniently summarized in Westfall (1962). Starting (as we have seen) from the obvious assumption that white light from the sun, or even the weak, yellowish gleam of a candle, is pure, natural, pristine, simple, and homogeneous, all philosophers before Newton regarded coloured light as white light whose nature had been changed in some way.

I believe him to have been truthful in declaring that his preference for an alternative hypothesis—that the variously coloured rays filling the length of the spectrum were real, each hue and allied refrangibility an elemental individual unsusceptible of change, and that the modifications of perceived colour were caused by variations in the combination of these elementals—to be one derived entirely from experiment. It is true that he supposed a mechanistic explanation to lie behind these phenomena, but in the 1660s he had no prejudice in favour of a particular explanation of that kind. Ten years later he himself regarded (in the "Hypothesis") a colour–wavelength correlation as one such feasible model—if there had not been an independent, overwhelming objection to light-waves.

Newton's views on colour-change impose no particular theory of the nature of light. They require only that the elemental rays be capable of separation out of their infinite mixtures (including white) by the natural properties of bodies. Newton's is a quantitative theory, essentially subtractive, though in some of his experiments beams of light were added by superimposing them. According to Newton's theory, when colour rather than white is seen at some place it is usually because certain rays have been abstracted from the beam reaching the eye.

Are the red rays swifter than the violet?

Nevertheless, for the remainder of his life Newton continued to speculate about possible mechanisms by which differential segregation and absorption of the rays might be effected. Since he disregarded the wave-hypothesis as unviable, he explored the alternative hypotheses already recorded in his early notebooks: the dependence of colour on either the velocity or the mass of the particle. Bechler (1973, pp. 3–6) has argued from Newton's account of refraction in the Optical Lectures that he then embraced the former hypothesis; however, his argument is general and uncertain, and in any case Newton did not openly advocate this correlation. During his last major period of work on *Opticks* in 1691–2 Newton devised an experimental test of its validity. If a very distant source of light is abruptly extinguished, in the time necessary for the last rays of its light to reach the eye the faster red should outrun the slower violet rays, which ought to be seen last; on the sudden re-appearance of a light the red rays should be seen first. At astronomical distances such extinctions and re-appearances of a light-source occur regularly when planetary satellites are occulted by the body of the planet. Accordingly on 10 August 1691, in a letter introducing David Gregory to the Astronomer Royal, John Flamsteed, with whom he had had no recorded contact for several years, Newton added the question: "When you observe the eclipses of [Jupiter's] satellits I should be glad to know if in long Telescopes the light of the Satellit immediately before it disappeares incline either to red or blew, or become more ruddy or pale than before." Gregory reported to Newton from Flamsteed 'that he never observed any change of Colour in the light of the appearing or disappearing Satellits of Jupiter' (Letters 369, 370). Though Gregory at one time heard from J. D. Cassini of the Paris Observatory that before immersion a satellite appeared *red* (which he was 'loath to beleeve'), a fact noted by Newton in a draft, the idea was finally quashed by Flamsteed's repeated negative (24 February 1692, Letters 373, 386; Shapiro 1992, p. 217).

The macro–micro analogy

As previous scholars have pointed out, in early calculations of the relative moments of the supposed light-particles Newton made use of the laws of elastic collision that he had already established (Bechler 1973, p. 2; Hendry 1980, p. 241). This is an early instance of his following the principle that the laws and computations found valid for macroscopic bodies may also be applied to microscopic bodies; if we did not follow such a principle, within such limits as may be appropriate, it would be impossible to proceed at all with investigation of the microscopic realm into which we cannot enter directly. Newton justified this principle—which is no more than a special-ized version of his reiterated dictum that Nature is ever consonant to herself—in the Third Rule of Reasoning of the second edition of the *Principia* (1713, p. 358):

Those qualities of bodies which undergo no changes of intensity and which occur in all bodies accessible to experiments, are to be held to be qualities of bodies universally.

   For the qualities of bodies are known to us only by experiments, and so those are to be held as general that generally agree with the experimental results; and what cannot be diminished cannot be removed ... The extension, hardness, impenetrability, mobility and force of inertia of the whole body arise from the extension, hardness, impenetrability, mobility and forces of inertia of the particles [composing it], and thence we conclude that all the least particles of all bodies are extended, hard, impenetrable, mobile and endowed with forces of inertia. And this is the ground of all philosophy [my translation].

Newton's reluctance to propose a material hypothesis of light

Unlike the velocity–colour correlation, the dependence of colour upon the mass of the rays continued to be explored privately by Newton into the period of the Queries. Not that he allowed any word of his interest in such hypotheses to emerge. From his early published papers he anxiously strove to eliminate any suggestion that his refraction-theory depended upon acceptance of a particular concept of the physical nature of light. As he wrote to F. Pardies in June 1672 (Letter 66):

the doctrine which I explained concerning refraction and colours, consists only in certain properties of light, without regarding any hypotheses, by which these properties might be explained . . . By light therefore I understand, any being or power of a being, (whether a substance, or any power or action or quality of it) which proceeding directly from a lucid body, is apt to excite vision.

He did, however, give Pardies an honest definition of a *ray* of light, which conveys a strong hint:

by rays of light I understand its least or infinitely small parts, which are independent of each other; such as are all those rays which lucid bodies emit in right lines, either successively or all together.

In the first printed optical letter, indeed, Newton had previously let fall another such hint, remaining in the printed *Philosophical Transactions* text; having summarized his deductions from the discovery of the varied refrangibility of the rays Newton remarks:

it can no longer be disputed, whether there be colours in the dark, nor whether they be the qualities of the objects we see, no nor perhaps, whether Light be a Body.

For (Newton continues) I have discovered colours to be qualities of light "having its Rays for their intire and immediate subject" and and accordingly its rays might properly be considered as substances (Letter 40, p. 100).

Robert Hooke, in his report to the Royal Society upon Newton's "New Theory of Light and Colours" exposed in this letter, was not slow to attack this point. In reply, Newton admitted that he preferred the material theory of light, but declared this to be "at most but a very possible *consequence* of the Doctrine [of colours] and not a fundamental supposition" (Letter 67, p. 173).

Foreshadowing future developments

In the same long answer to Hooke—which had taken some months to prepare, for it is dated 11 June 1672—Newton did offer him a view of further rich speculations:

assuming the Rays of Light to be small bodies, emitted every way from Shining substances, those, when they impinge on any Refracting or Reflecting superficies, must as necessarily excite Vibrations in the *aether*, as Stones do in water when thrown into it. And supposing these Vibrations to be of several depths or thicknesses, accordingly as they are excited by the said corpuscular rays of various sizes and velocities: of what use they will be for explicating the manner of Reflection and Refraction, the production of Heat by the Sun-beams, the Emission of Light from burning putrifying, or other substances, whose parts are vehemently agitated, the *Phaenomena* of thin transparent Plates and Bubbles, and of all Natural bodies, the Manner of Vision, and the Differences of Colours, as also their Harmony and Discord; I shall leave to their consideration, who may think it worth while endeavour to apply this *Hypothesis* to the solution of *Phaenomena* (ibid., p. 174).

Casually enough, Newton envisaged the possibility that light-corpuscles might vary in *both* mass and velocity, without going into details. In the next section of his paper he explained the wave- or vibration-theory of light (with the shorter waves violet and blue, the longer waves yellow and red), but then declared his inability to understand how it could be taken seriously as a physical theory:

For to me the fundamentall supposition it selfe seemes impossible, namely that the waves or vibrations of any fluid can like the Rays of Light be propagated in streight lines . . . I am mistaken if there be not both *Experiment* & *Demonstration* to the contrary . . . What I have said of this, may be easily applyed to all other *Mechanicall Hypotheses* in which light is supposed to be caused by any pression of motion whatsoever in the Aether excited by the agitated parts of luminous Bodies (Letter 67, pp. 175–6).

Obviously only the corpuscular, projectile, or emission theory remains for consideration.

If proof were needed that by June 1672 Newton had worked out the chief ideas explained in his "Hypothesis explaining the Properties of Light, discoursed of in my several Papers" (so often mentioned before), submitted to the Royal Society at the end of 1675, the former paragraph just quoted contains it amply. And indeed Newton quotes this paragraph at the opening of the 'Hypothesis'. Once again, when touching on the nature of light, he here spoke with the most tentative voice. Almost any hypothesis of light might be adapted to his exposition—except the wave-theory. Some might suppose light to be an aggregate of various peripatetic qualities:

Others may suppose it multitudes of unimaginable small and swift corpuscles of various sizes, springing from shining bodies at great distances one after another; but yet without any sensible interval of time, and continually urged forward by a principle of motion . . . Some would readily grant this may be a spiritual one; yet a mechanical one might be shown, did I not think it better to pass it by (Letter 146, p. 370).

Reflection and refraction are gradual changes of direction

Optical phenomena were conditioned by the reaction of the light-particles with the aether-waves that they themselves create, and by the interaction of both of these with matter: I have already outlined above these aetherial mechanisms devised by Newton for changing the direction of the light-ray at an interface, and producing colours. With Bechler (1973) we may again note the importance of the point that for Newton refraction is never an angular deformation of the ray, a sharp change of direction like the rebounding of an elastic ball. The region in which the change of direction occurs is always an extended one and even in the case of reflection the curvature (on the microscopic scale) is gradual. This point is well illustrated by the diagram in the *Principia mathematica*, Book I, Section XIV (Chaper 2, Section 5). Whatever the physical mechanism of what may be generally termed *inflection* (embracing reflection, refraction, and diffraction), whether it be an aether-gradient or a force, it invariably extends through a certain region with varying intensity, in such a way as to create this gradualness of action. Also with Bechler, we may note again that Newton now and for the future (at least in public) chose to call that property of the light-corpuscles that causes their dispersion when refracted strength, bigness, vigour, or magnitude.

Detailing the optical force

I have already alluded briefly to the passages in *Opticks* Book II, Part III in which Newton dealt fully with this matter of the interaction between light and matter, that is, in Propositions 8 and 9 (above p. 118). The arguments of these two propositions are essentially applicable to inflection effected either by an aether-gradient or by an optical force, the variant here adopted by Newton. In Proposition 8 he argues (in effect) that the interaction of light and matter cannot be directly between the particles of the one sort and the other nor between the particles of light and the pore-structure of matter. We must therefore suppose inflection to be caused by some general, diffused power or action of the medium (such as the optical force is); indeed, if a light-particle should happen to "impinge on the solid parts of Bodies [it is] not reflected but stifled and lost in the Bodies" (p. 266). Proposition 9 is a statement of the unity of inflections: "Bodies reflect and refract Light by one and the same power, variously exercised in various Circumstances" (p. 269). Although Newton did not here bring in diffraction—not so far mentioned in *Opticks*—there is ample reason to believe that he supposed its phenomena also to result from the same optical force. The evidence for the truth of this proposition is the smooth transition from transmission to total internal reflection, the correlation between high refractivity and high reflectivity, in transparent substances, and the fact that (in the phenomena of thin plates) the thickness of the plate "determines whether that Power by which Glass acts upon Light shall cause it to be reflected, or suffer it to be transmitted" (pp. 269–70).

As I have indicated on a previous page, the mechanical implementation of these ideas is to be found in the *Principia mathematica*, Book I, Section XIV. This piece of optical mechanics is a splendid example of Newton's complete transfer of his loyalty to force-physics from aether-physics, and its presence in a book universally taken to be devoted to the *gravitational* force becomes the less extraordinary when we remember that Newton intended his general theorems to apply to all bodies—that is, at the microscopic as well as the macroscopic level—and that it was his purpose to illustrate the utility of force-mechanics from as wide a range of examples as possible.

The correlation between colour and mass in Opticks

The Queries added to the later editions of *Opticks* contain further evidence of Newton's persistent efforts to present the mass–colour correlation in the strongest possible light. He carefully eliminated from his arguments any hint of the difficulties that might arise if the uniformity of the velocity of light of all colours were questioned; for example, in his dynamical proof (an experimental proof is also given) that the Snel law of the constant sine-ratios is true of every pure coloured ray, and not merely of the mean refracted ray (Book I, Part I, Proposition 6). Since it is the momentum—the product of mass and velocity—which determines the motion of the particle, it might seem (at least to a positivist) that the effort to decide whether, as between one particle of light and another having different momenta, it is the mass or the velocity which is different was somewhat redundant. Why try to force the issue? The answer lies in the theoretical implications of either choice. For one thing, as Bechler rightly remarks (1973, p. 33) in Newton's eyes the mass of a particle was one of its basic, inalienable characteristics. By contrast, the velocities of bodies are in general easily changed, by collision for example, as the theory of refraction had allowed from Descartes onwards. How could a light-particle change its velocity and retain its colour-potency, if colour be a function of velocity? But, as Bechler also points out (ibid., pp. 33–5) there is an equally grave conceptual obstacle telling against the mass–colour correlation, if this follows the gravitational model. A constant gravitational force (as at the Earth's surface) accelerates all bodies equally, as Galileo discovered with such pains, because its accelerative effect upon a body is proportional to the mass of the body, and the inertial resistance of the body is also proportional to its mass. Hence in the vacuum all bodies fall at the same speed, and (more to the present point) the trajectory of a projectile *depends only upon its velocity of projection* and not at all upon its mass. Hence a 'gravitational' optical force or aether could not discriminate between the masses of the light-particles when curving their paths, their velocities being the same.

What Newton needed (but he was two centuries too soon) was the example of the mass-spectrometer. In certain types of this instrument ions of varied composition ejected from the source with the same velocity are caused by electromagnetic fields to follow curved paths which separate them according to their various masses. In other words, discrimination between particles according to their mass is not only conceivable but experimentally attainable in physics, but not in any way accessible to Newton.

After traversing this background to the most speculative passages in *Opticks* we may return to the Queries in which they occur. The first group of Queries, making suggestions about diffraction, contain nothing of relevance here; the next group, concerned with heat and light, seem if anything almost opposed to the idea of light as particles. Query 8 asks whether incandescence is not "perform'd by the vibrating motions" of the parts of bodies; and if the vibration is not produced by heat, a cold "agitation" also can cause the emission of light. Other forms of agitation are fermentation and putrefaction. Queries 9, 10, and 11 continue this same theme; the emission and re-absorption of light by a hot body can heat it still more. Again, turning to physiology, it is vibration that is emphasized as conveying the sense of vision to the brain in Queries 12 to 16, just as Newton had hypothesized as long ago as 1675. (The two last Queries of the 1717 group, numbered 23 and 24, return to the same theme in an aetherial version, in which the aether becomes an 'animal spirit'.)

Then the first of the 1706 Queries, nos. 25 and 26, dealing with Icelandic spar and double refraction, tell us no more of the rays of light than that they have four sides—two pairs at right angles, it seems, as though the ray were of rectangular cross-section—and that somehow (by implication) they must be oriented so that this 'sidedness' of the rays can function. Query 27 insists yet again upon the "original and connate Properties of the Rays" while Query 28 contains Newton's heaviest denunciation of the wave-theory of light, as we have seen already: it is the next, Query 29, that provides the most open, clear and full account that Newton ever printed of his corpuscular theory of light (p. 138 above).

Query 29

Conceptually, this Query is the tip of an iceberg of speculation. From the invaluable investigations of Zev Bechler we can now form some idea of the highly intricate world of 'micro-forces' into which Newton plunged when he was induced by his fruitless attempts to explore diffraction by experiments to attempt a more complete theoretical review of the physical relations between light, matter, and force than he had essayed before. He started, surely, from his metaphysical confidence in the uniformity of Nature, from which he inferred that the optical force and the force of cohesion (in particular) were on the micro-scale analogous to gravitation on the macro-scale. (Electricity only seemed a force active on both scales.) But, as we have already seen, there are conceptual difficulties of some importance in the analogy and pitfalls into which (at least for a time) Newton fell. The avoidance of such mistakes partly explains the textual differences between the Latin Queries of 1706 and those of the subsequent English edition of 1717.

Query 22

Consider for example the passage of Query 22 in *Optice* omitted from Query 30 in 1717 (p. 140 above). Bechler (1974, pp. 201–2) has studied Newton's computations in the manuscripts and found them seriously flawed. Newton's evaluation of the force required to refract a hypothetical light-particle is too small by a factor of 10^7!* To that extent Newton weakened his argument for the great strength of such micro-forces. He could naturally make no experiment to confirm directly his highly arbitrary estimate of the optical force, but he was able to insert into *Optice* (and this remained in the 1717 edition) an experimental measure of the force of cohesion made by Hauksbee (p. 146 above) which is tantamount to saying that where the interval between two bodies is as small as one-half millionth of an inch the attractive force between them is equal to a pressure of about fifty atmospheres (*Opticks* (1952), p. 394).

'Weak' gravity, 'strong' micro-forces

Though it is not a point upon which Newton declared his opinion categorically, there can be little doubt that he regarded the optical force exerted by matter upon light, and that of cohesion, as being distinct from the chemical force and the electrical force. His problem was to explain how these various forces (and perhaps others yet unknown) might be unified in a single conceptual scheme, and to provide a justification for his, as it were,

---

* Newton assumes $V = 30$ ft/sec, i.e. 2.4 miles in 7 minutes; hence the radius of curvature of the projectile's orbit R is also 360 inches. Putting the speed of light v at 8.3×10^7 miles in 7 minutes, and r at 10^{-5} inches, we have $\frac{v^2}{r} : \frac{V^2}{R} = 4.10^{22} : 1$.

Newton, mistakenly taking the appropriate ratio to be $\frac{v}{r} : \frac{V}{R}$, arrived at the ratio of "more than 10^{15} to one".

instinctive belief that the smaller the particles, the stronger (relatively speaking) the force between them. Newton believed—as we now know correctly—that gravity is a 'weak' force, although it is also one that extends over cosmic distances, while the micro-forces directly associated with the particles of matter and light (he thought) must be vastly more powerful, though extending over minute distances.

He had, therefore, many problems. How was he to express the differences between 'weak' gravity and 'strong' micro-forces? How could their diverse laws of action be rendered mathematically? How could any theory dealing with these questions be justified experientially? Then there was a further set of problems in connection with heat in its associations with light and matter. It was easy enough to speculate that the vibration which is heat loosens and ejects the light-particles latent in bodies, and that the impact of these upon other bodies might heat them; but there remained other problems such as the radiation of heat without light and, seemingly, of light without heat; the intense and enduring radiation of heat and light from the sun and stars, and the question of the possible interconvertibility of heat and light.

It was not to be expected that Newton would make remarkable progress with all of these problems. Query 31 put the chemical force at least on a comparative quantitative basis in the sense that Newton is able to claim that

when a Solution of Iron in *Aqua fortis* dissolves the *Lapis Calaminaris*, and lets go the Iron, or a Solution of Copper dissolves Iron immersed in it and lets go the Copper, or a Solution of Silver dissolves Copper and lets go the Silver, or a Solution of Mercury in *Aqua fortis* being poured upon Iron, Copper, Tin, or Lead, dissolves the Metal and lets go the Mercury; does not this argue that the acid Particles of the *Aqua fortis* are attracted more strongly by the *Lapis Calaminaris* than by Iron, and more strongly by Iron than by Copper, and more strongly by Copper than by Silver, and more strongly by Iron, Copper, Tin, and Lead, than by Mercury? (pp. 380–1).

But this truly astonishing fragment of chemical theory still left the physical nature and laws of the chemical force unexplained, and in the end Newton's brilliant conception of an 'attractive affinity' between chemical corpuscles was to prove sterile. In other ways too Newton seemed to offer promising paths of development. Suppose (as the opening of Query 31 suggests) that matter and light are interconvertible, with the difference that the particles of light, being far more minute than those of matter, are also far more forceful (this is, of course, an idea that Newton might have imitated from Descartes). Then these highly active particles in matter might be imagined—no detailed account is given—to give to ordinary, inert matter much of its activity in phenomena. But if *little* is more active than *large*, it can only be if the little particle is capable of exerting (in proportion to its mass) more force than, say, the whole Earth does by its gravity in proportion to its mass. For in the theory of gravitation where the force between two bodies is proportional to the product of their masses divided by the square of the distance between them, there can be no change in the direct proportionality of mass and force.

Perhaps force increases inversely as the mass?

However, if we redefine the law of force so that for very small masses, and over very minute distances, the force increases in the *inverse* ratio of the mass, then the external force exerted can become very large in proportion to the size of the particle. Small particles with proportionately higher attractive forces will be accelerated vastly more than the larger ones, and so there will arise a discrimination between the motions of small and large, or between their forces of cohesion.

The eighteenth-century Newtonians, aware that Newton had long entertained the possibility of variations in the law of force from passages they noted in both the *Principia mathematica* and *Opticks*, were not slow to follow his example. J. T. Desaguliers in the synopsis of his *Physico-Mechanical Lectures* (1717) affirms without hesitation that the force of cohesion, which he identifies with 'the *Electrical Attraction unexcited*', is

very strong when the Parts of Bodies touch one another, but decreases (when the Parts of Bodies are at any sensible Distances) much faster than Gravity, so as to become almost insensible then (p. 2).

The rapid diminution of this force with distance is demonstrated by the oil of oranges experiment and other capillary effects, all borrowed from *Opticks*. Indeed, it is hard to understand why the law of the decrease of force with distance should be supposed to be the same for all forces, or why, when the force is not gravity, and the particles are extremely minute, we should not expect to find a statistical (if not a causal) correlation inversely between the size of the particle and the power of the force-function. On such a basis, gravitational mechanics might be held to provide not an exact similarity to particle mechanics, but an analogical model.

As for Newton himself, evidently he judged (from the simplicity of Nature) that the power of the distance expressing the force must be an integer, but that this was not necessarily two; it might be 1, 2, 3, or perhaps more. In the *Principia mathematica* the section on the 'elasticity of airs' demonstrates (Book II, Proposition 23) that Boyle's Law is consistent with a repulsion between the particles of the 'air' which varies inversely as the distance. Again, Book III, Proposition 6, Corollary 4 notes the qualitative differences between gravitation and magnetism and affirms that "the magnetic force is much stronger in proportion to the quantity of matter than is the force of gravity . . . [and] as one moves away from the magnet [the force] decreases in a ratio of the distance greater than two". When actual contact between magnet and iron occurs the force is much greater still

(*Principia* (1687), p. 411). In subsequent editions Newton averred that the law of force was nearly as the third power of the distance inversely (1713, p. 368). It is really not at all strange that Newton should have thought of the smallest particles of matter obeying a higher-order law of force.

It is in the abortive Book IV of *Opticks*, to which I have already alluded, that one finds Newton's most specific statement about the possibility (it is no more than that!) of there being such a higher-order law of force:

if they [the particles of bodies] have any forces decreasing in any ratio greater than the quadruplicate one of the distance from their centres, they may attract one another very strongly & yet great bodies composed of such particles shall not attract one another sensibly (Bechler 1974, p. 197).

Only hints of these speculations were to survive in the printed Queries. As Bechler has pointed out (ibid., p. 204) the passage in Query 31 on the hierarchical ordering of particles implies a higher-order law of force such as that indicated in the manuscript:

it may even be that the smallest particles of matter may stick together by the strongest attractions, and compose large particles in which the attractive force is weaker; and by many of these larger particles sticking together yet bigger corpuscles may be formed, whose attractive force is weaker still; and so on in a continuing series until at last we arrive at the largest of the those corpuscles upon which the operations of chemistry and the colours of natural bodies depend, and which by cohering together constitute bodies of such a size as to be perceived by the senses (*Optice*, 1706, p. 338, my translation).

Once again, the law of the proportionality of the gravitational force to mass precludes the possibility that this weak, long-range force could be that here described by Newton. The force of this last passage must be a higher-order force. If we imagine a relatively large mass composed of particles whose binding-forces are of a high order (and so of short range) only the particles in the outer shell of the body will exert any external effect; in other words, while the mass of such a body increases with the cube of the radius, the short-range force might increase only as the square of the radius. This point is somewhat concealed in the most obvious surviving reference to this matter, in Query 21 (added in 1717):

As Attraction is stronger in small Magnets than in great ones in proportion to their Bulk, and Gravity is greater in the Surfaces of small Planets than in those of great ones in proportion to their Bulk, and small Bodies are agitated much more by electric attractions than great ones; so the smallness of the Rays of Light may contribute very much to the power of the Agent by which they are refracted (pp. 351–2).

Here Newton seems, perhaps deliberately, to be obfuscating the issue by bringing in gravity (a square-law force) and electricity (whose law of force was not yet known).

Newton under pressure

Physically, all these assertions seem to be dubious. The clause about electricity, Bechler shows, was a late addition to earlier drafts on the same theme (Bechler 1974, p. 214). Its origin seems to lie in the rather trivial observation that small fragments of detritus are more readily attracted to a charged glass rod than are larger ones. The assertion about the planets may derive from Newton's earlier belief that small planets are denser than large ones; if this were so, it would be truer to say that 'gravity is greater in small planets than in large ones in proportion to their *volumes*', the ratio of gravity to mass being, as ever, constant. Newton's enthusiasm for an interesting speculation seems to have urged him to make strange claims. The final manifestation of the idea that force is inversely proportional to mass is, of course, in the aether-theory (Query 21, 1717) since only by supposing a fantastically high ratio of force to mass can such utterly minute particles as Newton postulates work the effects he attributes to them. But it is not clear to me that this repulsive force in the aether is to be envisaged as a short-range force.

Clearly in threading his way through these dark and intricate regions Newton was, as men then said, 'put to his shifts'. His drafts evolved rapidly and inconsistently between 1706 and 1717. I have remarked already that notes for an (abortive) longer Scholium Generale to the second *Principia mathematica* (1713) read like sketches for the late Queries in *Opticks*: Newton was already insisting that 'small is strong' and suggesting that 'attraction is of the electric kind', perhaps referring to an inverse ratio of proportionality between force and mass (Hall and Hall 1962, p. 361). One might almost say that he was grasping at straws. 'Mes yeux s'eteignent, mon esprit est las de travailler' Newton told the Fellows of the Royal Society according to a late French report (Home 1982, p. 202).

Doubts of Newton's meaning

We cannot hope, perhaps, to render fully consistent the various statements made by Newton at different times about the forces between particles, especially those relating to the aether on the one hand and electrical force on the other. Different passages, printed and manuscript, have suggested a range of different conceptual possibilities to different authors. Henry Guerlac in 1967 concluded that the electric and elastic spirit lying hidden in matter was for Newton the cause of

the short-range forces acting between the constituent particles of matter; it accounts for electrical attraction at greater distances; it heats bodies; it seems to explain the emission, reflexion, refraction and diffraction of light and the vibrations of this spirit, passing along the sensory nerves, yield our sensations, and passing from the brain through the nerves constitute the motor impulses sent to the muscles (Guerlac 1977, p. 127).

The aether of *Opticks* in 1717 is then the generalization of this conception, the spirit formerly found in the interior pores of bodies becoming a space-pervading aether. (But this point has also been doubted by others.) Joan Hawes, surveying the same body of evidence in the year after Guerlac, argued that Newton's

particles themselves possess an electric force which is effective over small distances and is active without the medium of an electric spirit (Hawes 1968, p. 205).

Did Newton mean that 'electric force' and 'electric and elastic spirit' are the same entity? Hawes, with some difficulty, thinks they are not and is supported (on this point) by R. W. Home (1982); Guerlac thinks that they are the same, as I have argued here (p. 152). Whereas the latter paraphrased the printed Scholium Generale, the former quotes in opposition the longer abortive draft:

As the system of the sun, planets and comets is put in motion by the forces of gravity and its parts persist in their motions, so also the smaller systems of bodies seem to be set in motion by other forces and their particles to be moved among themselves in different ways, and especially by the electric force. For the particles of very many bodies seem to be endowed with an electric force and to act upon each other at small distances even without friction, and those which are most electric, through friction, emit a spirit to great distances, by means of which straws and light bodies are now attracted, now repelled and now moved in diverse ways (ibid.; cf. Hall and Hall 1962, p. 353).

The fact that a draft and the printed version of the same document can readily bear opposite interpretations well illustrates the difficulty of Newtonian scholarship.

I do not think that Newton meant to resolve this issue sharply, preferring deliberately to leave uncertain and indeed contradictory his views upon the metaphysical question of the primacy of attractive force acting at a distance or of an aether whose mechanics remain vague. As Joan Hawes maintained, this irresolution at least had the merit of giving a soft answer to Newton's neo-Cartesian philosophical critics.

A single aether sufficient?

Setting aside this fundamental metaphysical issue, there is also (at a higher level) the question of the uniformity of explanation. Newton undoubtedly had a strong methodological preference for simplicity: perhaps a single spirit (or aether) could account for all (or most) of the phenomena of physics, or alternatively a single force (perhaps the electric force) might do so. Home quotes a draft perhaps only rejected finally from the Queries in 1717, beginning:

Do not electric bodies by friction emit a subtle exhalation or spirit by which they perform their attractions? And is not this spirit of a very active nature & capable of emitting light by its agitations?

Newton then went on to describe experimental effects—due to Hauksbee— proving the material, mechanical nature of this spirit. He concluded:

And since it easily emits light by agitation, why may it not emit light in all dense bodies heated red hot & thereby cause them to shine? (Home 1982, p. 195).

Here, at any rate, the electric spirit is as material as alcohol, and Newton thinks of it in a neo-Cartesian way as a mechanical effluvium. Home produces other evidence to show that Newton also believed magnetic attraction and repulsion to be caused by an effluvium or 'magnetic spirit' in the same manner. This makes it clear that, though Newton held Occam's razor to be the most useful of philosophical tools, and sought earnestly for uniformity in Nature, we can find in his writings not only an inevitable multiplicity of forces but at different times a multiplicity of spirits or effluvia and of aethers also.

One could go on with endless problems, for example, if the electric spirit should be supposed the substance of light, it can hardly also be the optical agent or force that causes matter to refract and reflect light. An even greater difficulty is gravity. Several scholars (including recently R. W. Home) have drawn attention to Newton's great hesitancy in bringing gravity within the scope of the aether theory of 1717, and Newton's general sense that while the long-range effects of magnetism and electricity might be attributed to effluvial mechanisms, though these also acted as short-range forces, no one could imagine such an effluvial mechanism applying to gravity. The uniqueness of gravity thus established by Newton seems to persist to this day.

Speculations are not 'doctrines'

Perhaps we should not attach too importance to Newton's intellectual twists and turns with respect to aether, fascinating as these are. Far more significant than the possibly doubtful and certainly subtle differences between the various aetherial hypotheses of 1675/79, 1713, and 1717 is the undoubted consistency in broad principles of explanation that they reveal. All these thoughts were tentative explanations, not "doctrine", belonging to Newton's early or late years. To say that Newton believed (from 1684 or so) that a proper theory of particles and micro-forces would be able to account for a large part of physics and chemistry is no more than the truth. This belief was the basis for a sound programme of investigation, and it was never forgotten. It would (in my view) be a misjudgement to suppose that he also thought his various aetherial attempts to extend this programme to a deeper level of explanation, accounting for the forces themselves, to be of equal value, or indeed to be truly well-founded hypotheses. I do not consider that Newton judged his speculations in the Queries to be near-certain truths, in the same sense that his demonstration of the oblate shape of the Earth or of the varied refrangibility of the rays of light were near-certain truths; some eighteenth-century Newtonians took the opposite view, and so perhaps do some modern scholars. When we look over the shoulder of this elderly mathematician and philosopher engaged upon his endless task of committing to paper the full import of his widely ramifying thoughts we have to make a guess—for we can only guess—at his own estimate of the significance to be attached to these drafts. Were they concerned with difficulties that (in Newton's judgement) more acute mathematical reasoning or experiments not yet devised might resolve? Or with matters so deep in the heart of things that knowledge of them was hardly to be hoped for? Newton was surely aware—though he was a man liable to be borne into over-confidence by the rich seductive flow of his own perception of things—that speculation about the ultimate forces of Nature was, despite all the suggestive analogy and comparison available to him, far advanced along a progression away from what would one day be called positivism.

In any case, Newton's failure to produce a convincing answer to the question 'What is light?' is, to my mind, less damaging to the system of physical knowledge conveyed in *Opticks* than is the theory of "fits", integral to it. To put it crudely, it might seem that a system requiring light to be particles, *or* a system requiring light to be waves, must be superior to a system requiring light to be *both*. (Twentieth-century wave-mechanics is irrelevant to this issue.) Newton could not do without waves (though he preferred to call them "fits") in any version of his ideas from 1675 onwards. True, the waves were never taken by Newton to be light; but they were essential to the manifestations of light as Newton described them. In fact, Newton's world would be largely colourless but for the waves. The theory of "fits" and all the wonderful consequences flowing from it in the quantitative explanation of how the colours of natural bodies arise from the various magnitudes of their surface particles—a notion previously proposed only in the loosest qualitative form—constituting the finest piece of 'microphysics' before Dalton's theory of atomic combination, was too massive a piece of work to be set aside by its author as something not essential to the physical nature of light. For how do we know what the nature of light may be, save from its phenomena, from which the "fits" cannot be separated? Surely Thomas Young was in the right here, in his insistence that the real essence of light was in its periodic motion, and that the question of its 'substance' intruded by Newton's metaphysics merely aroused illusory difficulties.

FOUR

Opticks *and its readers*

§1. The fate of *Opticks* in Britain

The immediate reception of Opticks

The most striking evidence of the success of *Opticks* in its native island is the fact that four editions were called for in twenty-five years. For the rest, the story is rather thin at first. We know that Newton's Optical Lectures had been sought out by a few zealous students at Cambridge even before the book was published, and that his optics were early taught in the Scottish universities, but the welcome accorded to either *Principia* or *Opticks* has yet to be investigated in detail. According to John Flamsteed, the Astronomer Royal and a far from impartial witness, by November 1704 'the book Makes no Noyse in Town as the *Principia* did . . ., for tho the experiments are very good & sincerely related, his deductions are many of them Mistakes . . .' (Letter 678, p. 424). Though Flamsteed permitted himself to be converted to Newton's view that the rays of light are differently refrangible, he rejected (as he always had) the concomitant assertion that all the coloured rays of the spectrum are essential to the reconstitution of white light; and he especially scorned Newton's computation that the minimum point of light visible through a telescope could not be less than five seconds of arc in diameter. The great majority of fixed stars visible through a telescope, Flamsteed retorted, 'have not one second diameter' but failed to explain how he had measured such a minute quantity (about one thousandth of a millimetre). Such technical and, it must be said, prejudiced objections against *Opticks* were, however, very rare.

One point at least is clear: Newton's two great works were treated by contemporaries in different ways, and as it were in different contexts. Early expositors of Newtonian science, or rather of the Newtonian world-view, like John Keill, William Whiston, and David Gregory, paid little or no attention to optics and light. For example, the last-named's chief work is entitled *The Physical and Geometrical Elements of Astronomy* (1702): no room for Newton's experiments on light there (Gregory 1715). Even Gregory's private notes make few allusions to *Opticks*, and then only to its future publication and, later, to Newton's more bizarre notions touched on in the Queries (Hiscock 1937). A generation passed before Robert Smith produced a textbook of optics embodying the Newtonian tradition: *A*

Compleat System of Opticks (1738), and in this generation little progress had been made towards achieving that synthesis of mathematical and experimental science which had certainly been among Newton's major objectives, though his own steps towards it had been somewhat tentative.

Contrast with the Principia

Some readers of *Opticks* responded warmly to the book because it was written in English, founded upon experiments, and (in the Queries) free-ranging in its speculation. At the limit, one might say that the *Principia* was frankly unintelligible to many men and women who could profit from *Opticks*. (A few women in the eighteenth century studied the *Principia* fruitfully: one was the Marquise du Châtellet, translator of the book into French (1756); another was Maria Gaetana Agnesi, whom Pope Benedict XIV appointed a professor at Bologna in 1750, the 'first woman in the world who can accurately be called a mathematician'.) It is thus tempting to distinguish—as Professor I. Bernard Cohen did thirty years ago—between 'experimental Newtonianism' and 'mathematical Newtonianism', with the former far more accessible to readers. The *Principia* in its own day was from the first regarded as a very difficult book. By contrast,

In an age of science characterized to some degree by experimental advances and the production of new concepts and theories based on experimental manipulation and observed data rather than mathematical deduction from axioms or "first principles", the *Opticks* was widely read as a classic of the experimenter's art—or, if you will, as a gadgeteer's delight. Many of the ingenious experiments of Newton had been performed only with a prism, a lens, a slit, and a straight edge: apparatus so simple that almost everyone who had the inclination could repeat the experiments, and many men did (Cohen 1956, p. 121).

Newton himself claimed—with a good deal of exaggeration of his clarity, it must be said—to have so described his experiments that the phenomena might be the more conspicuous and "A Novice the more easily try them". (Newton 1952, p. 25). Cohen goes on to find (p. 181) 'a continued sharp distinction between Newtonianism as a corpuscular philosophy and Newtonianism as a mathematico-deductive system of celestial dynamics' in eighteenth-century explanations of what the term 'Newtonian philosophy' signified. The 'corpuscular', or rather in Newton's case atomic, philosophy was, of course, necessarily speculative and was closely linked with the inductive (or experimental) rather than the deductive (or mathematical) road to the discovery of truth.

Desaguliers on Newtonian science

The same argument was well understood by Newton's younger contemporaries. J. T. Desaguliers, who had confirmed Newton's optical experiments in 1714, in his *Course of Experimental Philosophy* (1744) neatly stresses that *deduction* and *induction* are complementary processes in scientific investigation:

All the Knowledge we have of Nature depends upon Facts, for without Observations and Experiments, our natural Philosophy would only be a Science of Terms, and an unintelligible Jargon. But then we must call in Geometry and Arithmetick to our Assistance, unless we are willing to content ourselves with natural History and conjectural Philosophy.

He goes on to claim that Newton has excelled in both experiment and in mathematics: on the one hand, it was to his 'Application of Geometry to Philosophy, that we owe the routing of this Army of *Goths* and *Vandals* [the followers of Descartes] in the philosphical World; which he has enrich'd with more and greater Discoveries, than all the Philosophers that went before him.' On the other hand, our *'incomparable Philosopher* has discovered and demonstrated to us the true Nature of Light and Colours, of which the most sagacious and inquisitive Naturalists were entirely ignorant'. It would be a misrepresentation, however, to suggest that Desaguliers contrasts experimental *Opticks* with mathematical *Principia* in order to deny any grasp of the latter work to those unskilled in geometry. Quite the contrary is his purpose. Locke, he says, was the first non-mathematical reader of the *Principia*. Following his example, we can understand the physical principles of Newtonian mechanics by examining their experimental foundations, just as we can with Newtonian optics (Desaguliers 1763, pp. *v−vii*). And in fact in his big book, the *Course of Experimental Philosophy*, Desaguliers omitted optics altogether.

It was, he tells us, John Keill (like Gregory a Scot, and an associate of Newton's) who first inaugurated, at Oxford, the teaching of Newtonian

Natural Philosophy by *Experiments* in a mathematical Manner; for he had laid down very simple *Propositions*, which he prov'd by *Experiments*; and from those he deduced others more compound, which he still confirmed by *Experiments*; till he had instructed his Auditors in the *Laws of Motion*, the *Principles* of *Hydrostaticks* and *Opticks*, and some of the chief *Propositions* of *Sir Isaac Newton* concerning *Light* and *Colours*.

This was perhaps about the turn of the century. A few years later Francis Hauksbee in London publicly presented his own new experiments made with the air-pump, and upon electricity, but did not touch on optics. When after Hauksbee's death in 1713 his nephew of the same name continued these lectures, with the aid of William Whiston and others, he added a section on optics which included 'Sir Isaac Newton's Experiments, to shew the different Refrangibility of the Rays of Light, of the different Colours' and that 'White is a Mixture of all Sorts of colour'd Rays', among them the "crucial experiment" (Hauksbee ?1714). Also about the time of the elder

Hauksbee's death Desaguliers arrived in London with his systematic course derived from Keill, into which he introduced the technique acquired in vindicating Newton against Mariotte. In his *Physico-Mechanical Lectures: Or, the Account of what is Explain'd and Demonstrated in the Course of Mechanical and Experimental Philosophy given by J. T. Desaguliers* (London, 1717)—a small volume with a long title—he devoted seven of twenty-two lectures to optics. However, only the last of these described the experiments taken from Book I of *Opticks* and Newton's interpretation of them: 'Light consist of *Rays* of different Kinds, which are differently *refrangible* and differently colour'd' (p. 70).

Desaguliers also outlined Newton's contributions to the understanding of the colours of natural bodies seen by reflection, but entirely omitted the 'thin plates', and therefore also the theory of 'fits'.

The first sentence of these lectures on optics reads:

That *Light* is a Body, appears from its *Reflection, Refraction, Composition, Division, and moving in Time*; but especially from its being *propagated in right lines*, and being *stopp'd by an Obstacle*, (how thin soever, if not transparent) which shews, that it cannot be an *Action upon the Medium*, which wou'd be communicated beyond an Obstacle, as in the case of Sound (ibid., p. 42).

The arguments here in favour of Desaguliers's assertion are Newton's; but the flat dictum 'Light is a Body' is one that Newton hesitated to make. The step to certainty where Newton had remained conjectural is typical of the early eighteenth-century Newtonians, who held that Newton had 'known' much to be certain, that he had not alleged to be so in the absence of experimental or mathematical demonstration. So Desaguliers again, referring to the 'vast Fund of Philosophy; which (tho' he has modestly delivered under the Name of Queries, as if they were only Conjectures) daily Experiments and Observations confirm;' (Desaguliers 1763, pp. *vi–vii*). In this same spirit he also makes the positive claim that

The Physical Cause of Refraction is the Greater or Less Attraction of the new Medium [i.e. that into which the ray passes through an interface; Desaguliers 1717, p. 46].

Thus, passing from air into glass, a ray of light is bent towards the perpendicular by 'the Attraction of the Glass'; Newton had only hinted in the most delicate way that light might be thought of as very minute bodies upon which matter exerted mechanical forces.

Cheyne on light

We find the same confident, indeed rash assurance in other Newtonians. George Cheyne—an awkward and unconventional follower of the Master, it is true, much in dispute with him and his more loyal disciples over mathematical issues—in his *Philosophical Principles of Religion, Natural and Reveal'd* (1705, 1715) drew heavily upon *Opticks* while acknowledging that

Those who desire full Satisfaction in this wonderful Appearance of Nature [that is, the manifestations of light] must go to that late admirable Treatise of *Opticks*, written by Sir *Isaac Newton*; . . . That great Person having before shown how far *Numbers* and *Geometry* would go in *Natural Philosophy*, has now manifested to the World to what surprizing Heights, even vulgar Experiments duly managed and carefully examined in such Hands may advance it (Cheyne 1715, p. 85).

Like Desaguliers later and alleging the same reasons, Cheyne positively asserts that 'Light is a Body, or a material substance'. In addition, he makes the points that light 'acts upon the *Organs* of *Animals*, and upon all other Bodies, as other fluid Substances do, by striking upon them with a determin'd Force . . .;' it also warms bodies, and is 'yearly imprison'd in Fruits, Plants and other Vegetables'. More crudely than Newton, Cheyne claims that 'The parts of Light are endow'd with various *Original Colours* . . . as Sir *Isaac Newton* has demonstrated . . . Now all these are the Properties of Bodies, and can belong to nothing but Material Substances' (ibid., pp. 68–9).

Having spoken of light as a material fluid Cheyne also tells his readers that its particles must be extremely little or small because of their passage through dense transparent solids, borrowing (without acknowledgement) an experiment from Hauksbee to illustrate the passage of multiple fine beams of light through a single tiny pinhole without confusion or interaction. The speed of these tiny particles is so great that they travel 1 314 700 times more swiftly than a cannon-ball. Again taking the same line as the experimentalist lecturer Desaguliers later, Cheyne the mathematician and natural theologian is confident that attraction can be adduced as the physical cause of the phenomena occurring in the associations of light and matter, such as refraction, referring now to *Principia*, Book I, Section XIV. Moreover, in this long summary of Newtonian discoveries and theories, drawing extensively on the Queries but also making some use of geometry to demonstrate his arguments, Cheyne seems almost unwittingly to advance an interesting notion that was not Newton's. His discussion, invoking the action of light as a movement of particles, and also as a fluid, is certainly far from lucid; but then his model in *Opticks* was not very clear either. According to Cheyne, light falling upon bodies heats them, that is to say, it puts them into a certain mode of rapid vibration, while conversely bodies that are very hot (and therefore vibrating vigorously) emit light, as we see it shining from a white-hot iron. The bodies of the sun and stars are no more than matter that is hot, vibrating, and radiating intensely. He seems to indicate that the same vibration which is heat is that which, in association with a ray of light, imposes 'fits' upon its motion in the manner described by Newton and used by him to account for the colours of thin plates and solid bodies. This seems to be an elegant and economical hypothesis, since it accounts for the experiential linking of light and heat and removes the arbitrariness from the theory of 'fits' as stated by Newton in *Opticks*. Experiments to be made in the future would have confirmed it by showing that radiant heat has optical properties. But Cheyne does not appear to have realized that this hypothesis was not put forward by Newton.

Stephen Hales inspired by Opticks

George Cheyne, yet another Scot who was a peripheral member of Newton's London circle, was exceptional among British natural theologians in allotting so much space in his book to an almost technical exposition of optics, a branch of science not usually regarded as offering rich materials for the demonstration of providential creation—with the exception of the eye and the rainbow, of course. Another writer, one of the founders of experimental physiology, who found inspiration in the method and philosophy of *Opticks* rather than its technicalities, opened his influential book with an invocation no less pious than any passage to be found in Ray, Derham, or Cheyne:

The farther researches we make into this admirable scene of things, the more beauty and harmony we see in them: And the stronger and clearer convictions they give us, of the being, power and wisdom of the divine Architect, who has made all things to concur with a wonderful conformity, in carrying on, by various and innumerable combinations of matter, such a circulation of causes, and effects, as was necessary to the great ends of nature.

Stephen Hales, author of *Vegetable Staticks* (1727), acquired a love of natural science at the University of Cambridge, where he was one of a Newtonian group that included William Stukeley, William Whiston (Newton's successor in the Lucasian Chair), John Francis Vigani, John Waller, and Roger Cotes (editor of the second edition of the *Principia*). The first three of these had known Newton during his last Cambridge years, but he had left before Hales arrived as a student. He was to meet Newton later in London, as President of the Royal Society.

Though it is hardly to be expected that technical studies in optics should be relevant to the physiological researches pursued by Hales in the last years of Newton's life, the physical speculations and methodology of *Opticks* provided a model of inquiry and a framework of explanation. For example, in Query 31 of *Opticks* Newton mentioned an experiment (in fact performed by Francis Hauksbee) on the capillary ascent of water up a column of wood-ash packed into a glass tube (1952, p. 391). Newton regarded this phenomenon as being, like the cohesion of solids, an instance of corpuscular attraction. Hales applied his idea to the ascent of fluid through the stems of plants:

by the same principle it is, that we see in the preceding Experiments, plants imbibe moisture so vigorously up their fine capillary vessels; which moisture as it is carried off in perspiration [from the leaves], (by the action of warmth) thereby gives the sap vessels liberty to be almost continually attracting of fresh supplies . . . (Hales 1961, p. 56).

Hales adapted Newton's concept of attractive force to account for the absorption of fluids by dry materials and the pressure of sap in plant stems (which he measured meticulously) against the force of gravity, the upward attractive force exerted by the particles being stronger than the downward pull. So again, he writes

We see, in the Experiments of this chapter, many instances of the great efficacy of attraction; that universal principle which is so operative in all the very different worlds of nature; and is most eminently so in vegetables, all whose minutest parts are curiously ranged in such order, as is best adapted by their united force, to attract proper nourishment (ibid., p. 54).

In the course of his experiments on the movement of sap in plants Hales observed that the fluid contained bubbles of air, and he satisfied himself that leaves absorbed air, as well as transpiring water. He made a special study of air in plants and of the air evolved in chemical reactions that furnished nearly one-half of *Vegetable Staticks*. Others before him had shown that organic materials, when dissolved in acids for example, yielded gases ('factitious airs') in great quantity, as did fermenting fruits. Hales measured the quantities of gas produced in his experiments, and ascertained that it was elastic like ordinary air. Again he quotes Newton for the idea that attractive force binds the air into the solid from which, when released, repulsive force causes its particles to fly apart forming an elastic 'air'.

The illustrious Philosopher, Sir *Isaac Newton*, in accounting how air and vapour are produced, *Opticks Quer.* 31 says, "The particles when they are shaken off from bodies by heat or fermentation, so soon as they are beyond the reach of the attraction of the body [by] receding from it as also from one another with great strength and keeping at a distance, . . . sometimes . . . take up above a million times more space than they did before in the form of a dense body, which vast contraction and expansion seems unintelligible . . . by any other means than by a repulsive power." The truth of which is further confirmed by these Experiments, which shew the great quantity of air emitted from fermenting bodies . . . (Hales 1961, p. 119, quoting *Opticks* (1952), p.396).

After demonstrating in a variety of ways that organic materials could emit large quantities of air, Hales effectively passed (as we might say) from physiology to chemistry when he also examined the evolution of 'air' from gold dissolved in aqua regia. Such evolutions of air had been known long before, but no one had devised, as Hales did, techniques for collecting the gases and measuring their volumes. He also found chemical reactions in which 'air' was absorbed, and others in which 'air' might be produced and re-absorbed for days on end. When he repeated the experiment made by John Mayow (*c.* 1670) in which a small animal was enclosed in a volume of air over water, he noted (like Mayow) the rising of the water and the diminution of the air, as also in an experiment he devised involving his breathing in and out of a moist bladder. Hales thought that what was involved was not so much absorption of the air in his lungs as a reduction of its elasticity. By this he meant, following Newton in Query 31 once more, that the formerly separate, mutually repulsive particles of air had coalesced into a fluid or solid. The particles of air, he thought, might (when thus coalesced) be 'very instrumental as a band of union in those bodies', referring to a passage of Query 31 where Newton opines that the "Bodies which chemists call fix'd . . . being rarified by Fermentation, become true permanent Air; those Particles receding from one another with the greatest Force, and being most difficultly brought together, which upon Contact cohere most strongly" (*Opticks* (1952), p. 396). Moreover,

Sir *Isaac Newton* calculates from the inflection of the rays of light, that the attracting force of particles, near the point of contact, is 10000,0000,0000,0000 [times] greater than the force of gravity (Hales 1961, pp. 170–1).

Thus Hales, with Newton's assistance, found an explanation of his physiological experiments in the most profound principle of Newtonian philosophy.

The influence of Opticks upon chemistry

As Henry Guerlac pointed out long ago, *Vegetable Staticks*, translated into French by Buffon in 1735, provided the chemists of the eighteenth century, especially those of France, with the basic laboratory technique and many important conceptual clues for understanding the role of the common gases in chemical combination:

Because of Buffon's translation, and such references [to *Vegetable Staticks*] as those of Buffon, Musschenbroek and Macquer, Hales's work, unlike that of [Joseph] Black which was virtually unknown in France, had enjoyed an early *succès d'estime* and had by no means disappeared from sight. It was available to Lavoisier, who drew inspiration from it at [a] critical moment of his career and who gratefully refers to it at one point as 'un fonds inépuisable de méditations' (Guerlac 1977, p. 274).

In this unlikely and roundabout way Newton's physical speculations as recorded in *Opticks* exerted a formative influence upon the chemical revolution brought about by Antoine Laurent de Lavoisier and his colleagues, who were (nevertheless) very far from sharing Newton's notions about the atomic structure of matter and the decisive part to be played by the theory of atomic and molecular forces in accounting for chemical reactions; indeed, Lavoisier's revolution may be seen as a triumphant revulsion from the endeavour to interpret chemistry as a branch of physics (Thackray 1970).

John Freind

But to return to England in the early eighteenth century: Hales was by no means the only natural philosopher to write Newtonian chemistry. He himself acknowledged a debt to John Freind, author of *Praelectiones chymicae* (1709 = *Chymical Lectures*, 1712). Freind, a physician, came under the Newtonian influence second-hand, through his studies with John Keill at Oxford (above, p. 182). He did not settle down to practise in London until about 1709. Freind's object in his little book was to account for 'the several Operations in Chymistry' mechanically, that is, by 'the Principle of Attraction'. This 'Way whereby Chymistry might be examin'd and illustrated by Mechanical, that is, true Principles, was first shewn to us by Mr. John Keill . . .'. That the greater figure of Newton stood behind Keill is soon evident from such sentences as

Cohesion is deduc'd from, and is always proportionable to an *Attraction*, that necessarily resides in the Matter. But the Attractive Force being strongest at the Point of Contact, is the cause, why the Surfaces of the Parts are more firmly united . . . (Freind 1712, p. 17).

Or again, when Freind writes of 'fermentation' (the reactive solution of one body in another):

This Motion [of fermentation] may very well be accounted for, from an *Attractive Force*, which is so very extensive in *Natural Philosophy*, that there is no kind of Matter in the whole Universe, but what is subject to it (ibid., p. 71).

Freind noted that a solvent would rise by capillation into a heap of dry material, and so dissolve it; this he thought 'an ocular demonstration' of attractive force at work. So, 'we find how the Solution of Salts is to be accounted for, from an *Attractive Force*.'

Freind was well acquainted with the idea of substances' having a differential attraction, or affinity, one for another. Speaking of the amalgamation of mercury with metals, he deduces that mercury in uniting so strongly with them must have

a very strong *Attractive Force*. Therefore [its] Particles, when mix'd with *Copper* or *Silver*, in as much as they exceed in an Attractive Force, cause the Particles of either Metal to attract one another less; and by that means the Force of Cohesion, which was before in the *Copper* or *Silver* is abated, and grows weaker (ibid., p. 30).

Or again, when Freind explains the fact that salts will dissolve in water but not in alcohol:

because the *Aqueous* Particles are more strongly attracted by the *Saline Corpuscles*, than they are by one another. [Whereas] the Particles of the [alcohol], upon account of the minuteness of their Bulk, attracting one another more strongly, than they do the *Salts*, are not able to break the Cohesion of the Particles of Salt (ibid., p. 82).

It is difficult to believe that Newton's very effective use in a similar way of the concept of differential attraction (or affinity) in Query 31 was wholly unknown to Freind; unlike him, however, Freind did not employ it to explain the precipitation of substances out of solution.

Although Freind made no reference to *Opticks* throughout the *Chymical Lectures*, which were printed five years later, presumably because the lectures had been prepared before 1704 and were never revised, it can hardly be doubted that he was informed of Newton's extension of the principle of attraction to chemistry by John Keill or David Gregory, for the latter's private memoranda indicate that Newton's ideas were in circulation among his friends before they were committed to print in *Opticks* (Hiscock 1937). Freind's acrimonious rejoinder to the anti-Newtonian, hostile review of the Latin version of the lectures (perhaps from the pen of Leibniz, and printed in the *Acta Eruditorum* in 1710), which was added to the English text of Freind's work in 1712, makes his own commitment to Newton's method and Newton's philosophy completely clear.

Peter Shaw

Further evidence of the powerful effect of the Queries in *Opticks* upon the development of chemical speculation in Britain may be found in the translation (1741) by the physician Peter Shaw of Herman Boerhaave's *Elementa Chimiae*, a large work reprinted in 1753. Shaw added a large commentary and not a few purported corrections to his author in footnotes, many of which refer to the Queries, and especially Query 31. Shaw took so exaggerated a view of the science he had adopted that he declared chemistry to be 'in its extent, scarce less than the whole of natural philosophy' and that, in particular, 'It is by means of chemistry, that Sir *Isaac Newton* has made a great part of his discoveries in natural philosophy; and that curious set of queries, which we find at the end of his optics are [*sic*] almost wholly chemical.' Shaw's absurd distortions mark the acme of the British emphasis on these celebrated Queries, to the neglect of the substantive scientific content of *Opticks*. In his various notes to Boerhaave Shaw also quotes Newton on the explosion of gunpowder, the principle of chemical attraction, the heat of reaction, the conversion of matter into light and light into matter, the nature of fire and its relation to light, the action of bodies in attracting light, the absorption of light by black bodies, flame, the generation of airs by chemical reactions, the solution of salts as explained by attraction, and atoms. One of the longest of his notes summarizes the Newtonian doctrine of the diverse refrangibility of light, the relation between reflection and refraction, the 'fits' of easy reflection and easy transmission, and the 'sides' of the rays accounting for double refraction (Shaw 1753, pp. 363–4).

Herman Boerhaave

For Peter Shaw as for John Freind and Stephen Hales *Opticks* was the rich source of their most important ideas about the nature and behaviour of matter, and especially about the fundamental agents of phenomena, inter-corpuscular forces. Indeed, though to a less emphatic extent (for Robert Boyle was in his case a more constant fount of inspiration), the great Herman Boerhaave of Leiden himself also respected Newton as an authority in chemistry, making one or two allusions to *Optice* on his own account; thus,

it would be plain to any reader [of Shaw's translation] that Boerhaave particularly esteemed Newton for his contributions to the "corpuscular philosophy", his discourses concerning light and colour, and his speculations on the aether.

Even though Boerhaave's ideas of fire and light were far apart from Newton's, the former found occasion when dealing with this subject to elaborate upon the latter's mental abilities, and our

admiration, when, from these instances, we see what powers the Creator has given to the human mind; whereby, when duly cultivated, we can discover the laws he established in framing the world (Cohen 1956, pp. 229, 233).

Having a strong sense of the independence of the chemical tradition and theory, Boerhaave could never subscribe wholeheartedly (as the British writers did) to chemistry's subjection to the physical concept of mechanical force, but he was eclectic enough to appreciate Newton's contributions to the experimental, corpuscular treatment of chemical phenomena of which (rightly) he regarded Boyle as the chief progenitor.

It is of course obvious that the British writers discussed in this chapter were only too eager to subscribe to Newtonian doctrines, in order that Newton's name might add lustre to their expositions. By 1710 or thereabouts, when Newton was firmly in the saddle at the Royal Society, responding vigorously to the Leibnizian challenge, and despite his age showing no lessening of his intellectual powers (though he had given up mathematics!), the 'Newtonian bandwagon' was well worth climbing upon. But it cannot be doubted either that there was a great intrinsic force in the free-ranging and suggestive passages of the Queries, pointing the road to theoretical ideas far richer and more precise than those of Boyle, and uniting in a tighter theoretical framework—not despairing even of the rigour of mathematics, as Freind and others sought to demonstrate—the laws of physics and the phenomena that formed the subject of other experimental sciences: chemistry, physiology, even medicine. Newton's speculations in *Opticks* opened up wide vistas of creative research.

Misinterpretation by the Newtonians

With hindsight, one sees a great difference between Newton and those lesser mortals, his successors. Newton started from a solid and verifiable theory of mechanics, mathematically developed, and in optics from an equally solid experimental base. Though we are now aware that Newton's mind from youth onwards ventured far in both physical and philosophical speculations of which (until past his mature years) he endeavoured to keep the world ignorant, he made no overt use of them in his substantive scientific work. The quality and authority of this work were independent of his success or failure in wider speculations, and there were groups (like the French Academicians in relation to *Opticks*) to whom such speculative physical ideas as Newton favoured were intolerable, who nevertheless were compelled by objective evidence to admit the accuracy of Newton's substantive scientific work. Following this prudent policy—which after all observes the distinction drawn by modern philosophers between *discovery* and *demonstration*—Newton carefully distinguished the affirmations in the text of *Opticks* which he believed to be well-founded and virtually unimpugnable from the speculative content of the Queries.

His successors obliterated this distinction at their own risk, and in so far as they alleged that Newtonian substantive science depended upon the deeper 'truths' of the Queries, they betrayed Newton's own methodological principles. In proclaiming that their own writings flourished upon the assurance of the truth of concepts that Newton had labelled as merely conjectural, they renounced in advance the possibility of developing experimental sciences like chemistry and physiology along truly independent lines, starting from analysis of, and thought about, their respective phenomena. Hales was outstanding among them not because he was the most opiniated Newtonian, but because he demonstrated a number of new experimental truths. Within less than a century Hales's Newtonian theories of physiology were to vanish, just as Freind's Newtonian chemistry vanished; but physiologists even today remember Hales's experiments on sap and blood. In the long run the attempts of the Newtonians to reduce all systematic scientific inquiry to the discovery of theories of atoms and forces, for all the sanction given to their example by Newton himself, had to be abandoned.

The effective tradition of chemical atomism, the atomism of the nineteenth century, was created by John Dalton in a quite different mould (though he too had been a student of the Queries):

[This] theory was profoundly antiphysicalist and anti-Newtonian in its rejection of the unity of matter, and its dismissal of short-range forces. The triumphs of nineteenth century chemistry were thus built upon no reductionist foundation, but rather achieved in isolation from the newly emerging science of physics (Thackray 1970, p. 279).

Nevertheless, till Dalton put chemistry upon a new conceptual foundation, the Newtonian 'chemistry of forces' conditioned the thought of both philosophers and chemists, men as dissimilar as Boscovic, Lavoisier, and Priestley. The work of Keill and Freind had been presented to the Continent by an anonymous translator in a *Nouveau Cours de Chymie suivant les principes de Newton & de Stahl* (1723, 1737). And it is a curious paradox that the speculative chemical theory of atomic mechanics, derived in large part from *Opticks*, was replaced by the 'new chemistry', the chemistry of gases, whose distinctive origins may be traced back (as we have seen) to the writings of that committed Newtonian, Stephen Hales.

Optics in Britain after Newton

In the first volume of his *History . . . of Vision, Light and Colours* (1772) Joseph Priestley wrote:

The bulk of mankind, I may perhaps add of philosophers too, have a notion, that little or nothing has been done, on the subject of vision, light, and colours since the time of Sir Isaac Newton, imperfect as he left many of his experiments . . .

Readers, he continued, if surprised at the length of his history after Newton, would find in it pleasing entertainment; they

will find it a copious field, abounding not with trifling observations and frivolous minutiae, but with real and important discoveries, respecting the most fundamental principles of light, and of bodies respecting light (Priestley 1772, p. 355).

Setting aside the confirmation by James Bradley of Ole Roemer's determination of the speed of light—a discovery rather astronomical than optical—very little of the 'pleasing entertainment' foreseen by Priestley related to the quarter-century following Newton's death. After the need to defend it had passed, Newton's greatness had a stultifying effect on optics in Britain. The science stimulated almost no one after Desaguliers to authorship in the *Philosophical Transactions*, although accounts of Newton's work were widely diffused in a spate of compendious accounts— such as those of Worster (1722), Pemberton (1728), Rowning (1734, 1738), and Maclaurin (1968 [1748]). The more interesting work on the

Continent also either had no relation to light and colour or to any other optical question of interest to Newton (like Pierre Bouguer's development of photometry) or was actually opposed to it (like Leonhard Euler's insistent development of the wave-theory). The best British piece of work in this field was John Dollond's fabrication of an achromatic object-glass, but this was not until 1758 and, in spirit if not to the letter, it too seems to run counter to the Newtonian tradition (of which Dollond himself was, however, a faithful follower).

Smith's Opticks

As already mentioned, the chief early exemplar of this tradition was Robert Smith's *Compleat System of Opticks* (1738). Smith, a relative of Newton's editor Roger Cotes, professor of astronomy at Cambridge, Master of Trinity College, could hardly have been more firmly embedded in it. Yet it is at once obvious upon opening his large volumes that like his fellow-expositors Robert Smith was a revisionist. In part he was so because his purpose was different from Newton's. Just as the *Principia* is far from being a systematic textbook of rational and celestial mechanics, but is rather, and necessarily so, a statement of investigations into a series of particular problems as perceived at a certain point in time, so even more emphatically is *Opticks*. A great deal of what had passed under this label: geometrical optics, vision and the formation of images by lenses and mirrors, the eye, optical illusions, not to say the recent topic of the operation of optical instruments—such themes were largely omitted by Newton. Like the *Principia*, *Opticks* became a great growth from a small seed. For the former book, the seed was the successful mathematical demonstration of the force in an elliptical orbit. For the latter, the seed was Newton's first experience of looking through a prism. As the *Principia* grew in mathematical stature, *Opticks* grew in experimental stature. From his first crude but acute observations of the distortions of coloured lines seen through a prism, Newton went on swiftly and inexorably to those very complex experiments with multiple prisms described in Book I of *Opticks* (not least his delicate experiments on internal reflection and transmission) and the even more remarkably exact measurements of 'Newton's rings'. His manipulations of prisms and lenses were the first really delicate operations in the history of physics; without them, and the extraordinary skill in measuring and reasoning whereby Newton could ascertain the thickness of invisible films to the thousandth part of an inch, the precision of Newton's theory of auxiliary waves (or "fits") and of the surface colours of bodies could not have been attained—indeed, there could have been no quantitative wave-theory at all.

Unlike Newton, Robert Smith proposed to write a textbook. How greatly matters had changed in two generations is evident from the manner in

which, at the very first, Smith boldly enunciated what Newton had, before
the 1706 Queries, striven to keep in the shadows, the nature of light:

Whoever has considered what a number of properties and effects of light are exactly
similar to the properties and effects of bodies of a sensible bulk, will find it difficult
to conceive that light is anything else but very small and distinct particles of matter:
which being incessantly thrown out from shining substances, and every way
dispersed by reflection from all others, do impress upon our organs of seeing that
peculiar motion, which is requisite to excite in our minds the sensation of light.

After citing *Opticks*, Query 29, as authority for his assertion of the emission
or particle theory of light, Smith composed 70 pages without further
significant reference to the book; in a textbook he had to satisfy readers on
many topics that Newton could afford to ignore. With Chaper VI he takes
up the theory of colour, rather curiously adopting Newton's personal
pronoun without quotation marks: 'I placed a glass prism . . . I turned the
prism slowly . . .'. This chaper and the two following it are summaries of
Opticks, here reduced to 29 pages. Not surprisingly, the pedagogue re-
arranges the original into a simpler presentation and renders firmly positive
what was hesitant in it. After describing Newton's diffraction experiments
with a knife-blade (*Opticks*, Book III (1952), pp. 325–35) as evidence of
the action of matter upon light at a distance, Smith comments:

Our author has made it appear from these and some other experiments that bodies
act upon light in some circumstances by an attractive and in others by a repulsive
power . . . (Smith 1738, p. 88).

A brief account of the diffraction experiments made with a hair (*Opticks*
(1952), pp. 318–25) is followed by the further explanation:

And of these attractive and repulsive powers he [Newton] declares his sentiments
more fully in these words: Since metals dissolved in acids attract but a small quantity
of the acid, their attractive force can reach but to a small distance from them. And
as in algebra where affirmative quantities vanish and cease there negative ones
begin, so in mechanicks where attraction ceases there a repulsive virtue ought to
succeed. And that there is such a virtue seems to follow from the reflections and
inflections of the rays of light (Smith 1738, pp. 88–9; *Opticks* (1952), p. 395).

Smith continues with some further lines from Query 31, without giving
his readers any notice that he has moved without a break from the main text
to the Queries. With similar ingenuity he welds together various scattered
hints in *Opticks* to form a coherent theory of the optical force, which is far
more powerful than that of gravity, and decreases at a rate (unknown)
higher than the inverse square of the distance. Moreover,

According to this theory nothing more is requisite for producing all the variety of
colours and degrees of refrangibility, than that the rays of light be bodies of different
sizes; the least of which may make violet, the weakest and darkest of colours, and
be more easily diverted by refracting surfaces from its right course . . .

whereas in reflection, by contrast, light-particles of all magnitudes turn through the same angle, so that there is no segregation by colour or mass. (Smith does not apply this logic to the critical angle.)

Thus says our author will nature be very comfortable to herself, in performing all the great motions of the heavenly bodies by the attraction of gravity, which intercedes [comes between, i.e. links] those bodies, and almost all the small ones of their particles by some other attractive and repelling powers which intercede the particles (Smith 1738, pp. 92, 93).

Robert Smith compressed the whole of Book II into a mere five pages, with the total loss of all Newton's careful work in measuring the coloured (interference) rings, and of his suggestions about the sizes of the corpuscles forming the surfaces of bodies, derived from those measurements. His summary is bare and general. The whole of the original 1675 "Hypothesis" is reduced to a single bald and unintelligible sentence:

the origin of the different coloured rings in the open air [that is, when formed by white light] is manifest: namely, that the air between the glasses, according to its various thicknesses, is disposed in some places to reflect and in others to transmit the light of any one colour; and in the same place to reflect that of one colour where it transmits that of another.

Which is as much as to say that matters are so arranged that in thin films the coloured rings appear.

Smith's is a highly competent textbook. It contained some useful prescriptions in practical optics. Its geometrical demonstrations were sound, though no references seems to be made to the more highly mathematical content of the Optical Lectures. But Smith evidently felt it inappropriate or unnecessary to lay before students the more speculative of Newton's ideas about light, or even to make clear the entire dependence of Book II of *Opticks*, in its theoretical explanation of the phenomena discovered, upon an auxiliary wave-theory. By no means all the richness of *Opticks* was captured by Smith in fulfilling his own more limited purposes.

§2. The fate of *Opticks* in Europe

Newton and the Academy of Sciences

Newton's scientific writings made a poor first impression upon the world of learning across the Channel (Brunet 1926). In the last year of the seventeenth century, when a reorganization of the Académie Royale des Sciences in Paris was taking place, it was decided to appoint besides the regular members eight *Associés Étrangers*. Of these, Leibniz was the first to be chosen, Newton the last—or so it was until Vincenzo Viviani was added as a ninth. If the record made by Newton's nephew-in-law, John Conduitt, is true—that Newton had declined the offer of a pension as a full Academician—then he was indeed intended a high honour. Perhaps the incident inspired Voltaire to write (addressing the dead Louis XIV in the Epistle Dedicatory to *Zaire*):

> Et quelque forte pension
> Vous aurait pris le grand Newton,
> Si Newton avait pu se prendre.

We can be sure that whatever the precise degree of merit assigned to Newton by the French Crown and its academicians, they would have regarded Newton as a *mathematician*. There is a curious paradox in this, because virtually nothing of Newton's highly original mathematical work had yet been published; what had been published—the dynamical philosophy of the *Principia* expressed in near-orthodox geometry and the sketches of his optical investigations—had as yet been universally rejected by the Continental mathematicians. Newton himself attached so little importance to his election as *Associé Étranger* that he accorded it no acknowledgement, and ignored the Académie completely for many years. We may be confident that he would have disowned any responsibilities associated with the honour intended him with the plea that he was a servant of the English Crown, and had no leisure to pursue natural philosophy.

The Royal Society and the Academy

It is extraordinarily difficult to realize the extent to which Britain was still in the late seventeenth century a remote offshore island of whose indigenous inhabitants, uncouth, ill-mannered, and so ill-educated that even in Latin their speech was incomprehensible, the rare European traveller wrote much as the nineteenth-century voyager wrote of the Tahitian or the Eskimo. True, a few young Britons of good family spent months acquiring taste and culture in Europe, and others with fewer resources went to acquire a hasty medical degree at Angers or Leiden; their journeys only flattered the Europeans' sense that on all questions of art or music, philosophy, and learning, the British were apprentices still. William Harvey had found his great anatomical discovery in Padua, Christopher Wren his urbane architecture in Paris. Francis Bacon was the sole British hero of the century endowed with truly individual merit. The esteem accorded to the Royal Society was not a little due to the belief that it was Baconian in its aims: proceeding according to a fact-gathering plan that was modest, useful, and suited to the capacities of an industrious, tough, but not very sophisticated people. The French themselves, though conscious of the strength of their philosophical tradition and its schools, pursued in their Academy a programme that was in part Baconian. Indeed, the Académie Royale des

Sciences and the Royal Society had many ideas and ambitions in common, and maintained a close if largely unofficial exchange of inspiration and information, in which (for example) Newton's telescopes and Newton's experiments figured. In the 1670s these two scientific societies were the only major ones active in Europe, and as equals they were also to some extent rivals. Only they enjoyed an established institutional basis and royal patronage—however much a broken reed the latter proved to be in England. Only they were conducting organized research. Only in the French and English languages were widely-circulated scientific journals published, satisfying a wide variety of interests. In general, events on the intellectual scene in France were far better known in Britain than those in other countries, though the same was not reciprocally true of the French. An important element in all aspects of British intellectual and artistic life at this time was therefore a kind of running skirmish with the French—how far were their trends to be emulated in Britain? In science, the core of this skirmish during Newton's early years was the plausibility of Cartesianism (that is, one kind of debate between rationalism and experimentalism, among other things), while in the early eighteenth century the question became the plausibility of Newtonianism.

Travellers sought out Newton

Though perhaps few Europeans came to England in search of intellectual stimulation, for a number of those who braved English speech, roads, and inns the Royal Society was an important objective. It was the chief interest in London of Christiaan Huygens, who had met some of its founders as fugitives from the English Revolution. The Duke of Tuscany was entertained by the Society in the course of the Grandest of Tours. But the majority of early foreign Fellows never actually visited the Society. However, when Newton with his already great reputation became President, a host of learned travellers came to London in the hope of meeting him, and Newton gratified many by procuring their election to the Royal Society. He had sufficient charm and address to win over even those foreigners who came, like the Abbé Conti, with a bias against him; and where Newton's intelligence failed (Voltaire wrote wickedly) the bright eyes of Catherine Barton, his half-niece and hostess, were sure to prevail. So far as the French were concerned, war forbade such visits between 1702 and 1714.

The ascendancy of Descartes

Under Louis XIV, Paris was the pivot of Europe, French the language of civilization from St Petersburg to Madrid. The moment at which Newton published his "New Theory of Light and Colours" coincided with the zenith of Cartesianism; this was the time of the publication of Jacques Rohault's *Traité de Physique*, and of the introduction of Cartesian philosophy to the Dutch and German universities. Not that Descartes's philosophy lacked critics: there were academic conservatives, who met with some success in banning Descartes's writings; there were atomists who opposed Descartes's theory of matter, the essence of his science; there were theologians who regarded Descartes as a proponent of atheism; there were alchemists and other esoteric authors who took a different view of Nature altogether; there were Baconians who complained of the strong element of speculation in Descartes's science. And there were mathematicians who agreed that Descartes's methodology and philosophy were correct in principle, but lacked mathematical validification, except in optics.

Nevertheless, though there were critics of Descartes in the Académie Royale des Sciences and Baconians in French provincial learned Societies, the voice of Descartes had become during the last third of the seventeenth century the preponderant voice in natural philosophy, and so wherever the French cultural writ ran. In particular, though the mathematician Christiaan Huygens regarded Descartes as the author of scientific romances, he also believed that the basic philosophical principles underlying his mechanistic explanations of phenomena were correct. The ultimate physical reality consisted, he thought, of particles in motion. Phenomena resulted from the changed groupings of the particles and alterations in their motion, which could only be caused by the mutual impact of one upon another. Since it seemed absurd to him that one minute part of matter should affect another save by direct contact, there could be no 'action at a distance' by attraction or repulsion. The goals of natural philosophy were (1) to establish the laws of the transfer of motion in mathematical terms; and (2) to account for what happens in Nature by applying these laws to the particles of matter, also mathematically. Since the particles had not yet been isolated or investigated by experiment, and since the properties of particular kinds of them could only be inferred from large-scale phenomena, it was necessary to make hypotheses about them, in the manner of Descartes; but such hypotheses ought to be mathematical.

Huygens and optics

In actual fact, Huygens's early successes in science—his discoveries of the nature of Saturn's ring and of the first satellite of this planet, his successful study of the motion of the pendulum and his successful application of it to time-keeping—had little relevance to such a programme as this. And while Huygens was the leading light of the Académie Royale des Sciences during its early years, its members engaged in many equally unprogrammatic inquiries into astronomy, anatomy, chemistry, and mechanics. There is some irony in the fact that this body, rather than the 'Baconian' (but less well-endowed) Royal Society, sent out global expeditions of terrestrial enquiry. By the late 1660s, however, Huygens had developed a neo-Cartesian theory of light exemplifying his ideals. Postulating, like Descartes, a lumeniferous aether, he gave it instead of Descartes's motion of translation a motion of vibration, or waves. He was able to demonstrate geometrically that if the beam of light were a train of waves, it would satisfy the laws of reflection and refraction. After he had experimented with a piece of calcite received from Bartholin he worked out a geometrical process, related to a supposed structure of the crystal, whereby the extraordinary as well as the ordinary refracted ray could be generated, but he could not account for the phenomena of polarization which he discovered (as Newton's hypothesis did), nor did he have anything to say about interference and diffraction.

The posthumous publication of Huygens's work on dioptrics came too late to interest Newton.

Huygens was not very taken with Newton's miniature reflecting telescope—his own attempt to duplicate Newton's instrument on a larger scale failed, like those of the London artisans—nor was he greatly impressed by the discovery of dispersion and the unequal refrangibility of light. Well and good, Newton had elucidated a new fact of optics, but he had contributed nothing to an account of what light is and how its phenomena arise from its nature:

What you have put in your last Journals [he wrote to Oldenburg] from Mr Newton, confirms still further his theory of colours. Nevertheless, the matter could very well be otherwise, and it seems to me that he ought to content himself if what he has put forward is received as a very likely hypothesis. The more so since if it were true that the rays of light were, by their origin, some red, others blue, etc., there would still remain the great difficulty of explaining by mechanical physics what this diversity of colours consists of (Hall and Hall 1965–86, IX, pp. 247–9).

Newton's claim that light contained elements was barely intelligible to Huygens, an English aberration; as well say that motion has elements, since it was so clear that light must be a motion, and a very swift one. Colour as such did not interest him, nor did he repeat Newton's experiments. It is of course imaginable that Huygens was one of those men whose sense of colour is defective (an obvious physiological fact not to be discovered for another century). If ever he knew of Newton's suggestion (as *advocatus diaboli*) that colour might be a function of frequency of vibration, so easily assimilable into his own mechanical theory, he paid no attention to it.

The religious Orders

If Huygens represented the considerable group of mathematicians and experimenters in continental Europe who carried Descartes's natural philosophy further along progressive lines, teachers of the religious Orders, especially in Italy and the Iberian peninsula, opposed all change. There were, however, notable exceptions among them, especially among the mathematicians; in Italy and in France there were distinguished priests who strove for freedom to discuss the new ideas about the world, or who while defending the traditional positions did useful work in the mathematical sciences. The Society of Jesus, with its major role in education, whose authors still thought it important to avow the agreement of their texts with the writings of St Thomas Aquinas, was only moving very slowly through the second half of the seventeenth century towards acceptance of a purified Cartesian science. The English Jesuits at Liège who criticized Newton so persistently were still maintaining Aristotelian notions about light being a quality and colour an effect caused by the strength or weakness of this quality. Nevertheless the Jesuits published creditable work in mathematics and astronomy; they agreed that statements about Nature should correspond with experience or experiment, and indeed the disagreement of the Liègeois with Newton arose from conflicting matters of fact (as they saw them).

In Paris, Ignace Gaston Pardies (1636–73) of the Collège de Clermont (or Louis-le-Grand) was the most distinguished Jesuit mathematician. Although he gracefully withdrew criticism of Newton's assertion of the spectrum's elongation, it is clear that his ideas about light were wholly different from Newton's. Influenced by F. M. Grimaldi SJ and Robert Hooke, Pardies formulated a vibration theory in which black and white were taken to be elemental 'colours', all (other) colours being shades of these, corresponding to the harmony of the vibrations. Since Pardies died too soon to perfect a treatise on optics he had in preparation his ideas were published in *Optique divisée en trois livres* (1682) by Pierre Ango SJ. In Huygens's opinion this priest spoiled Pardies's manuscript (which he had read).

Among the experimenters in the Académie Royale des Sciences the most esteemed was a Benedictine prior appointed to that body in 1668, Edmé Mariotte. His *Traité de la nature des couleurs* (1681) was communicated to the Académie in 1679, and had been in preparation for some years before. In this puzzling treatise (Acloque 1986; Hall 1986; Guerlac 1981, pp. 98–100) Mariotte expressed his dissatisfaction with such major predecessors in optics as Descartes, Grimaldi, and Newton. He failed to confirm Grimaldi's experiment, and so rejected his concept of diffraction; he failed to confirm Newton's crucial experiment, and so rejected his concept of the segregation of colours in the spectrum by their discrete refrangibility; this he called an 'hypothèse fort surprennante'. In (as it seems) a rather careless repetition of Newton's work as described in the 1672 paper Mariotte separated violet light by means of a hole in a diaphragm, then refracting this violet ray a second time and letting it fall upon a screen, he found 'du rouge et du jaune dans la convexité de la courbure'. Hence, he declared, Newton was mistaken, because light is always capable of fresh modification by refraction. To posterity, it seems strange that this refutation based upon a single experimental trial stood unchallenged for so long, the more so because what Mariotte had to offer by way of a theory of light and colour was vague and incoherent, a fact which 'semblerait devoire rendre ambigu tout jugement général que l'on voudrait porter sur cet auteur à partir de l'examen de son ouvrage dans le domaine de l'optique' (Acloque 1986, p. 153).

No early welcome to Newton's "New Theory of Light and Colours" accorded by foreign readers of the *Philosophical Transactions* has been recorded, though they were not few in number. Those writers who, like Jacques Rohault, developed orthodox Cartesian science inevitably had nothing to say about it. Indeed, so far as France was concerned, after Huygens's return to his own country in 1683 and Mariotte's death in 1684 no one was actively interested in optics until after the publication of Newton's book in 1704.

The Oratory: Nicolas Malebranche

By this time the intellectual situation in France was much altered. The liveliest scientific—or one should rather say philosophical and mathematical —group in France now clustered about Nicolas Malebranche, a priest of the Oratory (Robinet 1961). He and his leading followers (the Marquis de L'Hospital, Charles-René Reyneau, Pierre Varignon, Joseph Sauveur, Pierre Rémond de Montmort, and others) became members of the Académie Royale des Sciences at its reorganization in 1699. It was a group moving towards innovation in two ways. In the first place, it had adopted from about 1690 onwards the new mathematics of Leibniz, the differential and integral calculus. On the former branch the Marquis de L'Hospital published the first textbook in 1696, *L'Analyse des infiniment petits*. This work in fact (but without saying so) followed closely the written teaching provided for the Marquis by the Swiss mathematician Johann Bernoulli, with whom the Marquis had made a private bargain that (in return for certain rewards) Bernoulli would share the fruits of his very great abilities with the Marquis alone. Bernoulli was the foremost mathematician of his generation (considerably younger than Newton), not excepting his brother Jacques, from whom Johann had gained his introduction to the Leibnizian calculus, or even Leibniz himself. He and the Bernoullis became close allies and frequent correspondents; Leibniz's freindship with Johann—who always recognized Leibniz as master—lasted through nearly twenty years until Leibniz's death in 1716. The French group could not have had a better instructor to bring them to the forefront of the subject; but, as it happened, though several of the French (including Malebranche himself) were competent students of mathematics, none was absolutely of the first rank.

The other way in which the Malebranchists broke away from the earlier generations of the Académie was in their attitude to Descartes. Here their position was analogous to that of Huygens, and indeed of Leibniz, both of whom like the Malebranchists may be classed as neo-Cartesians: that is, while differing from Descartes on many points of detail, they believed his concept of the mechanical explanation of phenomena to be correct. At heart, they were rationalists rather than experimentalists. As with Huygens in optics, and both Huygens and Leibniz in mechanics, Malebranche's solution to many problems of metaphysics and natural science rejected Descartes's reasoning in preference for an independent line. Notably (in the present context) Malebranche's explanation of the phenomena of light in the successive editions of *La recherche de la verité* from 1672 onwards demonstrated considerable originality. He preferred to postulate an aether of dynamically elastic particles in place of the hard particles of Descartes, and like Hooke and Huygens he saw the transmission of light as a vibratory motion of this elastic aether.

Malebranche's later theory of light

In the sixth edition (1712) of *La recherche de la verité* Malebranche, replacing the exposition of light he had favoured for more than ten years, put forward a distinctly 'Newtonian' type of vibrational hypothesis; it is indeed identical with that suggested as conceivable by Newton in his "Hypothesis" of 1675 (unknown to Malebranche, of course). To a given degree of rapidity of the vibration (that is, frequency) 'que je ne crois pas qu'on puisse déterminer exactement' corresponds, he thinks, each of the simple, homogeneous or primitive colours, red, yellow, blue, and so on. If the light contains vibrations of a variety of rapidities composite colours result, or else whiteness:

. . . white which is the most compounded of all. I say that white is the most compounded of all because it is compounded of the sum of the vibrations, differing in frequency, that each different particle of the flame produces in the aether. Because the universe is full and infinitely compressed each ray preserves throughout its length the same frequency of vibration as the little particle of the flame that produced it. And because the particles of the flame have diverse motions, the rays forming the colours are necessarily vibrating differently and undergo different refractions. On this one should consult the experiments to be found in the excellent work of Mr Newton.

Evidently, Malebranche has here furnished a hypothesis about the origin of the variety of motion in white light, about which Newton had been silent. He continues with an analogy from sound familiar to Newton:

I believe that I have clearly proved that the *different colours* consist only in the different *frequency* of the vibrations of the pressure in the aether, just as the *different tones* in music arise only from the *different frequency* of the vibrations of the coarser air, as experiment teaches us, whose vibrations also intersect without annihilating each other.

Malebranche was, besides, aware of Newton's comparison between the musical and the optical 'octave' (Malebranche 1712, pp. 330, 335, 361).

Malebranche reads Optice

Accordingly, before 1712 Malebranche had read *Opticks* or *Optice*, was convinced that Newton's experiments were sound and those of Mariotte unsound, and had logically so modified his own theory of light that it accommodated the new information. The positivist exposition of *Opticks* enabled him to do so. Malebranche by no means shared Newton's idea of the investigation of Nature, nor his notions of the plenum and attractive force.

In a letter of 1707—indicating an interest in *Optice* soon after its publication—Malebranche summarized his views neatly:

Although Mr Newton is no physicist his book is very curious and very useful to those possessing sound physical principles. He is moreover an excellent geometer. All my views on the properties of light adapt to his experiments (Robinet 1961, pp. 771–2).

At so early a date this was as much an invasion of French territory as the Newtonian forces had been able to achieve.

Geoffroy's translation of Opticks

While we may presume Malebranche's own reading of Newton's text to have depended upon the Latin translation, his introduction to it was based upon the English original. For he had attended meetings of the Académie Royale des Sciences at which (in August 1706 and January 1707) Étienne-François Geoffroy had read his own partial translation, or rather précis in French, of *Opticks*. Geoffroy, a visitor to London in 1698, when he was elected a Fellow of the Royal Society, was competent in the English tongue. He had become a correspondent of Hans Sloane, then Secretary of the Royal Society, later Newton's successor as President. Like Newton also, Sloane was to become an *Associé Étranger* of the Académie Royale in 1709. Geoffroy had received his copy of *Opticks* as a gift from Sloane, but not until late in 1705 (the two countries were at war!). Altogether, the reading of Geoffroy's manuscript occupied ten sessions of the Académie spread over ten months; Malebranche was not present at all of these, but we know of other auditors who, like him, were to play a part in effecting the recognition of Newton's optical discoveries in France (Cohen 1964).

How had Malebranche and his friends managed to put aside Mariotte's confutation of Newton's 1672 paper? A final vindication of Newton would rest, it seems, on a successful repetition of his experiments. Meanwhile, the quantity, consistency, and evident sincerity of Newton's testimony in *Opticks* was enough to put Mariotte in the shade, despite the fact that about this time support was given to him by his former colleague and friend, Philippe de La Hire. Of this intervention by a now elderly mathematician we know only from the correspondence of Leibniz, who was far from Paris and relied on an unknown French correspondent. He passed on to Johann Bernoulli the news that La Hire claimed to have been present when Mariotte long ago investigated with great care the changes of colour that light undergoes when it is refracted, with a result unfavourable to Newton. Leibniz wished

that in the Académie Royale accurate experiments about this matter were undertaken, for it is one of great importance . . . I am of opinion that if these experiments on colours were undertaken, many points would be met with that have as yet remained undiscovered by either Newton or Mariotte. He who pursues this business will have performed no inglorious task (Leibniz—Bernoulli 1745, II, p. 213, 25 April 1709).

In a later letter (15 October 1710, ibid., p. 234) Leibniz again reported that the members of the Académie Royale des Sciences were giving their support to Mariotte's observations; but, despite Leibniz's pressure for reliable experiments, Fontenelle (the Secretary of the Académie) would do nothing because of other business: 'as though they could do anything more useful than to establish principles of great moment!'

Newton's experiments confirmed (1716)

While the Académie was inert the young Malebranchists had confirmed Newton's accounts, especially of the crucial experiment. The story is somewhat complex, but it appears that a disciple of Malebranche, J. J. Dortous de Mairan, was led from his master's adoption of the Newtonian principle of segregation to study *Optice* and then to repeat privately some experiments in 1716 (Guerlac 1981, pp. 113–15). It is certain from his published work that Mairan was familiar with the book by this time: a brief but correct aside about Newton's theory was inserted into his *Dissertation sur la cause de la lumière des phosphores et des noctiluques* (Bordeaux, 1717) with the comment:

the ingenious experiments which he used to prove it, could serve by themselves to immortalize a name less celebrated than his (Guerlac 1981, p. 115).

This order of events makes it clear that Malebranche's change of opinion in no way depended upon the testimony of the senses. An authenticated, open submission of Newton's experimental claims to a test was still to be deferred for a few more years, in France.

The Germans support Newton's experiments

From what has been said of the close connection between the Malebranchists and Leibniz's mathematical circle in Germany, in which Johann Bernoulli was next senior to Leibniz himself, it will be quite evident that if Leibniz and his friends had firmly taken a position hostile to Newton as regards the accuracy of his optical experiments, they might have influenced the French against him. But in fact, after some hesitation, they supported Newton. Despite their annoyance at Newton's claim for priority in the discovery of the differential calculus, their astonished rejection of his supposed philosophy of 'attraction', and the many mathematical errors they found in the *Principia*, they did not fail to recognize his first-class abilities as an experimenter and a mathematician. Johann Bernoulli had replied to Leibniz's news about Philippe de La Hire's intervention on behalf of Mariotte:

I *fear* that this may detract from Newton's very elegant theory about the colours of the rays [of light] (Leibniz – Bernoulli 1745, II, p. 216, my italics).

A few months later still (on 10 December 1710) he admitted that

about the non-mutability I fully agree with Newton, having made my own observations on the point, which I would send you if they did not exceed the bounds of a letter, and I think I can even show, where Mariotte was mistaken when asserting the contrary. That is, as can easily happen to the observer unless he proceeds with great care, by taking another ray for that whose colour is supposed to be changed (ibid., p. 242).

Similarly Leibniz, after at first being scarcely able to 'believe that Newton could have fallen down on a matter so capital, which he had gone into so carefully', at a later date in their correspondence assured Bernoulli (on 10 February 1711):

I too think Newton's experiments are more to be trusted, because he repeated them so often through many years, even though La Hire adds his testimony to Mariotte (whose diligence is not to be despised) (ibid., p. 245).

Such an opinion could only have rested upon a careful study of *Opticks*. In January 1704 Leibniz had told Bernoulli that he was glad to learn of the coming publication of Newton's theory of colours, while a year later the book had reached his desk:

Newton's work on colours seems profound, but I have not yet been able to examine whether, by its means, we may have some hope of explaining the fixed colours, as they are called.

Reviews of Optice

When a copy of *Optice* also reached Leibniz, somewhat more quickly than the original edition had done, he passed it on to Bernoulli along with two English mathematical books (ibid., pp. 106, 159). Obviously in the German world as in the French *Opticks* had a tremendous effect in turning men's minds to Newtonian ways of understanding things. A long, fair, and capable summary of the book had been published in the influential Leipzig periodical, *Acta Eruditorum*, in February 1706. Accurately reporting Newton's experiments and his deductions from them, this factual analysis is approbatory in tone and makes frequent reference to Newton's repeated appeals to exact experimentation as justifying his ideas; but the review carefully abstains from setting Newton's work in any sort of intellectual context. It may be presumed to have come from Leibniz's own pen or that of the editor of the *Acta*, Otto Mencke.

The French analogue to the *Acta*, the *Journal des Sçavans*, the oldest learned periodical in Europe, took no notice of the English *Opticks*, which in the circumstances is not surprising. Since copies of *Optice* did reach France despite the war it was possible for the journal to consider it, the review appearing in October 1707. It is of twelve pages, of which the first reproduces Newton's "Advertisement" to the reader. His purpose is stated to be, not the application of hypotheses to explain phenomena, but simply to propose properties which have not hitherto been observed, to prove them by experiments and reason, and reveal their consequences. 'To gain this end, our illustrious mathematician uses the method of the geometers.' After describing, fairly enough, what Newton meant by compound, heterogeneous white light and a primitive, homogeneous coloured ray, the review recalls at some length Mariotte's 1681 rebuttal of Newton's experiments; like Leibniz the reviewer would welcome the resolution of the conflict in a matter of experiment between two observers, each with a reputation for accuracy. He then passes on to Newton's preference for the reflecting telescope, its construction, and his accounts of the rainbow and of natural colours. Books II and III of *Optice* are then quickly summarized, with the remark that Newton's conclusions 'confirm our physicist more and more strongly in his belief touching colours'. The review touches lightly upon Newton's theory of "fits" and agrees with him that

it would be a major discovery in physics if, as Mr Newton holds, one could guess from the colour of natural bodies the magnitude of the particles of which [their surfaces] are composed (*Journal des Sçavans*, 38, 137–49).

The remaining portions of the book, its incomplete state, and the addition of the Queries are noted without any indication of their content. Indeed, both this review and that in the *Acta Eruditorum*, perhaps respecting the positivism of Newton's methodological pronouncements, rather than his actual (occasionally incautious) practice, are scrupulous in *not* raising questions about Newton's ideas on the nature of light, or the physical mechanisms underlying the phenomena of refraction and so forth. They give a correct if narrow picture of the book from which the readers of these journals could have gained (no later than the autumn of 1707) a shrewd idea of Newton's principal discovery in optics, and some of its applications, while perhaps gaining little sense of the richness of the work in experiment, in physical theory, and in methodology. The extent of Newton's speculations about the secrets of Nature in the Queries would have quite escaped them.

Newton should be validated

To reach the conclusion that in relation to a single optical experiment (or indeed several) Newton had been right and Mariotte at fault was not to commit oneself to a new physics of light, still less to become a Newtonian. Neither Malebranche, Leibniz, Bernoulli, nor Dortous de Mairan was ever in danger of conversion to 'English' physics. The adoption by the French of Newtonian natural philosophy as a whole was still some way in the future. Even the verification of Newton's experiments in a public manner was still some way ahead; that was followed by the translation of *Opticks* into French, once more in the context of the Malebranchist group.

This later part of the story again begins with Leibniz, who returned to his desire for a final resolution of the important question of experimental fact in dispute between Newton and Mariotte in a review of another work by Samuel Clarke, published in the *Acta Eruditorum* for October 1713; having received no satisfaction from the French side, he in effect now challenged the English to vindicate Newton publicly (Guerlac 1981, p. 117). 'Sir Isaac Newton . . . upon reading what has been cited out of the *Acta Eruditorum*, desired Mr Desaguliers to try himself the Experiment', in public needless to say. So wrote Desaguliers in a *Philosophical Transactions* narrative of his justification of Newton's assertion of long before, against Mariotte (vol. 29, 1715, p. 435), which had taken place early in the summer of 1714, with several Fellows of the Royal Society present. In fact Desaguliers quoted a substantial extract from Leibniz's review in the course of explaining the context of his own trials, which were a complete success. John Theophilus Desaguliers was a practised experimenter. He had learnt from John Keill in Oxford the art of lecturing with experimental illustrations, later becoming (in 1713) a professional teacher of natural philosophy in London. He was well aware of the need to be 'particular in mentioning such things as ought to be avoided in making the Experiments', remarking that 'some Gentlemen abroad [had] complained that they had not found the Experiments answer, for want of sufficient Directions in Sir *Isaac Newton's Opticks*; tho' I had no other Directions than what I found there' (ibid., p. 447). Desaguliers's arrangements for the experiments did, nevertheless, differ in detail from those Newton had described; unlike Newton, Desaguliers was meticulous in describing exactly how Newton's results might be duplicated.

Desaguliers's demonstrations convince the French, 1715

When, in the following year, soon after the Peace of Utrecht, a party of French savants arrived in London Desaguliers was well prepared to satisfy their curiosity about Newtonian optics. The reason for this scientific incursion was an eclipse of the sun in 1715, visible in London but not in Paris. The party consisted of Rémond de Montmort, Claude-Joseph Geoffroy (younger brother of Étienne-François, already mentioned), and Jacques-Eugène d'Allonville, Chevalier de Louville, who was to play an enigmatic role in introducing Newtonian mechanics into France. The Malebranchist connection was strong. Desaguliers in his account recorded the repetition of the experiments for the benefit of the French visitors, and it was mentioned also by Pierre Coste in his introduction to the Paris translation of *Opticks* (1722). Since they were all predisposed in favour of Newton, we may guess that Desaguliers's successful demonstration was completely convincing. 'We can conclude, without serious risk of error, that it was the informal reports of these three academicians, warning of the precautions that must be observed, which led, under more or less official auspices, to successful repetitions of these famous experiments in France' (Guerlac 1981, p. 136).

Successful repetition in France of Newton's optical experiments

The involvement of other figures, men of political importance, in the validation of Newtonian optics is not at all clear, however. Perhaps some benevolent outside force was required to outflank the obstruction within the Académie Royale des Sciences, which Leibniz had found in Fontenelle. These were the Chancellor of France, Henri-François Daguesseau; the Cardinal de Polignac, whose particular keenness was noted; and Jean Truchet (Fr. Sebastien), a Carmelite friar, who was actually the first to repeat the experiment in France, in 1719, at his house in Paris. The witnesses included the Cardinal, the mathematician Pierre Varignon, M. Jaugeon, and M. Jussieu; the Chancellor had to wait two more years, when there was another demonstration by Nicolas Gauger.

Equally mysterious is the origin of the project to re-issue the French text of *Opticks* in Paris. The translation had been made by Pierre Coste (like De Moivre and many more, a Huguenot refugee in London) for publication at Amsterdam in 1720. Pierre Varignon was given the task of examining this printed version critically, and in fact took charge of the edition, entering into correspondence with Newton himself. The Chancellor helped to overcome the difficulties in the progress of the book and received Newton's thanks. The result was a very handsome example of French printing, reproducing Newton's only sketch of the famous 'crucial experiment', drawn expressly for the purpose.

The documents concerned with these various ventures suggest the formation of quite a large group of Frenchmen who had knowledge of Newton's work, and were inclined to accept it as accurate. The inclusion among them of the Cardinal de Polignac is puzzling, for he is otherwise known as a fervent Cartesian. A member of the Académie Royale des Sciences since 1714, Dortous de Mairan in his *Éloge* of the Cardinal wrote:

Newtonianism, as he understood it, had always seemed to him a dangerous doctrine because of its conformity with the fundamental points of the physics of Epicurus.

He also reported that the Cardinal drafted some lines on the optical experiments of Newton for his pro-Cartesian poem, *Anti-Lucrèce*; but there are none in the printed text. Not only did he stimulate Fr. Sebastien to the test, but he met the expenses himself, according to the historian Montucla. Others in the group, like Louville, Levesque de Pouilly, and just possibly C.-R. Reyneau, either accepted the Newtonian theory of universal gravitation already, or at least regarded it with a benevolent neutrality. Others, like Malebranche, Mairan, and perhaps the brothers Geoffroy, continued to support the Cartesian theory of aetherial vortices, but nevertheless accepted the experimental truth of the work described in *Opticks*, though individuals varied in the extent to which they also accepted Newton's interpretation of the experiments. Others again like Varignon and Rémond de Montmort, who were on the best of terms with Newton, were far from dismissing his scientific ideas as nonsense, and indeed recognized many of his mathematical and experimental results as correct; yet it is doubtful whether they could be called 'Newtonians'. Fontenelle was another witness of the Parisian experiments. In natural philosophy he remained faithful to Descartes to the end of his days, but he recognized (in his *Éloge* of Newton) that Mariotte had 'miscarried . . . even he who had such a genius for experiments, and had been so successful on many other subjects'. *Opticks*, he wrote, contained a science 'so perfectly new, that we may henceforward look upon that science as almost wholly owing to this Author.' As a last piece of evidence bearing on the complexity of the situation with respect to Newton in France at this time: Fr. Sebastien, writing (uniquely) to Newton about the success of his test, was careful to stress his rejection of Newton's primary theorem, that light is a heterogeneous mixture of rays!

Obviously Fr. Sebastien did not deny the fact of dispersion that he had himself just confirmed. Like others before, he wished to evade Newton's theorem by postulating a special physical condition, in his case the assumption that the rays coming from the periphery of the sun travel a greater distance, and are therefore weaker than those coming from its centre: the stronger rays have more inertia and are accordingly less refracted than the weaker. He might lament his lack of opportunity to meet Newton face to face, and flatter Newton as 'easily the Prince of all Physicists in our time', but like very nearly all his compatriots he was far from being a Newtonian, if to be a Newtonian was to adopt certain scientific concepts, certain patterns of scientific argument, and certain quite precise theoretical explanations.

Fontenelle and Newton

Bernard le Bovier de Fontenelle, the long-lived, erudite, and energetic Secretary of the Académie Royale des Sciences from 1699, who certainly had no high opinion of the Newtonian style of science, wrote of *Opticks* in his *Éloge* of Newton:

One advantage of this book, equal perhaps to that of the many new discoveries with which it abounds, is that is furnishes us with an excellent model of proceeding in Experimental Philosophy. When we are for prying into Nature, we ought to examine her like Sir Isaac, that is, in as accurate and importunate a manner . . .

Yet again one doubts whether Fontenelle thought experimental philosophy to be the highest form of natural philosophy, for all his handsome compliments. He deserves to speak the last word for France. Thanking Newton for a copy of the new French edition of *Opticks*, presented by the author to the Académie Royale des Sciences, Fontenelle wrote:

you know what the whole of the learned world of Europe thinks of a work so original, so ingenious, so worthy of yourself, but the Académie (which numbers you among its members) is conscious of its merits, and praises it, with a more particular concern.

To this Fontenelle added a private word on his own account, a hint of his generous treatment of Newton in the *Éloge* years later:

Take it kindly, Sir, that to the thanks of the Académie I add my own for the copy which I received from you; I cannot sufficiently express my sense of the honour done me by a man such as yourself, when he remembers me in so obliging a way. Even if you only knew my name I should be proud of the fact and would reckon it an extreme happiness that it had reached you . . . (Letter 1402).

The Secretary of the Académie was now genuinely happy to acclaim Newton as its member. As Henry Guerlac has rightly emphasized, French recognition of Newton's achievement in experimental physics had increased rapidly after 1715, and matured with the publication of the Paris *Optiques*.

But Pierre Brunet in his classical study, *L'Introduction des théories de Newton en France au XVIIIe siècle. Avant 1738* (Paris, 1931), was equally correct in holding that in the realm of mathematical and physical *theory* the transfer of the French allegiance from Descartes to Newton had scarcely begun by 1720. Before this date we have no evidence to indicate that Newton was admired in other than a positivist manner, as a discoverer of facts and theorems. Newton was still not seen to possess the true principles of Malebranche's sound physicist. And important as this positivist welcome to Newtonianism in France certainly was, we must distinguish it from the dawning sense (still to come) that Newton's works, both *Principia* and *Opticks*, truly represented the nature of things.

Newtonianism in Italy

The emergence of Newton's scientific work in print seems to have caused far less trauma in Italy than in France. This was not, alas! because in the former country intellectual life was more free and uninhibited than in France; quite the contrary was the case (Torrini 1979). All over Italy the anti-Copernican dogma was rigorously enforced, and 'liberal' ideas with regard to the interpretation of phenomena were regarded with deep suspicion, above all such as involved the abhorred tenets of atomism. It was impossible in Italy, before the end of the seventeenth century, openly to approve any of the philosophy of Galileo, though a collection of his writings was issued from Bologna in 1655–6. In that city, as in Naples and Tuscany, there were men eager to follow the new paths of learning, albeit *sub rosa*, and to take advantage of an inefficient machinery of repression. The clerical authorities did not frown upon experimentation as such, nor upon astronomical observation steering clear of the question of the Earth's motion; hence Vincenzo Viviani, Geminiano Montanari, Giovanni Domenico Cassini, and Marcello Malpighi—Italian savants whose names were known throughout Europe—pursued their investigations without hindrance. Mathematical books generally passed the censorship easily, leaving plenty of scope even for such a man of the new age as Giovanni Alfonso Borelli. Cartesian philosophy, with its strong metaphysical and moral elements, was a different matter. It is clear that Italians studied Descartes's writings, but officially they could be neither read nor taught. This worked to Newton's advantage, for there was no entrenched Cartesian orthodoxy to overcome, as there was in France.

When the merits of Galileo as a founding father of modern science and as a precursor of Newton were more clearly perceived in the eighteenth century, and especially when it became possible in Italy to acknowledge these things in print (as it increasingly was after the publication of Viviani's life of Galileo in 1717), Descartes began to be cast in the unenviable role of the philosopher who had led the world astray, beguiling it with fables, in the age between Galileo and Newton. Voltaire particularly spoke of Galileo as 'the first matter of knowledge, whom Descartes had the ill-luck never to quote', the master who had first demonstrated the power of the mathematical and experimental methods that Newton had brought to their full fruition with such beneficial results for human knowledge. The same point was made by Francesco Algarotti, one of the most successful early popularizers of Newton's works:

This great philosopher [Newton] and Galileo his predecessor met with almost the same fate. Both replaced the dreams of the Schoolmen by experiment and geometry. The latter thereby triumphed over Aristotle, so formidable because of the antiquity of his empire, the former over Descartes who was no less formidable on account of the number and strength of his supporters. Both totally altered the appearance of physics (Hall 1979*a*, p. 389).

Although these passages were written long after Newton's death, it can hardly be doubted that Italian mathematicians and experimenters were moved by the Galileo–Newton parallelism before the close of the seventeenth century.

Opticks *sent to Italy*

It is probable that copies of the *Principia* reached Italy within ten years of its publication, and certain that some Italians had read the book by then (Casini 1978, p. 85). When *Opticks* was published Newton was already acquainted with learned Italians, to whom he presented copies. One such was Guido Grandi, to whom Newton sent *Opticks* with a polite note in May 1704 (ibid., p. 87 note; Letter X.673.2, p. 434). Another was Francesco Bianchini, visiting London in 1713, when he attended three meetings of the Royal Society. This copy is now in the Bibliotheca Apostolica Vaticana at Rome. It seems that Bianchini had already confirmed Newton's optical experiments. Even earlier (1707) a copy of *Optice* had reached Rome, where Celestino Galiani regarded it as 'a precious work' containing such novel theses and such strange propositions and considerations touching light and colours that not even that prince of mathematicians René Descartes could rival them (ibid., p. 87; Letter 734, p. 506).

At Naples, Galiani founded a private academy at which, we may presume, currency was given to his reading of Newton's books, and of others by authors in Newton's circle which he had received from London. Also in Naples Niccolo Cirillo published a book that reveals familiarity with Newton's discovery of the varying refrangibility of the rays of light in 1728. At Pisa, Alberto De Soria, professor of logic (1713), introduced *Optice* to his pupils, and taught the theory of attraction; he managed to survive intact a formal accusation of teaching atheism (ibid., pp. 93–4).

Newton confirmed at Bologna, 1729

The foundation in Bologna by the military commander, polymath, and hydrographer, the Marchese Luigi Marsili, of the Istituto dell'Accademia delle Scienze had created a lively centre for the activities of both mathematicians and physicians, continuing the tradition of Montanari and Malpighi, among them the brothers Eustachio and Gabriele Manfredi and Francesco Maria Zanotti. The last-named, who was Secretary of the Accademia, had for some years considered a repetition of Newton's optical experiments; in 1729 he reported on the satisfactory confirmation of them accomplished by his pupil, Francesco Algarotti. Meeting at first with unsuccess, he succeeded in the end in fully confirming Newton's statements using an 'English prism' (Tega 1984, p. 93, 1986, p. 77). His trials were in part a response to the doubts cast upon Newton's experiments by Giovanni Rizzetti, who published a 'refutation' of them, and of Newton's theory, in 1722. Rizzetti's contradiction of the very first experiment described in *Opticks* was noticed in the *Acta Eruditorum* and drawn to the attention of the Royal Society by an Italian visitor to London. Although his name is now wholly forgotten, Newton took his challenge seriously enough to draft an answer to him, and to have J. T. Desaguliers again repeat the first experiment in *Opticks* to demonstrate Newton's accuracy (Westfall 1980, p. 796). Rizzetti republished his confutation in 1727 and as late as 1741 (*Saggio dell' antinewtonianismo sopra le leggi del moto e dei colori*, Venice; Casini 1978, pp. 95–6).

The Abbé Conti and Opticks: Algarotti

Newton attributed responsibility for the Rizzetti affair to Antonio Conti, a Venetian priest whom he had received on friendly terms at London in 1715, but whom he later regarded as betraying his confidence. Rizzetti too was a Venetian; Newton called him "a Friend [of Conti] who denies many of my Optical Experiments, though they have been all tried in France with Success" (Westfall 1989, p. 811). Conti's greatest sin in Newton's eyes was being, as he supposed, partial to Leibniz in the dispute concerning the discovery of the differential and integral calculus. Despite his loss of Newton's friendship, Conti seems after his return to Venice to have disseminated Newtonian ideas in intellectual circles there, and to have made *Opticks* known as well as the *Principia* (Casini 1978, p. 90, 1983, ch. 8). Perhaps he informed, if he did not inspire, Rizzetti. There were of course by now mathematical Newtonians in the Venetian Republic, notably the Marchese Giovanni Poleni, successively professor of astronomy, physics, and mathematics in the University of Padua from 1708 onwards (and elected FRS in 1710), of whom Newton's friend Alexander Cunningham, the English envoy in Venice, wrote to him (1716):

As he approves your Synthetique way in the search of nature, soe he admires your happyness in finding 'em [*sic*] out, I see he does not only understand your works, but also knows yourself as if he had been frequently with you, by your way of writing (Letter 1183, p. 279).

There is no evidence, however, of Poleni's having a special interest in *Opticks*.

Of all Italians, Algarotti was to become the most popular expositor of Newtonianism, in *Newtonianismo per le Dame* (Chapter 4, §3). Though by no means a heavyweight philosopher he was to become a major figure of the Enlightenment, an associate of Voltaire and Frederick II of Prussia, and as great a European as a Venetian. The publication of his book— supposedly, at free-thinking Naples—marks the end of the twilight period of Newton's introduction to Italy. All those mentioned above as admirers of Newtonian science or readers of Newton's books were prudent in their public affirmations. Few published on typically Newtonian themes such as the theory of forces; none offered a challenge to the existing reactionary system. Belief in the fixity of the Sun, the demonstration of which by dynamical reasoning Newton had declared to be a chief object of his *Principia*, was still firmly forbidden. Several of those already named were priests (besides Conti: Grandi, Galiani, and Bianchini) for whom defiance was impossible. For the University of Bologna, lying within the papal state, the election of Pope Benedict XIV in 1740 marked the opening of a more liberal age. Before the general prevalence of such liberal views, mathematical or experimental obscurity provided a decent concealment for new principles. So too, perhaps, did the deliberately light, almost jocular style of Algarotti. Could so charming a book be dangerous?

§3. The popularizers

Henry Pemberton

It is amusing to contrast the slight and light-hearted volume of Algarotti (to which I shall return), at its first publication entitled *Il Newtonianismo per le Dame. Dialoghi sopra la Luce e i Colori* (Milan, 1737)*—for the discussion of Newton's world-view was added later—with the ponderous folio of Henry Pemberton, published only nine years before, a major landmark in the British popularization of Newton. This author had

---

* The titlepage, stating 'Napoli', was a deception.

previously acted on Newton's behalf as editor of the third edition of the *Principia mathematica* (1726), but it is said that he had begun to compose his readable *View of Sir Isaac Newton's Philosophy* (1728) some years before first making Newton's acquaintance. Pemberton's professional life was devoted to anatomy and medicine, which he had studied under Boerhaave in Leiden and then in Paris. As a young man, however, he was much interested in mathematics, on which he published a little book (*Epistola ad Amicum*, 1722). Newton presumably chose Pemberton as an assistant because he was competent but subservient; their joint task was begun (probably) in the autumn of 1723. It may have been reluctance on Newton's part to see *A View* of his philosophy in print that delayed the book's publication, a delay for which Pemberton apologized to his subscribers (Cohen 1963).

It is hardly surprising that he makes no direct reference to *Opticks* in his Preface to this book, perhaps, nor that, while he devotes over 300 pages to the *Principia*, Newton's great experimental work merits less than one hundred, though Pemberton does remark that 'our great author's genius discovers itself no less in the former book than in the latter, nay perhaps even more, since this work gives as many instances of his singular force of reasoning, and of his unbounded invention'. Nor (he adds rather quaintly) is optics less useful than celestial mechanics, since the light and heat radiated by 'all these immense globes, with which the whole heavens are filled' are essential to 'the more noble operations of nature in vegetation and animal life'. He continues with a remark that is prudent but unfortunately not also prescient: Newton has not made so plain a disclosure of the optical force by which matter acts upon light, as he has of the force of gravity

yet he has led us to the very entrance upon it, and pointed out the path so plainly which must be followed to reach it; that one may be bold to say, whenever mankind shall be blessed with this improvement of their knowledge, it will be derived so directly from [Newton's] principles . . . that the greatest share of the praise due to the discovery will belong to him (Pemberton 1728, pp. 317–18).

Pemberton follows Newton's plan in giving an easy account, illustrated by experiments described, of the different refrangibilities of the rays forming the seven colours of the spectrum and of the distinct existence of these rays in the white light before their segregation by the prism, or after their recombination by a lens. The rays may also be separated from a white beam by reflection near the critical angle (after refraction). These discoveries of Newton suggest the reason for the apparent colours of bodies: selective absorption and reflection of the rays. In explaining how this can come about, says Pemberton, we meet with notions almost surpassing belief:

For it is proved by our author, that bodies are rendered transparent by the minuteness of their pores, and become opake by having them large; and more, that the most transparent body by being reduced to a great thinness will become less pervious to light (ibid., p. 339).

The resolution of these paradoxes is taken from Book II of *Opticks*, from which Pemberton also sketches, with great skill, the theory of the sizes of the component particles of the surfaces of bodies. The qualitative considerations of Book II, Part III where Newton worked out his choices of the orders of particles for several colours are rehearsed at some length. Newton's contention that the densest substances contain little solid matter is expressed imaginatively by Pemberton:

this whole globe of earth, nay all the known bodies in the universe together . . . may be compounded of no greater a portion of solid matter, than might be reduced into a globe of one inch only in diameter, or even less (ibid., p. 356).

If Pemberton had thought of this globe of solid matter expanding to create the actual universe, he would have invented the Big Bang theory of cosmogenesis!

Postponing to the end of his text what Newton had to say about the impossibility of correcting chromatic aberration in lenses, and the improvement of telescopes by substituting reflection for refraction, Pemberton is very interested in Newton's treatment of the interaction of light and matter, to the extent of providing a version of Newton's difficult Proposition 10 of Book II, Part III. In their different ways Newton and Pemberton demonstrate that the refracting powers of transparent bodies— among which diamond possesses the greatest—are as the squares of their refractive indices, and in turn generally proportional to their densities. This point is qualitatively reinforced by observing that

sulphureous bodies, which are most readily set on fire by the sun's light . . . act more upon light in refracting it, than other bodies of the same density do. And farther, that the densest bodies, which have now been shown to act most upon light, contract the greatest heat by being exposed to the summer sun (ibid., p. 369).

Pemberton now returns to the point that the power of reflection is the same as that of refraction, and explains how, for example, when light shines through transparent plates, the ability of the second surface to either reflect or refract the beam is caused 'by some power propagated from the first surface' in a periodic way, that is, by "fits". This formulation, naturally enough, corresponds to the more narrowly phenomenalistic one given by Newton in Book II, Part III, Prop. 12 rather than the more hypothetical, generalized idea of Prop. 13:

Light is in Fits of easy Reflexion and easy Transmission, *before* its Incidence on transparent Bodies. And probably it is put into such Fits at its first emission from luminous Bodies, and continues in them during all its progress (Newton 1952, p. 282, my italics).

If Pemberton found it difficult to reconcile this statement with the former, and the use to which that was put, he is hardly to be found wanting. However, 'what the power of nature is, whereby this action between light and bodies is caused our author has not discovered,' though he has hinted his opinion. Pemberton means the aetherial hypothesis, the hypothesis of 'some very subtle and elastic substance diffused through the universe, in which such vibrations may be excited by the rays of light, as they pass through it' indicated in the Queries. Pemberton made no mention of the diffraction experiments and their bearing on the concept of optical force.

The Lexion Technicum *(1704, 1710)*

The rather pompous though fluent Pemberton was not of course the first author to try to set Newton's optical discoveries before the wider public. Because the first Newtonians in the field of popularization (John Keill, David Gregory, William Whiston) were debarred from embarking on this branch of physics by Newton's long silence since 1675, the earliest commentator was John Harris, whose large dictionary, *Lexicon Technicum or a Universal Dictionary of Arts and Sciences* (vol. I, 1704) was in the press when *Opticks* appeared. Harris was a divine and public lecturer on natural philosophy, to be briefly Secretary of the Royal Society five years later. Newton allowed him to print in the second volume of his dictionary (1710) the first of his chemical writings to come before the public, *De natura acidorum*. In Harris's first volume, turning to the article on LIGHT, one finds rather slight trace of Newton, the argument that it is a substance being taken from William Molyneux's *Dioptrica nova* (1692). Perhaps the article was in print before *Opticks* was published, for so (it is evident) was the first part of the article on COLOUR, where Harris summarizes Newton's first *Philosophical Transactions* paper of 1672, competently enough and often using Newton's own words, including the famous passage

These things being so, it can be no longer disputed, whether there be colours in the dark, nor whether they be the qualities of the objects we see, no nor perhaps, whether Light be a Body. For, since Colours are the *qualities* of Light, having its Rays for their intire and immediate subject, how can we think those Rays *qualities* also, unless one quality may be the subject of and sustain another; which in effect is to call it *Substance* (Cohen 1958a, p. 57).

'Thus far this wonderful Man', continues Harris, 'as long ago as the Year 1675 . . .'.

Next—and the step seems unique in the annals of Newtonianism—he gives a narrative of experiments in confirmation of Newton's theory by a certain Mr John Perks in Worcestershire, who also contributed two mathematical papers to the *Philosophical Transactions*. After this follows a long analysis, proposition by proposition, of Book I of *Opticks*, wherein

Part II of this Book is described as Book II, indicating Harris's access to a pre-publication manuscript. The present Book II is very briefly dealt with:

he [Newton] takes into Consideration the Phaenomena of those Colours which are observed in thin transparent Bodies, showing how all our perceptions of colour must arise from the separation and combination of the homogeneous rays by refraction and reflection:
in this respect the Science of Colours becomes a Speculation as truly Mathematical as any other part of *Opticks* . . .

Accordingly, in this volume Harris made no reference to the theory of 'fits' nor (which is more surprising) to any other Queries in *Opticks* dealing with light. Under a variety of headings such as ATOM, ATTRACTION, CORPUSCLE, CHYMISTRY, Harris found as yet no occasion to revise what he had written before the Queries appeared, though under HEAT he inserted Newton's definition that flame is a red-hot vapour (Query 10).

The preparation of the second volume of his dictionary (published in 1710) gave Harris the opportunity to add to his Newtonian treatment of LIGHT, and to borrow more heavily from the Queries (extended in the 1706 *Optice*). Harris now firmly committed himself to the emission or projectile theory of light and its dynamical development:

The Rays of Light are certainly *little Particles*, actually emitted from the *Lucent Body*, and refracted by some Attraction, by which *Light* and the *Bodies* on which it falls do mutually act upon one another.

Harris also repeated Cheyne's arguments about the infinite smallness of these light-particles (see §1, p. 183). Unusually, he referred specifically to Newton's mathematical proposition in the *Principia* dealing with dynamical optics; if reflection, refraction, and inflection are all caused by some attractive force of bodies acting upon light-particles at a short distance, then

he shews in his admirable *Principia* that the *Sines of Incidence must be to the Sines of Refraction in a given Ratio*: as in fact we find the thing to be.

Harris made the point that such a dynamical account of light is consistent with the Newtonian theory of 'fits' in connection with the colours of thin plates; he [Newton]

judges that there is nothing more required than that the Rays should be very small Corpuscles of Matter, which either by their *Attraction or some other Force* do excite certain Vibrations in the *Bodies* on which they act.

However, the main part of Harris's summary of Book II of *Opticks* (omitted from the first volume of the *Lexicon*) comes under the word COLOUR. Only the briefest allusion is made to Hooke's rival theory—recently revived in his *Posthumous Works* (1705, p. 54)—that 'Newton's Rings' arise from the interaction of pulses in the aether.

Double-refraction comes into the main article on LIGHT, Harris describing Huygens's investigation and Newton's rival development of the hypothesis of 'sides', and himself suggesting—to modernize slightly—that the polarization of light may be the effect of an attractive force somewhat like the polarization of the magnet. INFLECTION is lightly touched on here, and then made the subject of a separate article in which Harris went through Book III of *Opticks*. Other articles making fresh use of non-optical matter in the Queries are those on ATTRACTION and COHESION.

Though Harris gave publicity at the earliest possible date to the more straightforward sections of Newton's recently issued volume, that is, those dealing with refraction as investigated in the prismatic experiments (Book I), his fuller exposition of the content of *Opticks* had to wait six years more, and even then *Lexicon Technicum* failed to exploit the wide range of physical speculation that Newton opened up, and which so much entranced later Newtonians (§1, p. 185). Such speculations admittedly seem alien to the factual, positivist spirit of Harris's volumes. Perhaps too he did not feel quite the firm confidence of his successors that it had been Newton's real, though unavowed, intention to convey as solid truths what he had formally expressed only in the guise of Queries.

W. J. 'sGravesande

Harris in 1704 and 1710 and Pemberton a generation later were alike in making few changes to Newton's own exposition, however much they might abbreviate and simplify it. The first member of a different group of Newtonians was the Dutch academic, Willem Jacob 'sGravesande. He assembled the pieces that Newton had provided into a new pattern. Exactly how 'sGravesande became a Newtonian is unfortunately not at all clear. He was well grounded in mathematics, but at first turned to the law as a profession. As a Leiden student, possibly influenced by Boerhaave, he may have been indirectly linked (through the Scot, Archibald Pitcairne, Boerhaave's predecessor) with the Newtonian group of Scotsmen, of an earlier date, the 1690s. Early in 1715, then aged twenty-seven, 'sGravesande travelled to London with a mission from the Netherlands, sent to congratulate George I on his accession to the British throne. He remained for a year, was elected FRS, and witnessed one of Desaguliers's repetitions of Newton's optical experiments, such as he was successfully to perform later himself. In fact, 'sGravesande must have familiarized himself thoroughly with the demonstrative teaching of Newtonian science in London, besides becoming acquainted with Newton and members of Newton's circle. Returning to Leiden, where he was appointed to a Chair of Mathematics, 'sGravesande developed an experimentally-based course of scientific instruction (for which indeed a precedent had been created previously by Burchard de Volder) founded upon the models of Desaguliers and Hauksbee: from the former he adapted mechanical and optical experiments, from the latter pneumatic and electrical ones. Some demonstrations were certainly original with 'sGravesande himself, such as his illustrations of Newton's Third Law of Motion—the equality of action and reaction—by the steam-jet propulsion of a toy car, a notion remotely stemming from Newton himself (Hall 1985). The object of the course was to explain and justify both the method and the content of Newtonian science, while omitting most of Newton's formal mathematical arguments.

The result is a more straightforwardly physical account of natural phenomena than Newton had provided; it is also one more fitted to the spirit of the times. Newton had not declared *why* there are laws of motion; 'sGravesande confidently asserts that the laws of nature were laid down by God and immediately depend upon His will. Continuing, 'sGravesande steers an unhesitating course through all sorts of metaphysical minefields that Newton had been happy to avoid, such as the nature of body, the real existence of the vacuum and the non-existence of atoms, the reality of forces of attraction and repulsion, and the infinity of the universe. Again, writing as a physicist rather than as a mathematician, 'sGravesande devotes separate sections of his book to the properties of ordinary incompressible fluids and of 'elastic fluids', airs or gases, which are very different from Newton's propositions. For he was eclectic enough to bring into Newtonianism much that did not originate with Newton—for example, he draws upon Robert Boyle. There may not have been much in the *Mathematical Elements* that Newton would have expunged; but there was much there to which Newton would have hesitated to subscribe his own name.

Popular experimental optics

The *Mathematical Elements of Natural Philosophy confirm'd by Experiments or An Introduction to Sir Isaac Newton's Philosophy*, to give the book its full title, appeared both in Latin and in English (by J. T. Desaguliers) in 1720. Clearly, its author had wasted little time since his return from London. Broadly speaking, the subject of 'sGravesande's first volume is mechanics; volume II deals with optics and celestial mechanics. Evidently 'sGravesande aimed at a unity of treatment closer than that attained by Newton. The price of unification seems at times rather high, as when he treats heat, fire, electricity, and light as all one. True, he says, there can be heat without fire and light without heat; but these are not the characteristic manifestations. So light is fire that moves—though 'sGravesande seems less certain than Newton that light moves in time; and both fire and light are attracted by matter. Contrary to all previous tradition in optics, he chooses this interaction as his fundamental phenomenon, demonstrated by the knife-edge diffraction experiment showing the attraction of light by matter. The same interaction is the cause of refraction (II, p. 26), and its law are to be learned not by experiment but are to be 'deduc'd from the Acceleration which the Attraction generates' (II, p. 32). Consideration of refraction leads 'sGravesande into discussion of vision, the eye, the action of lenses, and many matters properly considered by writers upon optics but not systematically by Newton.

With reflection he returns to *Opticks*, still with many ingenious experiments not borrowed from that book, to prove that light rebounds from the empty space within transparent mediums, not from the solid particles, and that reflection 'is made by the same Power by which the Rays are refracted, which produces different Effects in different Circumstances' (II, p. 85). How the optical force or forces operate, especially when a ray is partially refracted and partially reflected at an interface, is not very clear; there is an attractive force extending beyond the body (as in the mathematical model of *Principia*, Book I, Section XIV) but 'sGravesande seems also to suggest (as Newton does) a repulsive force acting beyond the body, whence

we deduce that *Light is driven back at a certain Distance from the Bodies*, in the same manner that the refracting Power does also act at some Distance from the Body (II, p. 87).

In the theory of colours and its application to the rainbow 'sGravesande closely follows the arguments and experiments of his original, only entering into greater detail about the experimental contrivances. Like other popularizers, 'sGravesande brought Book II of *Opticks* within brief but intelligible limits, without giving Newton's exact measurements. His statement of the periodicity of intervals producing Newton's rings is even more strictly phenomenalistic than Newton's own:

If there are Plates of the same Medium, whose Thicknesses answer to the odd Numbers 1, 3, 5, 7, &c [they will] reflect the Rays which the others transmit, whose Thicknesses answer to the even Numbers 2, 4, 6, 8 &c (II, p. 140).

No explanation of any sort is given as to why this should be; the theory of "fits" is suppressed. 'sGravesande makes the point that the distance through the plate to the eye may vary with the eye's position, and therefore as the head is moved the colours may appear to alter. Following Newton, he asserts that the particles of transparent bodies must be much denser than the medium between them, and the density is less in those

in the Tails of Peacocks, and in some Silks, and in general in all Bodies, whose Colour varies according to the different Situation of the Eye (II, p. 146).

This iridescent effect does not appear to have been mentioned by Newton.

The aether rejected

The Queries in *Opticks*, so far as I can discover, had a negligible effect upon 'sGravesande's textbook. It seems inconceivable that he had not read the Queries numbered 25 to 31 in the final text, added by Newton to *Optice* in 1706; in no. 25 was Newton's treatment of double-refraction, an aberrant phenomenon not considered by the popularizers. It is, however, possible that 'sGravesande did not take cognizance of Queries 17 to 24 (final numbering), in which Newton described his idiosyncratic highly tenuous, highly elastic aether, because these first appeared in the second English edition of *Opticks* in 1717. At any rate, Newton's arguments there left 'sGravesande unscathed. As a staunch anti-Cartesian he was opposed to all talk of aetherial mechanics, though he speaks of a *medium* occupying the wide spaces between the solid particles of bodies. His view is well expressed in a passage explaining that we are simply ignorant of the cause of gravity:

We have said that the Gravity, which we have hitherto explained, is to be taken for a Law of Nature, because we don't know the Cause of it; and because it depends upon no Cause that is known to us . . . Besides that, if Gravity depend upon any known Law of Motion, it ought to be referred to a Stroke [impact] from an extraneous Body; and because Gravity is continual, a continual Stroke would be required.

If there be such a Sort of Matter continually striking against Bodies, it must of Necessity be fluid, and very subtile, so as to penetrate all Bodies; for Bodies, that are any how shut up in others, are heavy.

Now let a Mathematician consider, whether a Fluid so subtile as freely to penetrate the Pores of all Bodies, and so rare, as not sensibly to hinder the Motion of Bodies (for in a Place void of Air, the Motion of a Pendulum will continue very long) can impel vast Bodies towards one another with so much Force? Let him explain how this Force increases in a ratio of the Mass of the Body towards which it is carried . . . (II, pp. 215–16).

It might almost seem that 'sGravesande was challenging Newton, the supreme mathematician, to make sense of the hypothesis of Newton the speculative physicist!

The Clarkes's Rohault

A popular work on natural philosophy in English nearly contemporary with 'sGravesande's was *Rohault's System of Natural Philosophy illustrated with Dr. Samuel Clarke's Notes Taken mostly out of Sir Isaac Newton's Philosophy Done into English by John Clarke*. The original of this verbosely titled book, a digested, simplified version of Cartesian astronomy, physics, and physiology by Jacques Rohault, had been published in French at Paris in 1671. It had been given wider currency by a Latin translation (1674), read even in the English universities. In 1697 Samuel Clarke published a fresh translation into Latin, to which he added explanatory Newtonian notes on, or one might better say refutations of, specific points in Rohault's text. This proved a popular book in England, and its Newtonianism increased in successive editions up to 1739 (Hoskin 1961). That of 1710 incorporated material from *Optice* (1706), of which Samuel Clarke had been the translator. The book was translated back into English by Samuel's brother John in 1723. Naturally, Rohault's Cartesian discussion of light and physical optics furnished many matters upon which the opposing Newtonian views had to be emphatically asserted (Casini 1969, pp. 125–36).

No sooner does the text touch upon light in Chapter 26, defining 'Original Light [as] a certain Motion of the Parts of luminous Bodies whereby they are capable of pushing every Way the subtil Matter which fills the Pores of transparent Bodies' than Clarke contradicts it in order to assert the emission theory. The motion in the luminous body shakes off 'some very small Particles from [it] which are sent forth all Ways with a very great Force', the radiation consisting of these particles 'receding every Way from the luminous Body in streight lines with incredible Swiftness'. Clarke quotes Newton at length on the impossibility of light's being a pressure in the aether, on its velocity of motion, and on the forces of particles (Clarke 1723, I, p. 201). Rohault's statement that light rays pass through the straight pores penetrating transparent bodies stimulates a long quotation of Newton's opinions about the paucity of solid matter in bodies and his argument that opacity is caused either by unequal density or the great width of the pores. Rohault's innocent-looking remark that light 'when it falls upon the Surface of a solid Body ought to be *turned back* or reflected' provokes a dissertation in small print on the Newtonian theory that reflection is not caused by solid particles of the reflecting body but by 'a certain Power equally diffused over [its] Surface . . . whereby it acts upon the Ray to attract or repel it, *without immediate Contact*' (ibid., p. 209). How could the reflection and transmission of light striking thin plates be effected by the "fits" described by Newton, and how could the transition from one to the other occur at the critical angle if everything depended upon the rays meeting with pores or particles?

It is perhaps surprising that Clarke allowed to pass without comment Rohault's statement that 'we certainly know, that one Body cannot act upon another without immediate Contact' but his assertion that 'the whole Action of the coloured Body [with respect to vision] consists in giving [light] some Modification which it had not before' does not similarly escape. No Newtonian could pass this! Clarke interprets Newton's original discovery of the varied refrangibility of the coloured rays produced by the prism in a mechanical form:

it is found by Experience, that the Rays of Light are compounded of Particles different from one another: that is, which are (as is highly probable) some larger and some smaller.

(The distinction between the *fact* and the *probability* is intriguing.) When
the beam of light containing these diverse particles approaches an interface,
'those Particles of light which are smallest, are the easiest of all, and the
most turned out of a straight Line', that is, refracted. These small, readily
diverted particles 'make a small Ray of a violet Colour [and] . . . (as is very
likely) . . . excite the shortest Vibrations in the *Tunica Retina*' of the eye
(ibid., p. 228). The largest particles, least refracted, make red by creating
long vibrations:

Much in the same Manner, as the Vibrations of Air, according to their different
Bignesses, cause Sensations of different Sounds.

Because he follows Rohault's plan of exposition rather than Newton's
Clarke comes last in his anti-Cartesian corrections to a description of
Newton's prismatic experiments and the conclusions he derived from them.
These are, writes Clarke, 'the Touchstone by which every Hypothesis, and
every Theory, concerning the Nature and Properties of Colours, is to be
examined and tried' (p. 224). In effect, he gives in this long footnote a clear
summary of Newton's first 1672 paper on light and colours, now explaining
(what has not come up before) how whiteness arises from the mixture of
the colours and requires the balance of the rays found in Nature. Rohault
is allowed then to proceed with his explanation of the eye and the
physiology of vision without much interruption drawn from *Opticks* by
Clarke, until in the chapter on 'Dioptricks' he necessarily corrects Rohault
on the improvement of telescopes, setting out the futility of Descartes's
hopes for major improvements from the adoption of aspherical lenses
(pp. 270–1). Clarke does not of course mention the relation of such
Cartesian "Glass-works" to Newton's preoccuption with the problem of
refraction, a relation suppressed by Newton himself after the 1672 paper.

Voltaire

Clarke's is from its plan an awkward and captious book, from which it is
a pleasure to turn to the smoother pages of Voltaire, whose *Lettres
Philosophiques* (or *Sur les Anglais*, as they are sometimes called) of 1734
was the first book addressed to Frenchmen in their own tongue to contrast
favourably the Newtonian philosophy with that of Descartes. During his
English exile (1726–9), though he never met Newton, he lived much
among Newton's friends, and attended his funeral in Westminster Abbey.
Neither experimenter nor mathematician, Voltaire nevertheless mastered
Newton's writings well enough to expound them in some detail (in his later
book devoted wholly to this topic).

Optics forms the subject of the sixteenth letter. Voltaire opens tactfully
with the remark that it was Descartes who had shown an almost divine
sagacity in subjecting the rainbow to calculation; what would he say,
however, if informed that he had been quite mistaken in his conception of

light? For it was false to suppose that light is directly reflected by rebounding from the solid particles of bodies; false also that bodies with large pores in them are transparent; one day a man would demonstrate such paradoxes as these, and would anatomize a single ray of light with more dexterity than that of the most skilful artist in the dissection of the human body. This man, Voltaire went on, was Isaac Newton, who, with the aid of nothing more than his prism, had demonstrated that light is a mass of coloured rays, which, all together, make whiteness.

All these points had been stressed by Samuel Clarke, with whom Voltaire was certainly acquainted in London. Like Clarke, Voltaire, after giving more details of the famous prism experiments, devotes a few sentences to thin plates and the theory of "fits". They are confusing enough:

[Newton] has found the secret of seeing the vibrations and tremours of light, coming and going endlessly, which either transmit the light or reflect it according to the thickness of the particles they meet. He has been so bold as to calculate the thickness of the particles of air that is necessary between two glasses (one flat, the other convex on one side) placed one upon the other, in order to effect such transmission or reflection, and to make this colour or that.

Returning secretly from his London exile to France late in 1728 or early in 1729, then permitted to reside in Paris, Voltaire wrote the *Lettres* between 1729 and 1731. They first saw the light in an English translation in 1733. For the French edition (to be issued in the following year) extraordinary precautions were taken to ensure secrecy during its printing, and circumvention of subsequent attempts to suppress the edition. However, Voltaire was again forced to leave France for a time. In Paris the *Parlement* ordered copies of the *Lettres* to be torn to pieces and burnt by the public hangman in the courtyard of the Palais de Justice, 'as infamous, contrary to religion, good morals and respect for authority' (Voltaire 1946, p. *xxix*). A strange context for Newtonianism! Living in retirement at Cirey, conveniently only just inside the French frontier, with his mistress Mme. du Châtellet, translator of the *Principia*, Voltaire had leisure to study Newton's writings in detail with the assistance of such able mathematicians as Alexis-Claude Clairaut and P. L. M. de Maupertuis. He also (like his lady) engaged in an extensive correspondence for the benefit of his book, *Élémens de la Philosophie de Neuton Mis à la portée de tout le monde* (1738), written because 'La Science de la Nature est un bien qui appartient à tous les hommes (*Avant-propos*)'. Voltaire knew of Algarotti's parallel design before his own book was published.

Voltaire's Élémens

Unlike most Newtonian popularizers, though with good logic, Voltaire devotes the first part of the *Élémens*—fourteen chapters—to *Opticks*—nearly half the book, though he inserts much matter on the eye and vision not found in Newton. Descartes fell into error because he depended upon deceptive Reason. The century since Descartes has advanced as far beyond him, as he advanced beyond the Ancients, for whereas he declared that he knew nothing in philosophy if light did not travel instantaneously from the sun, we have measured the time taken to be seven or eight minutes. Voltaire quotes Newton's argument against Descartes's concept of light: if it were so, we would see in the dark, and he describes the discoveries of Roemer and Bradley establishing the speed of light. Mallebranche (so spelled), whose mind was more subtle than true and whose meditations did not always correspond to Nature, was as mistaken as Descartes. 'Must it be the case that those men who spoke only of *truth* write only works of fiction! (p. 24)'.

Voltaire asks, What is light? and returns an ingenious answer, not dissimilar to 'sGravesande's. It is fire. The swifter, coarser, more compact particles radiated by a burning body constitute heat; those that are slower, less compacted, but finer constitute light. Light-particles, though almost infinitely minute and vastly swift in motion, obey the laws of mechanics, and their law of force is the same as that of gravity. It is force, not direct physical impact of matter upon matter that causes light to be reflected by bodies. The same force in different circumstances also causes a beam of light to be refracted (p. 101). The beam is bent towards the perpendicular when it passes from a medium having less force (such as air) into another having more (such as glass), whereby it is accelerated.

Suppose now we were to find some new property of light apparently caused by attraction, should we not believe that the same effects possess the same cause? Such a property is inflection [diffraction] discovered by Grimaldi: 'There is a new universe opening itself to the eyes of those who choose to see it' (p. 108). However, though attraction is everywhere at work, it does not follow the same law at close distances as at those which separate the sun from the planets. When they are adjacent or almost so the attraction between two minute bodies is far stronger than that between planets. (This seems somewhat in contradiction of what was said before and, like Newton, Voltaire does not explain how particles can be adjacent when they are widely dispersed, or how light-particles can be in contact with matter upon which they do not impinge.)

Chapter 8 describes Newton's discovery of the unequal refrangibility of the various coloured rays, long disregarded in France because of the legacy of Mariotte's defective experiment. Even after its successful confirmation in that country prejudice against it continued. As for the cause of the dispersion of the beam during refraction, Voltaire, like 'sGravesande, has no doubt that it is the result of the more powerful attractive force of one medium pulling differentially upon the light-particles:

This is what experiment confirms in all media, in every case. The red ray is always that which is least turned from its path, the violet ray is always that which is most turned from its. Thus the red is the more substantial, the harder, the more brilliant, and the more tiring to the eye. The violet ray, which of all the coloured rays is most restful to the sight is also the most refrangible, and consequently is composed of the most minute and least gravitating particles (pp. 126–7).

Lest the reader dismiss this assertion as mere conjecture, Voltaire adduces another 'proof': exposure to fire causes certain bodies to gain weight; light is fire; therefore light has weight! The rainbow is in fact a natural spectacle of this mass spectrometry of the particles of light.

To complete the explanation of colour, it is necessary to tell why scarlet is red, grass green. Voltaire states incorrectly (but he was not alone in his error, which possesses obvious charm) that Newton first derived his notions about the colours of thin plates by watching the iridescence of soap-bubbles blown by children (p. 162). It was he who discovered and measured the dependence of colour in such a thin film, layer, or plate upon its thickness, and similarly (as Voltaire has it) with the particles of a vapour:

So the finest vapours which rise above the Earth and which tinge the cloudless air with colour, having very minute surfaces, produce this celestial blue which so gratifies the sight (p. 164).

Voltaire neatly explains how, when Newton's Rings are formed by light of a single hue, they are alternations of dark and colour, the ring that appears dark by reflection appearing coloured by transmission, and vice versa. What he has to say about this experiment is more enthusiastic than clear. The rings, these 'jets transmis & réfléchis', are the result of an interaction between bodies and light still difficult to explain: Newton's conjecture was that light is radiated from the sun and other sources 'par accès, par vibrations', by fits conditioning the light to be either reflected or refracted through the second surface of the film. He had planned experiments to discover how the 'fits' are related to the general principle of attraction, but could not carry them out. He has also conjectured that the luminous vibrations causing the 'fits' are borne by 'a very thin and rare matter, which becomes less and less rare as it becomes the more remote from opaque bodies . . .' But this conjecture, though it may bring attractive force into the picture, is a hypothesis merely and not to be admitted [*sc.* as a truth].

The last optical chapter of the *Élémens*, Fourteen, deals with the analogy between the seven colours and the seven tones of music, and with the optical harpsichord.

Voltaire, for all his allusions to experiments and his amusing (but quite uninstructive) little pictures of them, did not write a practical book, as we may suppose those of 'sGravesande or Pieter Musschenbroek to be. Possibly he had not seen the experiments himself; he does not seriously expect his readers to attempt them, or if they should wish to do so he honestly says they should read another book. Though like other popularizers he praises Newton highly for his experimental sagacity, dexterity, and pertinacity it is really the new Newtonian world-view with its atoms, its concept of forces, its idea of attraction extending majestically from the least particles of matter to the sun and stars, that captivates his imagination. He does not skimp the task of conveying descriptive information to his readers; but this is not the core of his design, which is to show that we, the enlightened eighteenth century, have a new natural philosophy. We may pride ourselves on the fact that it is not a philosophy of imaginary things created by deceptive Reason, but solidly verified by mathematical calculation and experiment. Voltaire is fully conscious, and makes it plain to his readers, that with Newton a new and sure methodology has entered the world of learning. To use modern language we might say that for Voltaire the new epistemological status given to natural philosophy by Newton—which was to transfer that study from the hands of 'philosophers' to those of 'scientists', for, as Voltaire expressed the point pithily, it is true philosophy to cease to speculate where the torch of physical science fails to illuminate (Guerlac 1965, p. 318)—is no less important than the changes that he introduced into the content of philosophy. The triumph of the divine Newton (as Voltaire does not scruple to call him) in raising men from the slough of self-deception is in Voltaire's eyes as magnificent as his creation of a new system of the world. Perhaps more so (Hall 1979*b*).

The influence of Voltaire

Voltaire's writings did more than those of any other individual in the first half of the eighteenth century to elevate Newton to a predominant position in European culture, partly because he perceived in Newton's work more than mathematics and experiment:

he was one of the earliest to perceive, or to stress, the vast ideological import of Newton's scheme, and more especially of Newton's method . . . This 'method of analysis', as it was called, was taken to be the necessary and indispensable instrument for all kinds of thinking (Guerlac 1965, p. 318).

By such correct thinking society as well as physics might be reformed. Paolo Casini points out that the *Élémens* were the products of Voltaire's desire to instruct, of the 'pedagogical vocation that animates all his career as a writer', just as the *Lettres Philosophiques* gratified his desire to amuse and scandalize. Casini quotes the contemporary *Memoires de Trevoux* (1738):

Not long after the new *Élémens* were issued, they were seen in the hands of all Paris, and in every kind of hand. They were even stolen. Everyone wished to read at least a chapter, to run over their titles and devour the book with his eyes . . . All wish to snatch away some scrap of Newton's teaching . . . M. Voltaire speaks at last and at once Newton is understood, or on the way to being understood; all Paris resounds with Newton's name, all Paris babbles Newton, all Paris studies and learns Newton (Casini 1983, pp. 96–7).

Mme. du Châtellet

It is not the least significant point about Voltaire's moulding of the Newtonian legacy that unlike some other popularizers he gave equality of treatment to *Opticks* and *Principia*, balancing experiment and geometry, though we may infer that he responded more warmly to the former. (With mathematics, Voltaire sought help from others.) Inevitably, Newtonians with a predominant interest in mathematical science, or in the metaphysical aspects of Newtonian science, tended to neglect *Opticks*. One of the latter group was Voltaire's hostess at Cirey, Mme. du Châtellet, who was herself earnestly studying philosophy and mathematics while he was working on the *Élémens*. Their association in the diffusion of Newton's philosophy ended only with her death from puerperal fever at the age of forty-three (1749). Her main work, the French translation of the *Principia mathematica*, lay in abeyance for ten years after her death, but an earlier book from her pen, *Institutions de Physique* (1740) was complete when the *Élémens* were published. A work of composite inheritance—for Madame was almost as much convinced by the writings of Leibniz as by those of Newton—the *Institutions* contain a great deal more metaphysics than does Voltaire's volume, and do not address Newtonian optical theory (Iltis 1977). Mme. du Châtellet did nevertheless begin an *Essai sur l'Optique*, unfinished and still unprinted, and it is certain that she fully accepted Newton's discovery of the varying refrangibility of the coloured rays, since she proposes it as an example of the true organization of Nature which our senses misrepresent to our understandings:

the colour white is a phenomenon arising from nothing other than the confusion of all the primitive colours which occurs at the retina of our eyes; the prism causes it to vanish away. Thus a being whose eyes would be (as it were) natural prisms would have no more idea of whiteness than a deaf person has of sound (*Institutions*, p. 168).

Algarotti

Many writers have claimed that Mme. du Châtellet and Voltaire were inspired in their Newtonian writings by the example of Francesco Algarotti, who paid a visit to Cirey in 1735 while already occupied with his *Il Newtonianismo per le Dame* (1737). Educated in science at Bologna University, where besides his precocious reduplication of Newton's prismatic experiments (in 1728—at the age of sixteen!) and association with Zanotti (p. 213) he assisted Eustachio Manfredi in exact observations of the positions of the stars, he then led for some years a wandering life which included a period in Tuscany during which he associated with the

Freemasons, regarded in Italy as virtual infidels. After its publication (with the place, Milan, disguised) his book was placed on the *Index Librorum Prohibitorum* (13 April 1739), and it was only after a submission to the Church acknowledging the validity of the anti-Copernican decree of 1616 that Algarotti was permitted to republish it (Casini 1983, p. 226). Again he lived much abroad; he was elected a Fellow of the Royal Society in 1738, was appointed a Count of Prussia (1740) and Court Chamberlain (1747) by Frederick II, but returned to Italy in 1754.

Il Newtonianismo per le Dame was begun while Algarotti was living in Bologna and finished during his residence in France. In 1752 he published a heavily revised version of the book, leaving scarcely a sentence unmodified. This was dedicated to the King of Prussia under the new title of *Dialoghi sopra l'Ottica Neutoniana*. Algarotti compressed the former six dialogues into five, adding a new sixth dialogue refuting objections against Newtonianism put by a new character, Simplicio (the name borrowed from Galileo). In what follows I adhere to the early text, translated into English in 1739; so far as I know the later *Dialoghi* were not translated.

In dedicating the first edition of *Il Newtonianismo* to Fontenelle, the aged but still active Secretary of the Académie Royale des Sciences, Algarotti had declared that his book had been inspired by Fontenelle's widely admired *Discours sur la Pluralité des Mondes* (1686). This book does indeed provide a close model for Algarotti's dialogues between a noble lady (intelligent but uninformed) and the author; addressing Fontenelle, Algarotti declared him to be the first who 'softened the savage nature of philosophy' and pointed to the analogy between their endeavours:

It was indeed just that the ladies, who by your work had been made acquainted with the great change introduced by Des Cartes into the thinking world, should not be ignorant of the new, and it is possible, the last change, of which the illustrious Sir Isaac Newton was the author (Algarotti 1765, *v–vi*).

Among other remarks, he noted that Newton's general system of attraction could not be set aside from his dialogue, as it has a natural connection with the particular attraction observed between light and bodies. Like Voltaire, Algarotti discerned in Newton's writings a single 'philosophy of attraction' of which optics and celestial mechanics were distinct but cognate branches (ibid., p. *ix*).

Algarotti's extensive familiarity with English poetry, that of Pope in particular, afforded him an easy entrance in imaginary conversation with his Marchesa to English scientific writings. A sketch of the history of learning in Europe and of the origin of the Schools where 'greybearded children built nothing more solid than a soap-bubble' serves to introduce the names of Galileo (who, 'with his compasses in his hand laid the foundations of the Temple of Learning, afterwards made so lofty by Newton') and of

Descartes, who, in order to compose his own system of optics, reasoned and dogmatized about light without first assuring himself by experiments whether 'it is simple or compound, and without knowing its chief properties'. The Bulk of Dialogue I is taken up with an account of Descartes's theory of the mechanical universe, especially its optical aspects. In Dialogue II, the *camera obscura* is not forgotten, making a picture inverted, it is true, but even brighter and more exact than a scene painted by Canaletto; this device leads on naturally to a consideration of the eye and vision, just as (much later) a conversation about the infinitely great and the infinitely small introduces a compliment to Newton, who at the utmost stretch of the human mind overthrew all previous ideas on this topic to establish his celebrated doctrine of fluxions (Algarotti 1765, p. 117). The transition to Newtonian optics takes place in the fourth dialogue, where (rather oddly to a modern reader) praise of Newton the historian precedes the introduction of Newtonian optics, another entirely new world enriched with the most shining truths (ibid., p. 150). *Opticks*, the product of thirty years of study and research, is praised by Algarotti as a model of the true philosophy. The Marchesa's objection, that we can understand nothing if we do not first know its nature, yet Newton has not told us what the nature of light is, Algarotti soon overcomes.

He gives a picturesque yet clear account of how a beam of white light is found to be composed of an infinity of distinct coloured rays, forming seven principal hues in the spectrum, rightly asserting that this discovery of the relation between colour and refrangibility was the fundamental rock upon which the Newtonian edifice of optics was built. Somewhat unhistorically, he contrasts this theory of the pre-existence before refraction or reflection of the variously coloured and refrangible rays with the theory of 'dispersion' which Algarotti attributed to Grimaldi: that is, a shattering, splitting, or dilatation of the beam into the variously coloured rays. The decision between these two theories is pronounced, in his view, by that experiment of Newton's (Book I, Part I, Exper. 5; *Opticks* (1952), p. 34) in which he shone a beam of light through two prisms placed successively and at right angles, and found that the spectrum was formed diagonally without any such 'splitting' of the light by the second prism. The rest of this dialogue and the Fifth consists of an easy exposition of *Opticks*, not forgetting the colours of soap-bubbles, until Algarotti returns to his principle philosophical contention that attraction is the Newtonian key to all true understanding of Nature:

This universal attraction of matter, of which the particular attraction between light and bodies is a special case, was suspected in all ages by those who considered the system of the world more inwardly; but it was really discovered, brought into a clear light and subjected to calculation by Newton; and for the future it may be looked upon as the key to physics (Bonora 1977, pp. 57, 92).

Algarotti, stressing the positive elements in Newton's philosophy, insists that attraction is a concept firmly based upon the phenomena, not an esoteric notion:

his [Newton's] purpose is solely to satisfy himself about the general properties of Nature [and] about the laws by which Nature governs the universality of things (ibid., p. 94).

Newton's later suggestions about a subtle, elastic, and electric aether did not commend themselves to Algarotti, even in the revised version of his book (ibid., pp. 100–1). In the original text he regretted that Newton had weakened his concept of attractive force: Newton, he thought, had given way to the prejudices of the Cartesians in allowing that attraction might perhaps be caused by the impulse of a subtle matter issuing from bodies. (Such, of course, was not Newton's notion of the elastic and electric aether.) Newton had proved the heavens to be empty in the *Principia*, Algarotti argued, so what room remained for subtle matter?

Is it not a great reproach upon mankind, that even the truths of Sir Isaac Newton were obliged to use some little artifice in order to meet with a reception among them? (Algarotti 1765, p. 219).

After a long excursion into the system of the world in the sixth and last dialogue he returns in his final pages to the optical applications of the concept of attraction, explaining how the phenomena of light are best accounted for by the indirect action of forces, rather than the direct impact of material bodies. For all his scepticism, Algarotti faithfully (if guardedly) followed Newton into the mysteries of the "fits" of easy transmission and easy reflection, observing that 'we are now arrived at the confines of nature, where our ideas grow dark and confused' (ibid., p. 275). His allusions to the Queries in *Opticks* allow Algarotti to contrast the over-confidence of those who gave a definite resolution to every problem with the caution of Newton who, 'guided by a slow yet sure experience', went no further than experiment would take him: 'and in the extent of his *own*, discovers the limits of the *human* understanding' (ibid., p. 276).

When she understands this, the Marchesa is indeed a Newtonian.

Aether re-affirmed: Maclaurin

The few books considered in this chapter are only those most significant for the reception of Newton's optical discoveries in Europe, which also possess some inherent interest. Many other popularizations were published, from Wells's *Young Gentleman's Course of Mechanicks, Optics and Astronomy* (1714) to Benjamin Martin's *Plain and Familiar Introduction to the Newtonian Philosophy* (1754; Maclaurin 1968, *xi*, note). Some, like Colin

Maclaurin's *Account of Sir Isaac Newton's Philosophical Discoveries* (1748) do not regard *Opticks* as containing philosophical discoveries.

Authors like Maclaurin, representative of a younger generation of Newtonians, no longer reflect faithfully the Newtonian 'revolution' against Cartesian rationalistic physics, neither experimental nor mathematical, in the way that 'sGravesande and Algarotti do. The younger writers were strengthening the true Newtonian faith in readers already converted, not proselytizing among the infidel. Moreover, some writers after 1744— Maclaurin among them, though he died young in 1746—were much affected by the publication of Newton's letter to Boyle in the edition of Robert Boyle's *Works* of that year. These made plain Newton's early evolution of an aetherial conjecture, in 1679. Whereas earlier expositors, like those considered in this chapter, accepted the existence of physical forces and of the motions of attraction and repulsion caused by these forces as empirically justified elements in natural philosophy, even though the nature and *modus operandi* of such forces could not be further resolved or accounted for in any way (unless by the direct action of the deity), many exponents of the Newtonian philosophy after 1744 (of whom Bryan Robinson is the egregious example) started from the assumption of a Newtonian aether as the fundamental *explicans* of every phenomenon in nature. So, for example, Maclaurin:

Sir Isaac Newton . . . has plainly signified that he thought that those powers [virtues, and forces] arose from the impulses of a subtile aetherial *medium* that is diffused over the universe and penetrates the pores of grosser bodies. It appears from his letter to Mr. Boyle that this was his opinion early; and if he did not publish it sooner, it proceeded from hence only, that he found he was not able, from experiment and observation, to give a satisfactory account of this medium, and the manner of its operation, in producing the chief phaenomena of nature (Maclaurin 1968, p. 111).

Maclaurin's self-imposed restriction upon the content of his volume excused him from the necessity of reconciling Newton's emission or projectile theory of light with his revived (and revised) aether-theory of his last years. Gravitation imposed no great speculative problem: it was only necessary to argue (in one way or another) that the motion or elasticity of an aether somehow caused bodies to approach one another according to the verified laws. The aether served to 'explain' attraction, whose phenomena remained as the writers on mechanics proposed. With light the case was less easy. The aetherial explanation of refraction, for example—as put forward by Newton in his letter to Boyle of February 1679—does not supplement the dynamical treatment of his later optical writings; it can only be read as an alternative. As *Opticks* proves—as much by what Newton did not care to publish, as by what he did publish—it is not at all simple to frame a theory of light that postulates moving light-particles interacting, not with matter, but with an ubiquitous aether.

Musschenbroek

The last word here may be given to a distinguished Newtonian, Petrus van Musschenbroek, one of the younger generation of teachers of Newtonian philosophy who did not turn against the idea of attractive force. His work appeared in English in the critical year 1744, having been first published at Leiden ten years before. *Elements of Natural Philosophy*, in two volumes, closely follows its Dutch precursor, 'sGravesande's *Mathematical Elements*, and was similarly derived from the author's lectures. Like 'sGravesande, Musschenbroek identifies fire and light; his section on optics opens with thermometry and the increase in the weight of some bodies caused by their calcination: 'What else is light but fire, moving in right lines, and entering our eyes?' (Musschenbroek 1744, II, §850). He teaches that light is a highly fluid, particulate matter capable of interacting with ordinary matter; the fundamental cause of the phenomena in which both are concerned is the attractive optical force discovered by Newton (ibid., §854, 864, 866). A specialized instance is the dynamic theory of refraction:

Because the red rays are refracted less than the rays of other colours, they keep their way [through an interface] more obstinately, and are less liable to be diverted from it by the attracting and refracting force; and therefore the particles that compose the red rays are moved with greater force, and [the velocity of all particles being the same] will be either greater, or more dense than the particles of other colours (ibid., §927).

However, unlike Newton but quite in accord with Newtonian ideas, Musschenbroek appears to find a *repelling* force necessary for reflection (§1026).

Envoi

With Musschenbroek this story approaches the high epoch of eighteenth-century experimental science, into which I do not mean to enter. *Opticks* was already a classic work, its author esteemed as a being possessed of superhuman abilities. To the generation of men active after his own death Newton became a dominant influence within European culture, a pillar of the new age of the Enlightenment, a prophet of man's understanding of his world. The heroic view of Newton then current involved, of course, a partial indeed serious misunderstanding of his intellect and beliefs, hardly to be corrected before Sir David Brewster first looked into Newton's manuscripts. For the mid-eighteenth century the Newton of the Trinity College statue (and Wordsworth)—calm, logical, analytical, precise, and dispassionate—was the only Newton.

That *Principia* and *Opticks*, two books with perhaps more in common than at first seems possible, together shaped the future of astronomy, chemistry, mechanics, physics, and physiology requires no emphasis here. The same books also moulded for some generations the thinking of philosophers, theologians, and poets as no specialist works concerned with the physical sciences have done since. Their unprecedented importance was universally recognized even in Newton's lifetime, nor denied by his critics, and it is lamentable that our knowledge of Newton's involvement in the intellectual life of his age is so limited. We have some awareness of his concern for certain issues in theology, yet his personal relations with (for example) Clarke, Cheyne, Tenison, and Whiston are almost wholly unknown to us. Newton's friendship with John Locke is better illumined; but our knowledge is full of gaps and, perhaps, misunderstandings. Newton's opinions on some points of economic theory are clear enough; but his place in this and other areas of thought in his time is quite uncertain.

Scraps of information suggest that Newton may have been less austere and remote than legend suggests. He may well have been more at home in coffee-houses with the Augustan wits than we imagine. His friend and patron Halifax moved among them, and was a Kit-Kat; Arbuthnot was Newton's friend; Swift came often to his house, and at least once recorded a conversation with Newton. Perhaps he was also acquainted with Addison and Steele. But we have no evidence that Pope's most famous couplet

> Nature and Nature's laws lay hid in Night;
> God said, Let Newton be! and all was Light.

reflects any degree of acquaintance.

Some post-Newtonians, notably the Romantics, feared (as indeed Swift and Pope had done) the death-giving touch of quantitative science. But for many others, no more numerate, *Opticks* opened a delightful vista of experimental discovery. Leeuwenhoek in microscopy, Newton in several branches of science, provided the bases for the typically eighteenth-century demonstrative presentation of natural knowledge to a wide public. *Opticks* was a rich source-book for the numerous successors of Newton's colleagues Keill, Hauksbee, and Desaguliers, as popular lecturers. It was the most accessible and best-read of Newton's books, quoted on almost every serious topic: 'the rich, gentle, personal English style of the *Opticks* was far more conducive to pleasure than the severe and formal Latin phrases of the *Principia*' (Cohen 1956, p. 123).

The warm glow of intellectual satisfaction suggested by Bernard Cohen was perhaps of only relatively short duration; longer-lasting, and of great force in the development of European thought, was *Opticks*' supplementation over broad and non-mathematical fields of thought of the lesson taught by the *Principia* that the rational, factual investigation of problems could lead to their satisfactory solution. Contrast *Opticks* with Newton's lectures on the same topic, or still more those of Isaac Barrow. The book shows how mastery of a field of inquiry increases by the methodical exploitation of accidental or discordant circumstances; still more (again reinforcing the *Principia*) how a single avenue of research could expand and extend until the whole universe is within its scope. Newton's books were not only models of methods of discovery, but fertile sources of inspiration also.

Appendix I

The early editions of *Opticks, or a Treatise of the Reflexions, Refractions, Inflexions and Colours of Light*

A. 1704: Two volumes quarto, the first containing Book I (144 pp.), the second Books II and III (137 pp.). *Opticks* is followed by *Enumeratio lineis tertii ordinis* (pp. 138–69) and *Tractatus de quadratura curvarum* (pp. 170–211).
Printed for Sam. Smith and Benj. Walford, Printers to the Royal Society.
The title-page bears no author's name, but the *Advertisement* to the Reader dated April 1, 1704, carries the initials I. N.

B₁. 1717: 'The Second Edition with Additions', one volume octavo, 382 pp., without mathematical treatises.
Printed by W. Bowyer for W. Innys.
The title-page carries Newton's name as author and a second *Advertisement* is dated 16 July 1717.

B₂. 1718: The same issue with a different title-page and slight modifications to the first *Advertisement*.
Printed for W. and J. Innys, Printers to the Royal Society.

C. 1721: 'The Third Edition Corrected', one volume octavo, 382 pp.
Printed for William and John Innys.

D. 1730: 'The Fourth Edition, corrected', one volume octavo, 382 pp.
Printed for William Innys.
This first posthumous edition contains a new *Advertisement* inserted by the bookseller claiming that it was printed from a copy of the third edition corrected by Newton.

Translations

1. Latin

1706 *Optice: sive de Reflexionibus, Refractionibus, Inflexionibus & Coloribus Lucis*, one volume quarto, 348 pp., followed by the two mathematical treatises, separately paginated.
Impensis Sam. Smith & Benj. Walford Regiae Societatis Typograph.
The title-page has Newton's name as author and Samuel Clarke's as translator. Clarke noted that all changes from the first edition were made on the author's authority. Important additions are contained in the list of *Errata, Corrigenda & Addenda*.

1719 'Editio Secunda, auctior', one volume octavo, 415 pp.
Impensis Gul. & Joh. Innys.
Contains the second *Advertisement*. The printing was completed in September 1718.

2. **French**

1720 *Traité d'Optique*. Traduite par Pierre Coste, sur la seconde édition Angloise. Amsterdam, two volumes duodecimo.

1722 'Seconde Edition françoise beaucoup plus correcte que la première', Paris, one volume quarto.

Appendix II

The Queries in Opticks

A, the *editio princeps*, contains 16 Queries (pp. 132–7).

Optice (1706) contains 23 Queries (that is, seven more following sequentially after the former 16; pp. 293–348) plus further matter printed in the *Addenda*.

B_1, the second English edition, contains 31 Queries (pp. 313–82). The eight new Queries were interpolated after the original 16, being therefore numbered 17 to 24. The revised texts of the Queries formerly published in Latin (numbered 17 to 23 in *Optice*) received the numbers 25 to 31 in this English edition.

Appendix III

A sample list of books on optics published in the seventeenth century. Titles marked with * also appear in the Bibliography. Works on artistic perspective are omitted. Books recorded as Newton's are marked with †.

Anon. *Elementa opticae nova*. London 1651.

†Barrow, Isaac. **Lectiones XVIII in quibus opticorum phaenomenon genuinae rationes explicantur*. London 1669.

Chales, Claude François Milliet de. *Optica*; in his *Cursus seu Mundus mathematicus*. Lyons 1674.

Cherubin d'Orleans. *La Dioptrique oculaire*. Paris 1671.

†Descartes, René. *La Dioptrique*; *Les Météores*, published with *Discours de la Méthode*. Leiden 1637.

†Dominis, Marcus Antonius de. *De radiis visus et lucis in vitris perspectivis et iride tractatus*. Venice 1611.

Eschinardus, Franciscus. *Centuria problematum opticorum*. Rome 1666.

idem. *Dialogus opticus*. Rome 1666.

†Fabri, Honoratus. **Dialogi physici*. Lyons 1669.

†Gregory, David. **Catoptricae et dioptricae sphaericae elementa*. Oxford 1695.

†Gregory, James. *Optica promota, seu abdita radiorum reflexorum et refractorum mysteria geometrice enucleata.* London 1663.

Grimaldi, Francesco Maria. *Physico-mathesis de lumine.* Bologna 1665.

Hartsoeker, Nicolas. *Essai de Dioptrique.* Paris 1694.

Hérigone, Pierre. *Optica,* in his *Cursus mathematicus,* vol. V. Paris 1644.

Hooke, Robert. *Micrographia.* London 1665.

†Huygens, Christiaan. *Traité de la Lumière.* Leiden 1690.

Kepler, Johannes. *Ad Vitellionem paralipomena, quibus astronomiae pars optica traditur.* Frankfurt 1614.

†idem. *Dioptrice.* Augsburg 1611.

Kircher, Athanasius. *Ars magna lucis et umbrae in x libris digesta.* Amsterdam 1671.

Maignan, Emmanuel. *Cursus philosophicus.* Toulouse 1653.

Marci, Marcus. *Thaumantias; Liber de arcu coelestis deque colorum apparentium natura, ortu et causis* (Prague 1648, repr. 1968).

Maurolyco, Franciscus. *Theoremata de lumine et umbra.* Lyons 1617.

†Molyneux, William. *Dioptrica nova, a treatise of dioptrics.* London 1692.

Niceron, Jean-François. *La perspective curieuse, avec l'optique et la catoptrique du R.P. Mersenne.* Paris 1651, 1663.

Risner, Fredericus. *Opticae libri iv, ex voto P. Rami olim conscripti, nunc in lucem producti.* Kassel 1606.

†Scheiner, Christopher. *Oculus, hoc est, fundamentum opticum.* Innsbruck, 1619; London 1652.

Sirturus, Hieronymus. *Telescopium* . . . Frankfurt 1618.

Tacquet, Andreas. *Opticae libri tres* . . . in *Opera mathematica.* Antwerp 1669.

Vossius, Isaac. *De lucis natura et proprietate.* Amsterdam 1662.

Zucchius, Nicolaus. *Opticae philosophia experimentis et ratione a fundamentis constituta.* Lyons 1652–6.

Bibliography

Acloque (1986). P. Acloque, 'Le traité de la nature des couleurs de Mariotte'. In Mariotte Savant et Philosophe (ed. P. Costabel), pp. 133–54. Paris 1986.

Algarotti (1765). F. Algarotti, The Philosophy of Sir Isaac Newton explained in six Dialogues . . . . Glasgow 1765.

Bechler (1973). Z. Bechler, 'Newton's search for a mechanistic model of colour dispersion: a suggested interpretation'. Archive for History of Exact Sciences, 11, 1–37.

Bechler (1974). idem, Newton's law of forces which are inversely as the mass: a suggested interpretation of his later efforts to normalise a mechanistic model of optical dispersion. Centaurus, 18, 184–222.

Bechler (1975). idem, "A less Agreeable Matter": The disagreeable case of Newton and achromatic refraction. British Journal for the History of Science, 8, 101–26.

Birch (1756–7). T. Birch (ed.), History of the Royal Society of London, Vol. III. London 1757, repr. 1968.

Boas (1981). M. Boas (Hall), The Mechanical Philosophy. New York 1981; repr. from Osiris, 10 (1952), 412–541.

Boas and Hall (1959). M. Boas and A. R. Hall, Newton's Mechanical Principles, Journal of the History of Ideas, 20, 167–78.

Bonora (1977). Francesco Algarotti, Dialoghi sopra l'Ottica Neutoniana a cura di Ettore Bonora. Torino 1977.

Boyer (1959). Carl B. Boyer, The Rainbow: From Myth to Mathematics. New York and London 1959.

Boyle (1664). Robert Boyle, Experiments and Considerations touching Colours . . . the Beginning of an Experimental History of Colours. London 1664.

Brewster (1855). Sir David Brewster, Memoirs . . . of Sir Isaac Newton. Edinburgh 1855.

Brunet (1926). Pierre Brunet, Les Physiciens Hollandais et la Méthode Experimentale en France au XVIIIᵉ Siècle. Paris 1926.

Burke (1983). John G. Burke (ed.), The Uses of Science in the Age of Newton. London 1983.

Cantor (1983). G. N. Cantor, Optics after Newton. Theories of Light in Britain and Ireland 1704–1840. Manchester 1983.

Casini (1969). P. Casini, L'universo-macchina. Origini della filosofia newtoniana. Bari 1969.

Casini (1978). idem, Les debuts du Newtonianisme en Italie, 1700–1740. Dix-huitieme Siecle, 10, 85–100.

Casini (1983). idem, Newton e la Coscienza Europea. Bologna 1983.

Charleton (1654). Walter Charleton, Physiologia Epicuro-Gassendo-Charltoniana, 1654; repr., ed. R. H. Kargon, New York and London 1966.

Châtellet (1740). Gabrielle-Emilie du Châtellet, Institutions de Physique. Paris 1740.

Cheyne (1715). George Cheyne, Philosophical Principles of Religion Natural and Reveal'd. London 1715.

Clarke (1717). Samuel Clarke, A Collection of Papers which passed between the late learned Mr Leibnitz and Dr Clarke in the Years 1715 and 1716. London 1717.

Clarke (1723). John Clarke (trans.), *Rohault's System of Natural Philosophy with Dr Samuel Clarke's Notes*. London 1723.

Cohen (1956). I. B. Cohen, *Franklin and Newton: An Inquiry into Speculative Newtonian Experimental Science*. Philadelphia 1956.

Cohen (1958*a*). idem (ed.), *Isaac Newton's Papers and Letters on Natural Philosophy*. Cambridge, Mass., 1958.

Cohen (1958*b*). idem, Versions of Isaac Newton's first published paper. *Archives Internationales d'Histoire des Sciences*, **11**, 357–75.

Cohen (1963). idem, Pemberton's translation of Newton's *Principia*, with notes on Motte's translation. *Isis*, **54**, 319–51.

Cohen (1964). idem, Isaac Newton, Hans Sloane and the Académie Royale des Sciences. In *Mélanges Alexandre Koyré* (ed. I. B. Cohen and R. Taton), I, pp. 61–116. Paris 1964.

Cohen (1966). idem, Hypotheses in Newton's philosophy. *Physis*, **8**, 163–84.

Cohen (1971). idem, *Introduction to Newton's Principia*. Cambridge 1971.

Cohen (1980). idem, *The Newtonian Revolution*. Cambridge 1980.

Crombie (1953). A. C. Crombie, *Robert Grosseteste and the Origins of Experimental Science 1100–1700*. Oxford 1953.

Crombie (1967). idem, The mechanistic hypothesis and the scientific study of vision. In *Historical Aspects of Microscopy* (ed. S. Bradbury and G. L'E. Turner), pp. 3–112. Cambridge, 1967.

Desaguliers (1717). J. T. Desaguliers, *Physico-Mechanical Lectures*. London 1717.

Desaguliers (1763). idem, *A Course of Experimental Philosophy* (3rd edn). London 1763.

Descartes (1672). René Descartes, *Opera philosophica*. Amsterdam 1672.

Dominis (1611). Marcus Antonius de Dominis, *De radiis visus et lucis in vitris perspectivis et iride tractatus*. Venice 1611.

Edleston (1850). J. Edleston, *Correspondence of Sir Isaac Newton and Professor Cotes*. Cambridge 1850, repr. 1969.

Fabri (1669). Honoratus Fabri, *Dialogi physici*. Lyons 1669.

Fauvel *et al.* (1988). J. Fauvel, R. Flood, M. Shortland, and R. Wilson, *Let Newton Be! A New Perspective on his Life and Works*. Oxford 1988.

Field (1712). J. Field, *Chymical Lectures . . . Read in the Museum at Oxford, 1704*, London 1712.

Gouk (1988). P. Gouk, The harmonic roots of Newtonian Science. In Fauvel *et al.* (1988), pp. 101–25.

'sGravesande (1731). W. J. 'sGravesande, *Elements of Natural Philosophy confirm'd by Experiments or an Introduction to Sir Isaac Newton's Philosophy* (4th edn). London 1731.

Gregory (1663). James Gregory, *Optica promota, seu abdita reflexorum et refractorum mysteria, geometrice enucleata*. London 1663.

Gregory (1695). David Gregory, *Catoptricae et dioptricae elementa*. Oxford 1695.

Gregory (1715). idem, *Elements of Astronomy, physical and geometrical translated*. London 1715.

Grimaldi (1665). Francesco Maria Grimaldi, *Physico-mathesis de lumine*. Bologna 1665.

Guerlac (1965). H. Guerlac, Where the statue stood: divergent loyalties to Newton in the 18th century. In *Aspects of the Eighteenth Century* (ed. E. R. Wasserman), pp. 317–34. Baltimore 1965.

Guerlac (1977). idem, *Essays and Papers in the History of Science*. Baltimore and London 1977.

Guerlac (1981). idem, *Newton on the Continent*. Ithaca and London 1981.

Guerlac (1983). idem, Can we date Newton's early optical experiments? *Isis*, **74**, 74–80.

Hakfoort (1988). C. Hakfoort, Newton's optics: the changing spectrum of science. In Fauvel *et al.* (1988), pp. 81–99.

Hales (1961). Stephen Hales, *Vegetable Staticks* (1727), reprinted with a preface by M. A. Hoskin. Cambridge 1961.

Hall (1948). A. Rupert Hall, Sir Isaac Newton's Note-Book, 1661–1665. *Cambridge Historical Journal*, **9**, 239–50.

Hall (1955). idem, Further optical experiments of Isaac Newton. *Annals of Science*, **11**, 27–43.

Hall (1960). idem, Newton's First Book. *Archives Internationales d'Histoire des Sciences*, **13**, 39–61.

Hall (1975). idem, Newton in France. *History of Science*, **13**, 233–50.

Hall (1976). idem, *La Rivoluzione Scientifica 1500–1800*. Milan 1976.

Hall (1979*a*). idem, Galileo nel XVIII secolo. *Rivista di Filosofia*, no. **15**, 367–90.

Hall (1979*b*). idem, Newton – the eighteenth century's marble image. *Vistas in Astronomy*, **22**, 405–12.

Hall (1985). idem, Isaac Newton's steamer. *History of Technology* (ed. Norman Smith), **10**, 17–29.

Hall (1986). idem, Mariotte et la Royal Society. In *Mariotte Savant et Philosophe* (ed. Pierre Costabel), pp. 33–42. Paris 1986.

Hall (1992). idem, *Isaac Newton: Adventurer in Thought*. Oxford 1992.

Hall and Hall (1962). idem and M. B. Hall, *Unpublished Scientific Papers of Isaac Newton*. Cambridge 1962, repr. 1978.

Hall and Hall (1965–86). idem and M. B. Hall, *The Correspondence of Henry Oldenburg*. Madison and London, 1965–86.

Hanson (1960). N. R. Hanson, Waves, particles and Newton's "Fits". *Journal of the History of Ideas*, **21**, 370–91.

Harrison (1978). J. Harrison, *The Library of Isaac Newton*. Cambridge 1978.

Hauksbee (?1714). Francis Hauksbee, jun., *A Course of Mechanical, Optical, Hydrostatical, and Pneumatic Experiments . . . the Explanatory Lectures read by William Whiston*. London n.d.

Hauksbee (1719). idem, *Physico-Mechanical Experiments on various Subjects* (2nd. edn). London 1719.

Hawes (1968). J. L. Hawes, Newton's revival of the aether hypothesis and the explanation of gravitational attraction. *Notes and Records of the Royal Society*, **23**, 200–12.

Heimann (1973). P. M. Heimann [Harman], "Nature is a perpetual worker": Newton's aether and eighteenth century natural philosophy. *Ambix*, **20**, 1–25.

Hendry (1980). John Hendry, Newton's theory of colour. *Centaurus*, **23**, 230–51.

Hiscock (1937). W. G. Hiscock, *David Gregory, Isaac Newton, and Their Circle*. Oxford 1937.

Home (1982). R. W. Home, Newton on electricity and the aether. In *Contemporary Newtonian research* (ed. Z. Bechler), pp. 191–213. Dordrecht 1982.

Hooke (1665). Robert Hooke, *Micrographia*. London 1665.

Hoskin (1961). M. A. Hoskin, 'Mining all within', Clarke's notes to Rohault's *Traité de Physique*. *The Thomist*, **24**, 357–63.

Huygens (1690). Christiaan Huygens, *Traité de la Lumière*. Leiden 1690.

Iltis (1977). C. Iltis, Madame de Châtellet's metaphysics and mechanics. *Studies in History of Physical Sciences*, **8**, 29–48.

Kepler (1682). Johannes Kepler, *Dioptrice*. Amsterdam 1682.

Koyré (1960). A. Koyré, Les Quéries d'Optique. *Archives Internationales d'Histoire des Sciences*, **13**, 15–29.

Koyré and Cohen (1961). idem and I. B. Cohen, The case of the missing tanquam. *Isis*, **52**, 555–66.

Leibniz – Bernoulli (1745). *Virorum Cel. G. G. Leibnitii et J. Bernoulli Commercium Philosophicum et Mathematicum*. Lausanne and Geneva 1745.

Lohne (1965). J. A. Lohne, Isaac Newton: the rise of a scientist 1661–71. *Notes and Records of the Royal Society*, **20**, 125–39.

Lohne (1968). idem, Experimentum crucis. *Notes and Records of the Royal Society*, **23**, 169–99.

McGuire (1968). J. E. McGuire, Force, Active Principles and Newton's invisible realm. *Ambix*, **15**, 154–208.

McGuire and Tamny (1983). idem and M. Tamny, *Certain philosophical questions: Newton's Trinity notebook*. Cambridge 1983.

Mach (1926). Ernst Mach, *The Principles of Physical Optics: an historical and philosophical treatment* (English trans. by J. S. Anderson and A. F. A. Young, 1926). Repr. New York, n.d.

Maclaurin (1968). Colin Maclaurin, *An Account of Sir Isaac Newton's Philosophical Discoveries* (1748) (ed. with introduction by L. L. Laudan). New York and London 1968.

Malebranche (1712). Nicolas Malebranche, *De la Recherche de la Verité où l'on traitte de la Nature de l'Esprit de l'Homme, et de l'Usage qu'il en doit faire pour éviter l'Erreur dans les Sciences* (6th edn). Paris 1712.

Mamiani (1976). M. Mamiani, *Isaac Newton filosofo della Natura. Le lezioni giovanili di ottica e la genesi del metodo newtoniano*. Florence 1976.

Mamiani (1986). idem, *Il prisma di Newton*. Roma – Bari 1986.

Marek (1968). Jiri Marek (ed.), *Thaumantias* by Marcus Marci. Repr. Prague 1968.

Martin (1735). B. Martin, *The Philosophical Grammar*. London 1735.

Metzger (1938). H. Metzger, *Attraction Universelle et Religion Naturelle chez quelques commentateurs anglais de Newton*. Paris 1938.

Mills (1981). A. A. Mills, Newton's prisms and his experiments on the spectrum. *Notes and Records of the Royal Society*, **36**, 13–36.

Mills and Turvey (1979). idem and P. J. Turvey, Newton's telescope. *Notes and Records of the Royal Society*, **33**, 133–55.

Molyneux (1692). William Molyneux, *Dioptrica nova, a treatise of dioptricks*. London 1692.

Musschenbroek (1744). Pieter van Musschenbroek, *Elements of Natural Philosophy*. London 1744.

Newton (1687). Isaac Newton, *Philosophiae Naturalis Principia Mathematica*. London 1687.

Newton (1952). idem, *Opticks: Or a Treatise of the Reflections, Refractions, Inflections and Colours of Light* (4th edn). Repr. New York 1952.

Pemberton (1728). Henry Pemberton, *A View of Sir Isaac Newton's Philosophy*. London 1728.

Priestley (1772). Joseph Priestley, *The History and Present State of Discoveries relating to Vision, Light and Colours*. London 1772.

Robinet (1960). A. Robinet, Le groupe malebranchiste introducteur du calcul infinitésimal en France. *Revue d'Histoire des Sciences*, **13**, 287–308.

Robinet (1961). idem (ed.), *Malebranche*, tome XIX: *Correspondance, actes et documents, 1690–1715*. Paris 1961.

Rosenfeld (1932). L. Rosenfeld, Marcus Marci Untersuchungen über das Prisma und ihr Verhaltnis zu Newton's Farbentheorie. *Isis*, **18**, 325–30.

Rowning (1734–38). J. Rowning, *A Compendious System of Natural Philosophy*. London 1734, 1738.

Sabra (1967). A. I. Sabra, *Theories of Light from Descartes to Newton*. London 1967.

Schaffer (1989). Simon Schaffer, Glass works: Newton's prisms and the uses of experiment. In *The Uses of Experiment: Studies in the Natural Sciences* (ed. D. Gooding, T. Pinch, and S. Schaffer), pp. 67–104. Cambridge 1989.

Scheiner (1652). Christopher Scheiner, *Oculus, hoc est fundamentum opticum*. Innsbruck 1619, London 1652.

Shapiro (1975). A. E. Shapiro, Newton's definition of a light ray and the diffusion theories of chromatic dispersion. *Isis*, **66**, 194–210.

Shapiro (1979). idem, Newton's "achromatic" dispersion law: theoretical background and experimental evidence. *Archive for History of Exact Sciences*, **21**, 91–128.

Shapiro (1980). idem, Huygens' kinematic theory of light. In *Studies on Christiaan Huygens* (ed. H. J. M. Bos *et al.*), pp. 200–20. Lisse 1980.

Shapiro (1984). idem, *The Optical Papers of Isaac Newton*, Vol. I. Cambridge 1984.

Shapiro (1989). idem, Newton's *Opticks* and Huygens' *Traité de la Lumière*: pursuing and eschewing hypotheses. *Notes and Records of the Royal Society*, **43**, 223–46.

Shapiro (1990). idem, The *Optical Lectures* and the foundations of the theory of optical imagery. In *Before Newton: the Life and Times of Isaac Barrow* (ed. M. Feingold), pp. 105–78. Cambridge 1990.

Shapiro (1992). idem, Beyond the dating game: watermark clusters and the composition of Newton's *Opticks*. In *The Investigation of Difficult Things*: *Essays on Newton and the History of the Exact Sciences in Honour of D. T. Whiteside* (ed. P. M. Harman and Alan E. Shapiro), pp. 181–227. Cambridge 1992.

Shaw (1753). Peter Shaw, *A New Method of Chemistry* (3rd edn). London 1753.

Shirley (1974). J. W. Shirley (ed.), *Thomas Harriot, Renaissance Scientist*. Oxford 1974.

Smith (1738). Robert Smith, *A compleat System of Opticks in four Books*. Cambridge 1738.

Smith (1927). D. E. Smith, Portraits of Sir Isaac Newton. In *Isaac Newton 1642–1727* (ed. W. J. Greenstreet), pp. 171–8. London 1927.

Stuewer (1970). R. H. Stuewer, A critical analysis of Newton's work on diffraction. *Isis*, **61**, 1970, 188–205.

Tega (1984). W. Tega (ed.), *Scienza e Letteratura nella Cultura Italiana del Settecento*. Bologna 1984.

Tega (1986). idem, *Anatomie Accademiche I. I Commentari dell'Accademia delle Scienze di Bologna*. Bologna 1986.

Thackray (1970). A. Thackray, *Atoms and Powers: An Essay on Newtonian Matter-theory and the Development of Chemistry*. Cambridge, Mass. 1970.

Torrini (1979). M. Torrini, *Dopo Galileo: Una Polemica Scientifica (1684–1711)*. Florence 1979.

Toulmin (1959). S. E. Toulmin, Criticism in the history of science: Newton on absolute space, time and motion. *Philosophical Review*, **68**, 1–29, 203–27.

Turnbull (1959–77). H. W. Turnbull *et al.*, *The Correspondence of Isaac Newton*, 7 vols. Cambridge 1959–77.

Van Helden (1977). Albert Van Helden, The invention of the telescope. *Transactions of the American Philosophical Society*, **67**, 1–67.

Voltaire (1946). F. A. Taylor (ed.), *Voltaire: Lettres Philosophiques*. Oxford 1946.

Westfall (1962). R. S. Westfall, The development of Newton's theory of colour. *Isis*, **53**, 339–58.

Westfall (1965). idem, Isaac Newton's "Coloured Circles 'twixt two Contiguous Glasses". *Archive for History of Exact Sciences*, **2**, 181–96.

Westfall (1970). idem, Uneasily fitful reflections on fits of easy transmission. In *The Annus Mirabilis of Sir Isaac Newton 1666–1966* (ed. Robert Palter), pp. Cambridge, Mass. 1970.

Westfall (1971). idem, *Force in Newton's Physics*. London and New York 1971.

Westfall (1973). idem, Newton and the fudge factor. *Science*, **179**, 751–8.

Westfall (1980). idem, *Never at Rest: A Biography of Isaac Newton*. Cambridge 1980.

Whewell (1860). Williams Whewell (ed.), *The Mathematical Works of Isaac Barrow*. Cambridge 1860.

Whiteside (1967). D. T. Whiteside, *Mathematical Papers of Isaac Newton*, Vol. I. Cambridge 1967.

Whiteside (1969). idem, *op. cit.*, Vol. III. Cambridge 1969.

Whiteside (1973). idem, *The Unpublished First Version of Isaac Newton's Cambridge Lectures on Optics, 1670–72*. Cambridge 1973.

Whiteside (1974). idem, *Mathematical Papers of Isaac Newton*, Vol. VI. Cambridge 1974.

Worster (1722). Benjamin Worster, *A Compendious and Methodical Account of the Principles of Natural Philosophy*. London 1722.

Ziggelaar (1971). August Ziggelaar, *Le Physicien Ignace Gaston Pardies S.J. (1636–1673)*. Odense 1971.

Index of names and works

Index of topics

aberrations 43–4, 62, 63, 102–5;
  chromatic 49, 60, 62, 108; spherical 36,
  49
absorption 24, 119–20
achromatism 105, 110–11, 133, 193
active principles 148, 153
aetherial hypotheses 74–8, 90, 118,
  153–62, 176–9, 202, 217, 222, 232–3;
  and gravity 159, 222, 233; and nerves
  160
air-pump 17, 24, 182
atomism 24, 135, 157

birefringence 24, 31, 58, 94, 127, 131–3,
  171, 190, 219, 222

calculus 201, 231
chemical reactions 129–30, 141–4, 173,
  188–9, 192
cohesion 144–5, 172, 219
colour and mathematics 28–30, 51, 95,
  113, 117, 122
colour-circle 115–16
colours of natural bodies 14–17, 73, 91,
  118–19, 206
colours of thick plates 72, 78, 92, 118,
  121–3
colours of thin plates 17–21, 24, 45, 58,
  68–72, 139
comb or wheel 44–5, 52, 62, 114
composition of white light 50–6, 61–2,
  95–102, 114–16
compound lens 63, 103–5, 107–8, 193
critical angle experiments 53–4, 69,
  98–100, 118, 215

diffraction 24, 31, 58, 68, 72, 78–80, 81,
  87, 90, 92, 124–6, 128–9, 157–8, 194,
  217, 219, 221, 226
'dilation' of spectrum 66
dispersion 107–13; calculated 105–6, 113;
  discovered 36–41, 49, 60, 62–3, 96;
  proved 96–100
double refraction see birefringence
dynamic philosophy 26, 34, 37–8, 80–3,
  87–9, 102, 109–10, 118, 124, 126–7,
  128, 138–49, 171–5, 178–9, 218, 234

electricity 129, 152, 159, 175, 176–7, 182
electroluminescence 24, 152, 155
experimentum crucis 41, 49, 54–5, 61, 66,
  67, 96, 98; verified 207–8, 213, 219

fire in Newton's papers 86
fire is light 220, 226, 234
"fits" 21, 26, 30–1, 77–8, 87, 90–2,
  117–18, 139, 158, 179, 206, 216, 218,
  225, 227, 232

geometrical optics 22–4, 46, 55
'Glassworks' 40–1, 104, 224
God and nature 135–8, 150–2, 162, 220
gravity 170, 172–5, 178, 195

halo 123
heat 129–30, 155–6, 184–5, 216, 218

inflection, see diffraction
iridescence 80, 221, 227

jet-propulsion 220

light, velocity of 24, 49, 192, 226
lignum nephriticum 15

matter largely void 72–3, 120, 215–16
methodology 26–7, 31–2, 59, 94–5,
  181–2, 206
microscopes 17, 119
modification of light denied 49–51, 67,
  100–1, 112, 133, 134, 223

'Newton's rings' 42–3, 45, 58, 68–73, 87,
  113, 116–18, 138, 195, 218, 221, 227
notebooks 33–43, 45, 163–4

optical force 25–6, 32, 80–3, 118,
  120–1, 126, 129–30, 138–40, 161,
  169–70, 172, 183, 194, 215, 220–1,
  226, 232; inversely as mass 174–6; see
  also Newton, I., Principia, Book I,
  section XIV

particle theory 11–12, 80–3, 120–2,
  166–8; colour and mass 138–9, 164–5,
  170–6, 223–4, 227; colour and velocity
  163–6